CRIMINAL LAW PROCEDURE FOR PRIVATE SECURITY

About The Author

Arthur C. Weinstock, Jr., graduated from Providence College, Providence, Rhode Island, with an A.B. Degree in 1950. After serving two years in the U.S. Army in Germany, he entered the formal study of law and graduated from Boston College Law School in 1956. He practiced law for several years in Boston, Massachusetts, and became a Special Agent of the Federal Bureau of Investigation in 1959. Mr. Weinstock resigned that position in 1962 to work in the private security industry for American Express Company, Texaco, and the Massachusetts State Lottery Commission, as Chief of Security until 1983, when he was appointed to the position he still holds, Associate General Counsel. Mr. Weinstock is also an adjunct lecturer in criminal law at Dean College in Franklin, Massachusetts. In 1984, he was inducted into the Providence College Athletic Hall of Fame.

Second Edition

CRIMINAL LAW PROCEDURE FOR PRIVATE SECURITY

By

ARTHUR C. WEINSTOCK, JR., A.B., J.D.
Member of the Bar, Commonwealth of Massachusetts
Member of the Bar, United States Supreme Court
Former Member, American Society for Industrial Security

CHARLES C THOMAS • PUBLISHER
Springfield • Illinois • U.S.A.

Published and Distributed Throughout the World by

CHARLES C THOMAS • PUBLISHER
2600 South First Street
Springfield, Illinois 62794-9265

ISBN 0-398-05997-7 (cloth)
ISBN 0-398-05998-5 (paper)

Library of Congress Catalog Card Number: 95-2366

First Edition, 1983
Second Edition, 1995

With THOMAS BOOKS *careful attention is given to all details of manufacturing and design. It is the Publisher's desire to present books that are satisfactory as to their physical qualities and artistic possibilities and appropriate for their particular use.* THOMAS BOOKS *will be true to those laws of quality that assure a good name and good will.*

Printed in the United States of America
SC-R-3

Library of Congress Cataloging-in-Publication Data

Weinstock, Arthur C.
Criminal law procedures for private security / by Arthur C. Weinstock. — 2nd ed.
p. cm.
Includes index.
ISBN 0-398-05997-7 (cloth). — ISBN 0-398-05998-5 (pbk.)
1. Police, Private—United States—Cases. 2. Criminal procedure—United States—Cases. I. Title.
KF5399.5.P7W44 1995
345.73'05—dc20
[347.3055] 95-2366
CIP

But Rabbi Akiba said: He who glories merely in his knowledge of the law is like the carcass of a dead animal lying in the road. To be sure, the rotting beast attracts the attention of all, but whoever passes by holds his hand to his nose, for it stinks.

Reprinted from *The Source*
by James A. Michener, with
permission of Random House, Inc.,
New York, New York.

INTRODUCTION TO THE FIRST EDITION

OFTEN I have shuddered when being told by private security persons that they know the law, proudly reciting verbatim a statute. They are totally unaware that there is more to the *law* than knowing a statute. While teaching criminal law to college law enforcement students, including both federal and local officers, I was struck by the lack of accent on case law in the textbooks. Where cases were used, it was generally a citation as authority for the general proposition of the law as stated by the author, with little or no recitation of case facts, issue or issues, or the logic and reasons for the decisions, i.e., the case law. I mused, here is a group of nonlawyers who are to be trained and taught what the *law* is, but little is being done to teach or help this group to apply their learning. They can recite law, but do not learn how to use it in their work; thus, I had the idea that the use of the case method to study law would be helpful to nonlawyers to relate general legal principles to fact situations. A review of textbooks on criminal law and other literature demonstrated the lack of attention to this subject matter for the private security field, and more particularly, the use of the case method to learn. From experience and hearsay I knew that law enforcement officers were often forced to make split-second decisions. Can I arrest this person? If he refused to go along with me, can I use my gun? Can I use my club to protect myself against a group of teenagers who have been drinking? No wonder there exists animosity on the part of law enforcement toward the judiciary when the officer's on-the-spot decision is denounced by an appellate court majority of justices, sometimes 5–4, as "unreasonable."

This book is intended to reach private security persons directly, to be read, reread, studied, and referred to for guidance, and indirectly through instructors in college private security programs and in vocational training schools, commercial or otherwise.

Hopefully, the case selections contained in this text will demonstrate the interaction of constitutions, statutes and case decisions in arriving at the current status of the *law,* and a recognition and an appreciation of the notion that law, in a rapidly changing society, responds to many varied political pressures developing from sociological, economical, and technological changes and therefore changes. Perhaps the readers will also become aware of some classic battles in the field of law. Most important is the clash between change and continuity; secondly, a look at the doctrine of judicial supremacy and when it becomes unwarranted legislation; and thirdly, the doctrine of stare decisis.

When the U.S. Constitution was ratified in 1788 and put into effect in 1789, it created a government with three basic departments: legislative, executive, and judicial, separating the governmental powers. The legislative power, i.e., statute making, was vested in the Congress; the executive in the president; and the judicial, i.e., power to decide cases properly before the court, in a "Supreme Court and in such inferior Courts as the Congress may . . . ordain and establish" (Art. 111.§1 U.S. Constitution).

In 1803, the U.S. Supreme Court, in deciding the case of *Marbury v. Madison,* 1 Cr. 137 (1803), ruled that a certain statute enacted by Congress was repugnant to the U.S. Constitution and that the court had the power to declare such a statute void. Thus, the doctrine of judicial supremacy was created, i.e., that the judicial branch of the government is supreme and can invalidate acts of the other branches of government, which, in its opinion, are contrary to the Constitution.

With regard to the battle between changing the law and continuity of law (seemingly essential to the ability of lawyers to advise clients as to proper action in advance), it is important to understand that the appellate decisions of the cases reported herein have been through a trial that must be conducted by a trial judge in accordance with the current law; that *findings of fact* have been made at the trial; and that an appeal to an appellate court has been made, questioning a *ruling of law* that had been made by the judge presiding at the trial.

To provide some continuity, there is the judicial doctrine of *stare decisis,* which means respect for judicial precedents set forth in prior appellate decisions in similar cases. Therefore, this doctrine expects that all judges will respect appellate judges' prior decisions, which have the force of law. Lawyers will argue that certain prior decisions are controlling and should be followed, if these favor their clients. If these prior decisions are not favorable to their clients, it will be argued that their case is different from the prior cases, and therefore it is not controlling, or that society has undergone change, and therefore the prior law should be changed. But, should the law be changed judicially because a few believe the social change to be so significant as to require a change in the law, or should the law be changed only by the legislative branch of government, which theoretically represents the will of the people, i.e., the many? Does legislative inaction justify judicial change, or does it really indicate that the people do not desire a change?

INTRODUCTION TO THE SECOND EDITION

In this the Second Edition of *Criminal Law Procedure For Private Security,* I have retained the cases which appear in the First Edition and inserted newer cases to demonstrate many of my comments in the Introduction to the First Edition concerning the changing dynamic nature of Law, the degree of respect by the Court for the Doctrine of Stare Decisis, i.e., respect for prior decisions, and whether there exists a justifiable legal reason to change the law, not a mere political purpose to accomplish that which has been frustrated by legislative inaction.

We can also begin to notice different legal results in seemingly similar factual situations, particularly between different jurisdictions.

We can note how in the chapter on Use of Force to Effect an Arrest, the confirmation of the concept of the Klein Case demonstrated by Tennessee v. Garner, now the Law of the Land by the United States Supreme Court concerning Governmental action.

CONTENTS

CRIMINAL LAW PROCEDURE FOR PRIVATE SECURITY

Chapter 1

LEGAL BASES OF PRIVATE SECURITY

A. SELF-DEFENSE

1. USE OF FORCE TO PROTECT ONESELF (SELF-DEFENSE)

The right of a private citizen or entity to protect itself is based on the law of self-defense, a doctrine which allows one to use as much force as is reasonably necessary to protect one's person. It is a legal right with limitations and conditions. The legal doctrine of self-defense can be defined as the use of force to prevent the improper application of force against one's person, that of another, or one's property. Deadly force is generally defined as the kind of force likely or intended to cause death or serious bodily harm. Nondeadly force is, naturally, that kind of force not likely or intended to cause death or serious bodily harm.

Commonwealth v. Kendrick
Supreme Judicial Court of Massachusetts, 1966
351 Mass. 203, 218 N.E. 2d 408

Facts of Case

Defendant Kendrick was found guilty by a jury of murder in the second degree and he appealed. Kendrick was charged with the murder of Thomas Giangreco. Kendrick had been maintaining an amorous relationship with Giangreco's wife and had fathered a child born to her. One evening, defendant went to the Giangreco home to discuss with the deceased the prospect of Mrs. Giangreco obtaining a divorce. Defendant armed himself with a seven and a half inch long knife. The front door of the deceased's house is in the recessed area or alcove. While waiting for deceased to answer the door, he turned to see the deceased with a fireplace poker in his hand. While still in the alcove, the deceased struck the defendant in the shoulder with the fireplace poker; the second blow the defendant deflected with his left arm, but was hit on the nose. Defendant grappled with the deceased and tried to hold him off with his fists, could not, and drew his knife. Deceased's body was found near some bushes at least fifteen feet from the door area.

Court Opinion

"Hovering over the case are the admitted facts that the defendant armed himself with a deadly weapon and went, unbidden, to the deceased's house for the purpose of discussing with him a subject which the defendant knew would arouse Giangreco's strongest emotions and might produce violence. On the other hand, there is the countervailing circumstance, if the jury believed the defendant, that the confrontation and the mortal affray occurred before the defendant had an opportunity to mention the subject which he feared would provoke Giangreco to anger. Another circumstance which the jury could find was that a meeting of the two men in the Giangreco household was planned by the defendant but was neither sought nor expected by the deceased. They could find, however, that the actual place of the confrontation was a surprise to both. Giangreco had last seen the defendant, if indeed he had recognized him, at the kitchen window. He had no reason to suppose that the defendant had a knife in his pocket or belt. The defendant, on his part, expected Giangreco to meet him by opening the front door, unarmed. Instead, it could be found, Giangreco armed himself with the poker, left the house by the back door, and came around the end of the house to the front lawn. On the defendant's version, the clash in the recessed area of the front door could be found to have been a sudden combat in which the deceased was initially the aggressor. Commonwealth v. Baker, 246 Mass. 107, 117, 119. If the deceased initiated the assault with the poker while the defendant was cornered in the areaway of the door so that the defendant in fact feared and reasonably feared that he was in danger of being killed or suffering grievous bodily harm at the hands of Giangreco, he had the right to use whatever means were reasonably necessary to avert the threatened harm. Commonwealth v. Woodward, 102 Mass. 155, 161–162. In order to create a right to defend oneself with a dangerous weapon likely to cause serious injury or death, it must appear that the person using the weapon had a *reasonable apprehension of great bodily harm* and a *reasonable belief that no other means would suffice to prevent such harm.* Commonwealth v. Houston, 332 Mass. 687, 790, and cases cited. If the jury found that the circumstances immediately preceding and attending the killing created in the defendant the right to use the deadly weapon to defend himself against Giangreco, the homicide was excusable and the defendant was entitled to a verdict of not guilty. In substance the judge so instructed the jury. His instructions were correct as far as they went. The jury, however, should have been instructed further, upon the assumption that the deceased was the original assailant, that if the use of the knife by the defendant as a means of averting harm to himself was unreasonable and clearly excessive in light of the existing circumstances they should conclude that the defendant himself became the attacker and, since death resulted from his use of excessive force, he would be guilty of manslaughter. Ordinarily the question how far a party may go in self-defense is a question for the jury, not to be judged of very nicely, but with due regard to the infirmity of human impulses and passions. Monize v. Bagaso, 190 Mass. 87, 89 quoted in Commonwealth v. Huston, 332 Mass. 687, 790. The judge's charge left it to the jury to accept wholly or to reject self-defense as an excuse for the killing. We think that the legal consequence of using manifestly *disproportionate violence* in the supposed exercise of the right of self-defense should likewise have been known to the jury.

In passing upon the reasonableness of the force used by the defendant, again on the hypothesis that he was acting in self-defense, the jury should consider evidence of the *relative physical capabilities of the combatants, the characteristics of the weapons used,* and the *availability of maneuver room in, or means of escape from, the doorway area.* In addition, the distance from the doorway to the spot where the deceased's body was found could be a significant factor in determining who was doing the attacking when the deceased was felled.

Indeed, the place where the body was found might well be of significance in determining whether the defendant had the right of self-defense at all. If in fact, the confrontation and fight took place on the front lawn where the body was found, the right of self-defense might not be available to the defendant, since it might then appear that the defendant had a clear field to escape before delivering the lethal blows. The *right of self-defense does not accrue to a person until he has availed all proper means to avoid physical combat.* Commonwealth v. Peterson, 275 Mass. 437, 478. Commonwealth v. Trippi, 268 Mass. 227. Commonwealth v. Hartford, 346 Mass, 482, 490. The right of self-defense arises from necessity, and ends when the necessity ends.

The judgement was reversed, defendant's conviction of murder in the second degree was set aside, requiring a new trial.

Commonwealth v. Shaffer
Supreme Judicial Court of Massachusetts, 1975
367 Mass. 508, 326 N.E. 2d 880

TAURO, C.J. The defendant, having been indicted for murders, was tried and convicted of manslaughter and appealed pursuant to G.L. C. 278—section 33A–33G. The Appeals Court affirmed the judgement. Commonwealth v. Shaffer, 2 Mass. App. Ct. 658 (1974). We granted the defendant's application for further appellate review and we affirm the judgment of the Superior Court.

From the evidence, the jury could have found the following:

The defendant, who was separated from her husband and in the process of being divorced, resided with her two children in a one-story ranch house since 1971. The defendant had received several severe beatings at the hands of the victim, and on at least one occasion he had threatened to kill her and the children when asked to leave the defendant's home. Although the defendant loved the victim, she feared for herself and the children, and had persuaded him to seek psychiatric help.

On the morning of the homicide, the defendant was having breakfast with the victim when an argument ensued. At one point, the victim rose, saying "Never mind. I'll take care of you right now." The defendant threw a cup of tea at him and ran downstairs to the basement playroom, where the children were having breakfast and watching television.

Shortly thereafter, the victim opened the door at the top of the basement stairs and said, "If you don't come up these stairs, I'll come down and kill you and the kids." She started to telephone the police, but hung up the telephone when the victim said he would leave the house. Instead, he returned to the top of the stairs, at which time the defendant took a .22 caliber rifle from a rack on the wall and loaded it. She again started to telephone the police when the victim started down the stairs. She fired a fatal shot. More than five minutes elapsed from the time the defendant went to the basement until the shooting took place.

1. The defendant's principal argument for reversal is that the judge erred in his instructions to the jury regarding self-defense. She contends that the judge in effect instructed the jury that she had a duty to retreat

from her home and this was error. A review of the charge in its entirety discloses no error.

The defendant asks us in this case to adopt the majority rule that one assaulted in his own home need not retreat before resorting to the use of deadly force. See, e.g., People v. Tomlins, 213 N.Y. 240 (1914). See also the cases collected in Perkins, Criminal Law, 1005–1012 (2d ed. 1969) and in LaFave and Scott, Criminal SS 53 pp. 395–396 (1972). This has never been the law of the Commonwealth, and we see no reason to adopt it now. We prefer instead to follow our long-established rule that the right to use deadly force by way of self-defense is not available to one threatened until he has availed himself of all reasonable and proper means in the circumstances to avoid combat, Commonwealth v. Peterson, 257 Mass. 473, 478 (1926); Commonwealth v. Trippi, 268 Mass. 227, 232 (1929); Commonwealth v. Houston, 332 Mass. 687, 690 (1955); Commonwealth v. Hartford, 346 Mass. 482, 490 (1963); Commonwealth v. Kendrick, 351 Mass. 203, 212 (1966); Commonwealth v. Leate, 352 Mass. 452, 456 (1967); Commonwealth v. Decaro, 359 Mass. 388, 390 (1970), and *hold that this rule has equal application to one assaulted in his own home.*

This rule does not impose an absolute duty to retreat regardless of consideration of personal safety. The proper application of this doctrine does not require an innocent victim to increase his own peril out of regard for the safety of a murderous assailant, Perkins, op.cit., at 1010, because one need only retreat as far as necessary in the circumstances, until there is no probable means of escape. Commonwealth v. Crowley, 1168 Mass. 121, 126 (1897). Our rule gives due recognition to the value of human life, and requires that all available means for escape be exhausted. "The right of self-defense arises from necessity, and ends when the necessity ends." Commonwealth v. Kendrick, supra. See Bealte, Retreat from a Murderous Assault, 16 Harv. L. Rev. 567 (1903).

To what extent one who is threatened may go in defending himself and whether he has availed himself of all proper means of escape, ordinarily are questions of fact for the jury, to be decided in light of all the existing circumstances. Commonwealth v. Kendrick, 351 Mass. at 211 (1966). The jury must receive complete instructions from the trial judge, including an explanation of the proper factors to be considered in determining the issues of self-defense. The fact that one is threatened in his own home or in a place where he has exclusive right to be is one of the more important factors in making such determination, but this factor is not without limitations in this application. We stated in the Kendrick case that, "in passing upon the reasonableness of the force used by the defendant, . . . the jury should consider evidence of the relative physical capabilities of the combatants, the characteristics of the weapons used, and the availability of maneuver room in, or means of escape from, the . . . area (in which confrontation occurs)." 351 Mass. at 212 (1966) (fn. added). We would add that in determining whether all proper means have been taken to avoid the use of deadly force, the jury should be instructed that the location of the assault is an element of major importance in their consideration. We hold that one assaulted in his own home does not have the unlimited right to react with deadly force without any attempt at retreat. However, the importance of the location of the assault and the surrounding circumstances should be stressed to the jury.

In the instant case, the judge charged the jury that, in order for there to have been a proper exercise of self-defense, "It must appear that the defendant endeavored to avoid any further struggle and retreated as far as she could until there was not probable means of escape. In this connection, you may consider that the assault, if you find one took place, by the deceased took place in the home of the defendant where she had a right to be." This instruction, especially when considered with the charge as a whole, Commonwealth v. Pinnick, 354 Mass. 13, 15 (1968); Commonwealth v. Benders, 361 Mass. 704, 707 (1972), made clear that the location of the assault in the defendant's home was a proper factor to be considered. Reading the instructions as a whole, there is no merit to the defendant's argument that, in the circumstances of this case, they were misleading.

The defendant further argues that even if we do not adopt the majority rule, in the circumstances of the present case, the judge should have instructed the jury that the defendant, having already run to the basement, had no duty to retreat further. In doing so, she places much reliance on People v. Tomlins, 313 N.Y. 240 (1914), and State v. Bonano, 59, N.Y. 515 (1971). However, these cases make clear that even where no retreat is required, there are limitations to the use of deadly force in self-defense.

In the Tomlins case, at 244, the court said, "We think that if the situation justified the defendant as a reasonable man in believing that he was about to be murderously attacked, he had the right to stand his ground." And in the Bonano case, at 518, the court said, "Self-defense may be successfully invoked only in the cases where the act of killing is necessary or reasonably appears to be so in order to preserve the defendant's life or to protect him from serious bodily harm."

In the instant case, the jury could have found that the defendant was not in imminent danger for her life or of serious injury at the hands of the victim. There was *no evidence that he had a dangerous weapon at any time.* He was only two or three steps from the top of the stairway when he was shot. The defendant had ample opportunity to call the police. *She could have left the basement with her children.* A period of five minutes had elapsed from the time the defendant first went down to the basement until the shooting occurred. *The defendant did not warn the victim that she would shoot* if he continued his descent down the stairway. There was evidence from the defendant's husband that she had considerable experience in the use of that rifle. One shot was sufficient to kill the victim.

In these circumstances, there was no error in the judge's instruction to the jury, on the question of reasonableness, that the jury could consider the means of escape from the basement area. This is clearly a part of the *totality of circumstances* which must be considered in every case.

The judge's instructions were in keeping with our own rule that "in order to create a right to defend oneself with a dangerous weapon likely to cause serious injury or death, it must appear that the person using the weapon had a reasonable apprehension of great bodily harm and a reasonable belief that no other means would suffice to prevent such harm." Commonwealth v. Houston, 332 Mass. 687, 690 (1955).

For reasons stated, we believe the judge correctly instructed the jury that "(a) precondition to assert the defense of self-defense is that the person claiming it must have been assaulted (threatened) by the deceased in order to give rise to this defense whatsoever. There must be some overt act by the deceased threatening in nature to commit a battery likely to produce death or serious physical harm to the defendant or her children."

There is no merit to the defendant's argument that the word "assault" means a battery on the defendant. The legal definition of assault is an attempt or threat to do bodily harm, and the judge made that clear to the jury.

In sum, the judge's instructions to the jury required them to consider the totality of circumstances in deciding whether the shooting was in self-defense. There was no error.

At Place of Business

Further, the case of Commonwealth v. Gagne, 367 Mass. 519, 326 N.E. 2d 907 (1975), decided at the same time as the Shaffer case, establishes that where one's place of business is the scene of attack, the rule requiring retreat still applies. In this case a pharmacist, after closing, shot an intruder in his place of business.

"The defendant next argues that the judge erred in charging the jury that the defendant had a duty to retreat before resorting to the use of deadly force. There is no merit to this contention."

Although the defendant recognizes that we follow the rules that a person attacked with deadly force must retreat whenever it is possible to do so in safety, Commonwealth v. Crowley, 168 Mass. 121, 126 (1897), Commonwealth v. Houston, 332 Mass. 687, 690 (1955), Commonwealth v. Kendrick, 351 Mass. 203, 211–212 (1966), he urges us to create an exception where one is attacked in his place of business. See, e.g., State v. Sharpe, 18 N.C. App. 136 (1973); Commonwealth v. Johnson, 483 Pa. 485 (1970). See also anno. 41 A.L.R. 3d 584 (1972). In Commonwealth v. Shaffer ante, 508, 511 (1975), we were asked to adopt a similar exception where one is threatened in his own home. We declined to do so, holding that the location of the assault is just one of the factors, although an important one, to be considered by the jury. See Commonwealth v. Barton, ante, 515, 518 (1975). The reasoning of the Shaffer case applies equally to the instant case. Accordingly, there was no error in the judge's instruction that the right of self-defense does not accrue unless a person has reasonably availed himself of all proper means in his power to avoid the combat.

The defendant argues that even if there is a duty to retreat, the trial judge erred in failing to charge the jury specifically that they should consider that the assault took place in the defendant's place of business. Although we stated in the Barton case, supra, at 518, fn. 2, that the best procedure is for the judge to explain specifically what factors are to be considered, we cannot say that, taken as a whole, the charge in this case constituted reversible error. The judge instructed the jury to consider all the circumstances in determining whether the defendant was justified in using deadly force. He distinguished between an attack in the home and one on the highway, and left it for the jury to determine what the facts of this case required. In the light of all the circumstances, we find no error in the judge's charges.

1981 Regular Session

Crimes and Offenses—Killing or Injuring Person Unlawfully in Dwelling

Chap. 696. AN ACT PERMITTING THE KILLING OR INJURING OF A PERSON UNLAWFULLY IN A DWELLING.

Be it enacted, etc., as follows:

Chapter 278 of the General Laws is hereby amended by inserting after section 8 the following section:

Section 8A. In the prosecution of a person who is an occupant of a dwelling charged with killing or injuring one who was unlawfully in said dwelling, it shall be a defense that the occupant was in his dwelling at the time of the offense and that he acted in the reasonable belief that the person unlawfully in said dwelling was about to inflict great bodily injury or death upon said occupant or upon another person lawfully in said dwelling, and that said occupant used reasonable means to defend himself or such other person lawfully in said dwelling. There shall be no duty on said occupant to retreat from such person unlawfully in said dwelling.

Approved December 24, 1981.

Comment

The opinion of the appellate court in the Kendrick case discusses the legal principles of the law of self-defense, which can be memorized, but, very importantly sets forth certain factors considered to be significant by this court: in this case on the questions, (1) whether there was a right to use force in self-defense and (2) the reasonableness of the degree and amount of force used, to wit,

1. relative physical capabilities of the combatants,
2. characteristics of the weapons used,
3. availability of maneuver room or means of escape, and
4. location of the deceased's body.

The Shaffer and Gagne cases both decided on the same day in 1975, affirmed the duty of every person to use any and all reasonable means to avoid deadly combat before exercising the right of self-defense, and confirmed that this duty applies even if one is confronted at home or at one's place of business.

Over five years later, the legislature, apparently responding to political pressure caused by increasing crimes of violence, particularly in victims' homes passed a statute "permitting the killing or injuring of a person unlawfully in a dwelling." Governor Edward King signed this bill into law on December 24, 1981, effective March 24, 1982.

One of the functions of an appellate court is to decide on the proper application of a statute, raised as a defense. Assume that this statute was in effect at the time deadly force was used in the Shaffer and Gagne cases. In the Shaffer case, was the deceased "one who was unlawfully in said dwelling"? In the Gagne case, was the defendant an "occupant—in his dwelling at the time of the offense"?

Commonwealth v. Gregory
17 Mass. App 651
461 N.E. 2D 831 (1984)

BROWN, Judge.

The defendant appeals from his conviction of manslaughter on an indictment charging murder. At trial, the defendant admitted that he had killed the victim, but claimed that he acted in self-defense. The incident which gave rise to the indictment took place in the defendant's bedroom in his home. The defendant claims that the judge's charge on self-defense incorrectly implied, contrary to the recently enacted so-called "castle" law (G.L. c. 278, section 8A), that the defendant had a duty to retreat from an assailant while in his own home. The defendant also raises two less substantial evidentiary questions. We think that the judge misstated the law now applicable to the circumstances here. We reverse and remand this case to the Superior Court for a new trial.

Prior to the enactment of G.L. c. 278, ss 8A, the law imposed a duty on the occupant of a dwelling, to retreat before resorting to the use of deadly force for self-defense. Commonwealth v. Shaffer, 367 Mass. 508, 326, N.E. 2d 880 (1975). In *Shaffer,* the court was asked to adopt the majority rule that one assaulted in his own home need not retreat before resorting to the use of deadly force. The court declined, stating that "[w]e prefer instead to follow our long-established rule that the right to use deadly force by way of self-defense is not available to one threatened until he has availed himself of all reasonable and proper means in the circumstance to avoid combat [citations omitted], and hold that this rule has equal application to one assaulted in his own home." *Id.* at 511, 326 N.E. 2d 880. See also *Commonwealth v. Gagne,* 367 Mass. 519, 524–525, 326 N.E. 2d 907 (1975), and cases cited. With the enactment of section 8A the rule announced in *Shaffer* was modified so that now there is no obligation on the part of an occupant to retreat if he acts in a reasonable belief that a person unlawfully in his dwelling is about to inflict great bodily injury or death upon him.

[1] In the present case, the defendant made a timely objection to the judge's charge. The thrust of the defendant's claim is that because the incident occurred in his dwelling place the judge should have limited the instructions on self-defense merely to the question whether the defendant was reasonable in the use of the means by which he defended himself. In the defendant's view, therefore, it is not relevant whether he had exhausted all means of escape. The Commonwealth contends, however, that when the judge's instructions are read in their entirety, "it is clear that a reasonable juror would [have understood] that the defendant's obligation to avoid physical combat did in fact mean a duty to avail himself of all methods for doing so other than retreat." We, of course, must consider the charge as a whole in order to determine its adequacy and the over-all impact on the jury. *Commonwealth v. Sellon,* 380 Mass. 220, 231–232, 402 N.E. 2d 1329 (1980).

[2] The trial court's instructions here were substantially in accord with the law prior to the enactment of ss 8A. The following illustrates the language that permeated the charge on self-defense: "A person who is or reasonably believes that he is about to be attacked may repel deadly force with deadly force, so long as the danger appears to exist and *there is no* opportunity to avoid physical combat (emphasis supplied).2 Although a portion of the judge's instructions did track substantially the language of section 8A, it was immediately followed by the language: "The obligation not to retreat does not totally relieve a person from availing himself of all proper means to avoid physical combat. You are not required to retreat from your own home."3 This language may have confused the jurors. Moreover, the latter statement is flawed because the statute provides that there is no duty on the part of an occupant to retreat from *an unlawful intruder.*

[3] The Commonwealth maintains that by integrating established principles of self-defense with the new statutory provision the judge's instructions, when considered as a whole, articulated a clear and accept-

able definition of the right of nonretreat. The argument continues that the judge carefully avoided the use of such words as "retreat" or "escape." These arguments lack substance for two reasons. First, the trial judge's interpretation of section 8A was incorrect. The language of section 8A is not ambiguous. It states that "[t]here shall be no duty on said occupant to retreat from such person unlawfully in said dwelling." Second, the failure of the judge specifically to use the words "retreat" or "escape" is not determinative. Indeed, the court in *Shaffer* used the phrases "avoid combat" and "availability of maneuver room" interchangeably with "retreat" and escape." 367 Mass. at 511–513.

Judgment reversed verdict set aside.

Commonwealth v. Albert
391 Mass. 853, 466 N.E. 2D 78 (1984)

Before HENNESSEY, C.J., and ABRAMS, NOLAN, LYNCH and O'CONNOR, JJ. LYNCH, Justice.

The *defendant was convicted of murder in the first degree,* on November 24, 1982, and was sentenced to life imprisonment.

Although the two versions of the confrontation and the stabbing differ greatly up to this point, there is little dispute about what happened next. The police arrived soon after, and found the victim lying on the sidewalk outside the apartment building. A search revealed no weapons on the victim's person or in the immediate area. After speaking with Harvey and persons in a crowd that had gathered, the police approached the defendant, who was standing at the periphery of the group. Upon being informed of his rights, the defendant confessed to the stabbing, and directed the police to his apartment for retrieval of the knife. An officer went upstairs, noticing along the way bloodstains in the stairwell which extended into the defendant's apartment. After the knife was found, the defendant was taken to the police station and then to the hospital for treatment of the cut on his hand. No tests were done to determine whether the blood found in the defendant's apartment was his or that of the victim. The autopsy of the victim revealed that he had died of five stab wounds, of which two had been inflicted to his back, two to his forehead, and one to his chest.

---

[7] The defendant additionally contends that the judge employed an incorrect definition of "dwelling" in explaining the applicability G.L. c. 278, section 8A. The judge instructed the jury in accordance with that statute. The judge defined "dwelling" as a place where one is "temporarily or permanently residing and which is in [one's] exclusive possession." With reference to an apartment building, the judge stated that "a tenant's dwelling cannot reasonably be said to extend beyond his own apartment and perhaps any separate areas subject to his exclusive control."

This definition accords with our interpretation of the term "dwelling" in analogous contexts. *Commonwealth v. Seay,* 376 Mass. 735, 742, 383 N.E. 2d 828 (1978) (right to carry firearm without license while in one's dwelling). *Commonwealth v. Thomas,* 358 Mass. 771, 774–775, 267 N.E. 2d 489 (1971) (search of cellar did not invade area within the "curtilage" of defendant's apartment). As we observed in *Seay,* "[t]he interest of an apartment dweller in defending himself—the only apparent reason for allowing him to carry a firearm in his own dwelling in the first place—is clearly attenuated when he passes his doorway to enter a common area offering easy retreat." *Seay supra* 376 Mass. at 742–743, 383 N.E.2d 828. There was no error in the judge's instructions in this regard.

Judgment Affirmed

Comment
In Commonwealth v. Gregory

A Massachusetts intermediate Appellate Court reverses a manslaughter conviction because of an improper change to the jury by the trial judge, because it implied that the defendant had a duty to retreat from his own dwelling. This court clearly approved the statutory modification of the judicial rule of a "duty to retreat" before resort to deadly force in self-defense, to the legislative "no duty to retreat." Note well that the judicial system is now approving a legislative reversal of previous law, i.e., the duty to retreat from one's dwelling.

In Commonwealth v. Albert, the highest Appellate Court in Massachusetts impliedly accepts the statute as an established definition of "dwelling" as properly applied to this statute.

USE OF FORCE TO PROTECT ANOTHER PERSON

Since a private person has a limited right of self-defense, the next question which arises is whether a person may use force to defend *another person* who is being attacked unlawfully. A recent case, arising under rather bizarre circumstances, established that right, but as is quite common in law, with limitation.

Commonwealth v. Martin
Supreme Court of Massachusetts,
369 Mass. 640, 341 N.E. 2d 885 (1976)

KAPLAN, Justice. The defendant Daniel R. Martin appeals under G.L. c. 278—section 33A–33G, from his multiple convictions, described in the margin,1 arising from a clash between inmates and guards at Massachusetts Correctional Institution at Concord on October 15, 1972. The issue on appeal is whether the trial judge committed error in failing to instruct the jury with respect to the defendant's claimed justification or defense, namely, that the acts of which he was accused were part of an attempt on his part to come to the aid of a fellow inmate and friend, Gene Tremblay (tried and convicted together with the defendant), who was being unlawfully beaten by prison guards.

We sketch very briefly the facts as they appeared at trial. The prosecution was, of course, intent to show that the defendant's acts were simply aggressive attacks on the officers in a prison brawl, while the defendant strove to prove that he acted honestly and reasonably upon observing the inmate Tremblay being beaten by the officers.

The evidence on the part of the defendant, summarized above, was sufficient to lay a basis for a charge to the jury on the justification claimed by him.

The judge instructed the jury with respect to self-defense and even related these instructions to the question whether the defendant was privileged to use a dangerous weapon to protect himself from attack by Officer Quealey. But he gave the jury *no* instruction on the subject of the privileged use of force to protect *another.* This failure seems to have been due to the judge's belief that the claimed justification was not recognized in the law of Massachusetts.

We hold that a justification corresponding roughly to that quoted from the Illinois statute is recognized by the law of the Commonwealth.

Of course, the justification may exist although it is not found in so many words in our statute law: it may be read into the definition of a statutory offense or considered a common-law adjunct to, or qualification of, the offense. This is easily accepted and understood as to the more commonplace justification of self-defense. See Commonwealth v. Shaffer, —Mass.—, 326 N.E. 2d 880 (1975) and the many cases cited; United States v. Grimes, 413F. 2d 1376–1379 (7th Cir. 1969).

There is some, but not much, light in the decided cases in this jurisdiction about justified force and in aid of another. In Commonwealth v. Cooley, 6 Gray 350 (1856), H. and A. Cooley apparently interfered in the arrest of a relative, B. Cooley, by one Rice, an assistant marshal of Springfield, and they were indicted in a first count for assault on Rice as an officer, and in a second count for common assault on him. A majority of the court held the following charge proper (although possibly too favorable to the defendants): "If Harrison and A.M. Cooley, not knowing that Rice was an officer and acting in discharge of his duty, but interposed for the purpose of arresting or quelling a fight or breach of the peace, they would not be liable for so doing, unless they used more force or violence then would have been necessary for that purpose; and if they did interpose for the purpose of arresting a fight, and used more force than was necessary for that purpose, they would be liable on the second count (Id. at 354). Somewhat closer in point is Commonwealth v. Malone, 114 Mass. 295 (1873), where the defendant assaulted a young girl in the presence of her mother; the mother struck the defendant, and the defendant retaliated, for which assault he was charged. The defendant's request for an instruction that the mother was not entitled to use force to defend her daughter was held properly refused and the following instruction properly given: "... the law gives the right, if the defendant was inflicting great violence on the daughter's person. The mother had a right to use as much force as was reasonably necessary to protect her person from great injury, and if she did not use more force than was reasonably necessary for that purpose, the use of such force was no justification of the defendant's blow upon Mrs. Rennehan" (*Id.* at 296). These cases are suggestive but laconic. The paucity of direct authority is perhaps explained by the likelihood that one coming to the defense of another may himself be under attack, and may thus simply claim self-defense, a less esoteric justification.

Whatever the precise precedents, it is hardly conceivable that the law of the Commonwealth, or indeed, of any jurisdiction, should mark as criminal those who intervene forcibly to protect others; for the law to do so would aggravate the fears which lead to the alienation of people from one another, an alienation symbolized for our time by the notorious Genovese incident. To the fear of "involvement" and of injury to oneself if one answered a call for help would be added the fear of possible prosecution.

It became necessary to sketch the conditions justifying the use of intervening protective force. An actor is justified in using force against another to protect a third person when (a) a reasonable person in the actor's position would believe his intervention to be necessary for the protection of the third person, and (b) in the circumstances as that reasonable person would believe them to be, the third person would be justified in using such force to protect himself. The reasonableness of the belief may depend in part on the relationships among the persons involved (a matter to which we return below). The actor's justification is lost if he uses excessive force unwarranted for the protective purpose.

Of course, the subject cannot be exhausted in a paragraph. Without subscribing in advance to all the relevant provisions of the Model Penal Code of the American Law Institute, we recommended it for study. Accelerated by that Code, the trend, which is exemplified by legislation adopted in many states, has been to interweave closely the justification of defense of a third person with self-defense; to eliminate some earlier authority restricting the justification of third person defense to situations where the third person is seen retrospectively to have been entitled to use force in his own defense (regardless of the belief, which might be mistaken, of the "reasonable person" at the time); and to remove earlier artificial or factitious restrictions of the justification, e.g., restriction of protection of spouse, child, parent, master, or servant.

One such possible factitious restriction was rejected, we think correctly, in United States v. Grimes, 413 F. 3d 1376 (7th Cir. 1969), a case resembling the present. The defendant Grimes, an inmate of the federal penitentiary in Marion, Illinois, seeing (as he claimed) a fellow inmate Reid, being beaten by prison guards with metal flashlights, ran to Reid's aid and struck one of the guards. Grimes was indicted and convicted of assault upon an employee of a United States Correctional Institution (18 U.S.C. Section 111, 1114 (1970)). On appeal, it was held that the trial erred in refusing a jury instruction regarding justified use of force to protect a third person. The court spoke as follows to the point that, while the justification might be suitable generally, it should be rejected in the prison context because of its effect on institutional discipline: "We perceive no serious threat to prison discipline from a defense which merely protects inmates from unauthorized physical abuse by overzealous officials. Our decision in no way limits the power of prison officials to restrain or subdue unruly inmates, to carry out all reasonable orders necessary for the maintenance of prison discipline, or to cope with attempted assaults or escapes by prison inmates. See A.L.I. Model Penal Code ss 3.07, 3.08 (Proposed Official Draft 1962). The Government's concern that recognition of this limited defense will emasculate section ss 111 is belied by the fact that since 1905, when this statute was originally enacted, this is apparently the first such case."

We agree with the court in the Grimes case that the justification of defense of a third person does not necessarily stop short at the prison gates. But the fact that an episode occurs in prison may have considerable significance. So the question of the reasonableness of a belief that an inmate would be justified in using force against a prison guard, thus justifying intervening protective force, is conditioned by the fact that the guard, by the nature of his job, is himself privileged to apply force to inmates when necessary to preserve order in the institution. Therefore, the guard's mere taking an inmate to custody or holding him in custody would not be a proper occasion for intervening force. This may have an important bearing on the present case in the event of retrial. Judgements reversed. Verdict set aside.

Comment

The reader should note that in Commonwealth v. Martin the Supreme Judicial Court decided a rule of law allowing the use of force by a person in aid of another person not related to the actor, a point of law which had never been decided and on which there was no legislation. Was this judicial legislation?

Note also that this court did not subscribe to or adopt provisions of the Model Penal Code, but did "recommend it for study." The Model Penal Code is a recommendation of legal scholars as to what they think the law should be and a codification of the law in statute form. Do you think that the court's recommendation for study was addressed to the legislature to act further on this issue?

It is interesting to note that prior to Commonwealth v. Martin, decided in 1976, there was no firm legal authority, either case law or statute, allowing one person to use force to defend another person who was under attack. One wonders by what legal authority a bodyguard could act to defend the person who hired the bodyguard. In civil law (non-criminal) there is a doctrine known as RESPONDEAT SUPERIOR that imposes civil liability (i.e., money damages) on the MASTER for civil wrongs committed by a SERVANT in the course of the SERVANT'S employment. The test to determine whether or not a Master-Servant relationship exists is whether or not there existed a *right to control.* If "A" hires "B" to perform certain duties and "A" has the right to control "B", the Master-Servant relationship exists, and the doctrine of Respondeat Superior creates civil liability on the Master (in addition to the Servant) for civil wrongs (negligence, assault, battery, etc.) committed by the Servant in the course of employment.

One can reasonably wonder by what legal basis a person could, prior to 1976, grant to another person a right or privilege that did not firmly exist in law.

USE OF FORCE TO DEFEND OR REGAIN PROPERTY

There follows a case establishing one's right to use force to defend one's property (not person), but only reasonable nondeadly force. The use of deadly force or excessive, nondeadly force is not legally justifiable solely to defend one's property.

Commonwealth v. Donahue
Supreme Judicial Court of Massachusetts, 1889
148 Mass. 529, 20 N.E. 177

HOLMES, J. This is an indictment for robbery, in which the defendant had been found guilty of an assault. The evidence for the Commonwealth was, that the defendant had bought clothes amounting to $21.55 of one Mitchelman, who called at the defendant's house, by appointment, for his pay; that some discussion arose about the bill, and that the defendant went upstairs, brought down the clothes, placed them on a chair and put $20.00 on the table, and told Mitchelman that he could have the money or the clothes; that Mitchelman took the money, and put it in his pocket, and told the defendant he owed him $1.55, whereupon the defendant demanded his money back, and, on Mitchelman refusing, attacked him, threw him on the floor, and choked him, until Mitchelman gave him a pocketbook containing $29.00. The defendant's counsel denied the receiving of the pocketbook, and said that he could show that the assault was justifiable under the circumstances of the case, as the defendant believed that he had a right to recover his own money by force, if necessary. The presiding justice stated that he should be obliged to rule that the defendant would not be justified in assaulting Mitchelman to get his own money, and that he should rule as follows:

"If the jury are satisfied that the defendant choked and otherwise assaulted Mitchelman, they would be warranted in finding the defendant guilty, although the sole motive of the defendant was by this violence to get from Mitchelman by force money which the defendant honestly believed to be his own." Upon this the defendant saved his exceptions, and declined to introduce evidence; the jury were instructed as stated, and found the defendant guilty.

It is settled by ancient and modern authority that under such circumstances a man may defend or regain his momentarily interrupted possession by the use of reasonable force, short of wounding, or the employment of a dangerous weapon. To this extent the right to protect one's possession has been regarded as an extension of the right to protect one's person, with which it is generally mentioned (Baldwin v. Hayden, 6 Conn. 453; Y.B. 19 Hen. V1 31, pl. 59. Rogers v. Spence, EB Mees. Section W. 579; 1 Hawk. P.C. c. 60 SS 23; 3 Bl. Comm. 120, 131).

We need not consider whether this explanation is quite adequate. There are weighty decisions which go further than those above cited, and which hardly can stand on the right of self-defense, but involve other considerations of policy. It has been held that even where a considerable time had elapsed between the wrongful taking of the defendant's property and the assault, the defendant had a right to regain possession by reasonable force, after demand upon the third person in possession, in like manner as he might have protected it without civil liability. Whatever the true rule may be, probably there is no difference in this respect between the civil and criminal law (Blades v. Higgs, 10 C.B. (N.S.) 713, 12 C.B. (N.S.) 501, 13 C.B. (N.S.) 844, 11 H.L. Cas. 621; Commonwealth v. McCue, 16 Gray, 226, 227). The principle has been extended to a case where the defendant had yielded possession to the person assaulted, through the fraud of the latter (Hodgeden v. Hubbard 18 Vt. 504) (see Johnson v. Perry, 56 Vt. 703). On the other hand, a distinction has been taken between the right to maintain possession and the right to regain it from another who is peaceably established in it, although the possession of the latter is wrongful (Bob v. Bosworth, Litt.

Sel. Cas. 81) (see Barnes v. Martin, 15 Wis, 240; Andre v. Johnson, 6 Balckf. 375; Davis v. Whitridge, 2 Strob. 232; 3 Bl. Comm. 4. It is necessary to decide whether in this case, if Mitchelman had taken the money with a fraudulent intent, but had not repudiated the condition until afterwards, the defendant would have had any other remedy than to hold him to his bargain, if he could, even if he knew that Mitchelman still had the identical money on his person. If the force used by the defendant was excessive, the jury would have been warranted in finding him guilty. Whether it was excessive or not was a question for them; the judge could not rule that it was not, as a matter of law. Therefore, the instruction given to them, taken only literally, was correct. But the preliminary statement went further, and was erroneous; and, coupling that statement with the defendant's offer of proof, and his course after the rulings, we think it fair to assume that the instruction was not understood to be limited, or indeed to be directed to the case of excessive force, which, so far as appears, had not been mentioned, but that it was intended and understood to mean that any assault to regain his own money would warrant finding the defendant guilty. Therefore the exception must be sustained.

It will be seen that our decision is irrespective of the defendant's belief as to what he had a right to do. If the charge of robbery had been persisted in, and the difficulties which we have stated could have been got over, we might have had to consider cases like Reg. v. Boden, 1 Car. SS K. 395, 41 Iowa, 200 (Compare Comm v. Stebbins, ubi supra; Comm, v. McDuffy, 126 Mass. 467). There is no question here of the effect of a reasonable belief with regard to the facts.

Exceptions sustained.

Comment

This 1889 case may appear confusing. At the trial, the judge instructed the jury that if they believed that the defendant assaulted and choked Mitchelman, they could find him guilty of assault. The defense counsel argued that if allowed, he could prove that defendant was justified in assaulting Mitchelman. The judge indicated that defendant could not be justified in assaulting Mitchelman to regain his own money. Defense counsel objected to this ruling, and "excepted" (a legal term), thereby preserving his right of appeal to the Supreme Judicial Court to determine the correct law on the legal issue as to whether a person may use reasonable force to protect or regain property. Mr. Justice Holmes indicated that the correct law was that one may use reasonable force to defend or regain his momentarily interrupted possession of his property, but one may *not* use *excessive or deadly force.*

STATUTORY BASIS FOR COMMERCIAL PRIVATE SECURITY

Massachusetts General Laws, Chapter 147, Section 22 through 30, requires that any person engaging in the private detective business or the business of watch, guard or patrol agency must obtain a license to do so from the Commissioner of Public Safety. This licensing requirement applies to those commercial firms which engage in, or solicit, such business "for hire, fee or reward." Section 23 excepts certain persons, including those who are employed by a licensee, or by another business in connection with the regular and customary business of the employer and whose services are not let out to another for profit or gain. Sections 27 and 30 specifically prohibit certain activities by licensees, mostly in connection with labor conditions and strikes, including an undercover assignment for such purposes. An opinion of the Attorney General (June 7, 1976) indicates a person who has a private detective license may also engage in the "watch, guard or patrol business," but no such indication is available for the opposite, probably, because the private detective license requirements include specific prior experience in law enforcement.

It is also noted that this statute prohibits a licensee from hiring any person who has been convicted of a felony, or a misdemeanor "involving moral turpitude." However, the confidentiality of particular Criminal Records maintained by law enforcement agencies and most trial courts precludes a licensee from legitimately checking such records to determine if an applicant for employment is eligible for hiring. Some states have taken steps to address this apparent Catch-22.

Comment

It is extremely important that private security persons fully understand the law of self-defense, particularly with regard to protection of property only, where the use of deadly force cannot be justified. Deadly force cannot be used to prevent the pure theft of property. Even the 1981 Massachusetts statute permitting the killing or injuring of a person unlawfully in a dwelling requires that the lawful occupant act "in the reasonable belief that the person unlawfully in said dwelling was about to inflict great bodily injury or death . . . " Only reasonable, nondeadly force may be used to protect property only. The case of Commonwealth v. Klein (Chapter 3) definitely prohibits the use of deadly force in the apprehension and arrest of a criminal fleeing from a crime involving only property.

In concluding this chapter on the legal doctrine of self-defense as justification for otherwise criminal acts, it is clear that *the best defense is NOT a good offense!!*

Chapter 2

POWER OF ARREST

As stated previously, a private security person has the same legal rights and powers as a private citizen. Therefore, when inquiring as to the legal power of a private security person to arrest, without an arrest warrant, we must determine the law as to private citizens.

Generally, arrest can be defined as the taking into custody or restraining the freedom of movement of another person in order to bring the arrested person before a court to answer a criminal charge. For an arrest to be complete there should be an intent to make an arrest, communication of this intent to the person to be arrested, and physical restraint of the arrestee or submission by the arrestee.

For our purposes, crimes are broadly classified as felonies or misdemeanors. It is important to be able to distinguish whether a certain criminal act is a felony or misdemeanor. In Massachusetts, a felony is distinguished from a misdemeanor on the basis of the possible sentence for conviction for that crime. If, for a certain crime, the perpetrator can possibly be sentenced to any term in a state prison (as opposed to a house of correction or jail), that crime is a felony. If not, the crime is a misdemeanor.

MISDEMEANOR

The power to arrest for a misdemeanor without a warrant is the same for police officers and private citizens.

In 1925, Chief Justice William Howard Taft, writing for the United States Supreme Court in Carroll v. United States, 267 U.S. 132 at 157, stated:

> 'In cases of misdemeanor, a peace officer like a private person has at common law no power of arresting without a warrant except when a breach of peace is about to be committed in his presence or there is reasonable grounds for supposing that a breach of peace is about to be committed or renewed in his presence," Halsbury's Laws of England, Vol. 9, part III, 612.

Commonwealth v. Gorman
Supreme Judicial Court of Massachusetts, 1934
288 Mass. 294, 192 N.E. 618

The defendant contended that the right of an officer to arrest without a warrant for an offense relating to the operation or control of motor vehicles is limited by G.L. (Ter. Ed.) C.90, Section 21, to the arrest of an operator who does not have in his possession a license to operate motor vehicles; and that only an investigator or examiner appointed by the registrar of motor vehicles may arrest without a warrant, for the offense of operating a motor vehicle while under the influence of intoxicating liquor, one who possesses such a license.

We think, however, that the statute relied on does not by implication cut down the common law authority of an officer. State police officers have throughout the Commonwealth "all the powers of constable, except the service of civil process, and of police officers and watchmen." G.L. (Ter. Ed.) C.22, Section 9A. Constables have common law power as peace officers to make arrests without warrants in cases in which such arrests are permitted by law. Hartley v. Granville, 216 Mass. 38. Commonwealth v. Hastings, 9 Met. 259. In Sharrock v. Hannemer, Cro. Eliz. 375, 376, Beaumond (Beaumont), J., said, "A constable and sheriff are conservators of the peace at common law."

The offense of operating a motor vehicle while under the influence of intoxicating liquor is classified by our statute as a misdemeanor. G.L. (Ter. Ed.) C.274, Section 1; C.90, Section 24. St. 1932, C.26. For the common law, see Commonwealth v. Carey, 12 Cush. 246, 252; Jones v. Robbins, & Gray, 329, 347–350; Kurtz v. Moffitt, 115 U.S. 487, 499. *A peace officer, in the absence of statute* (Commonwealth v. Wright, 158 Mass. 149, 159;) *may arrest without a warrant for a misdemeanor which* (1) *involves a breach of the peace,* (2) *is committed in the presence or view of the officer* (Commonwealth b. McLaughlin, 12 Cush. 615; 81 Mass. 74; McLennon v. Richardson, 15 Gray, 74; Commonwealth v. Ruggles, 6 Allen, 588, 590; Carroll v. United States, 267 U.S. 132, 156, 157), *and* (3) *is still continuing at the time of the arrest or only interrupted, so that the offense and the arrest form parts of one transaction.* Commonwealth v. Hastings, 9 Met. 25, 263. Leddy v. Crossman, 108 Mass. 237. Scott v. Eldridge, 154 Mass. 25. Eldredge v. Mitchell, 214 Mass. 480, 483. Price v. Seeley, 10 Cl. & Fin. 28. Regina v. Light, 7 Cox C.C. 389. See also Am. Law Inst. Restatement: Torts, Section 119, 121, 140, 141. In Regina v. Tooley, 2 Ld. Raym, 1296, 1301; S.C. 11

Mod. 242, 250, Lord Chief Justice Holt states the rule as follows: "A constable cannot arrest but where he sees an actual breach of the peace; and if the affray be over, . . . he cannot arrest." In the same case, reported in Holt, 485, 490, sub nomine Case of the Reforming Constables, his statement reads, "A constable may arrest a man that breaks the law in his view, but if it be done out of his view he cannot." In the present case, the only point upon which there can be doubt as to the right to arrest without a warrant *is whether the offense involves a breach of the peace.*

The breach of the peace that justifies arrest for a misdemeanor without warrant must be something more than that which used to be alleged in indictments and complaints as a legal incident of every criminal offense. See G.L. (Ter. Ed.) C. 277, Section 33. Not every misdemeanor involves a breach of the peace. For example, *the possession of short lobster involves none,* Commonwealth v. Wright, 158 Mass. 149, 159, 33 N.E. 82, 19 L.R.A. 206, 35 Am. St. Rep. 475; *voluntary drunkenness in private,* though a crime (Commonwealth v. Conlin, 184 Mass. 195, 68 N.E. 207), is not of itself a breach of the peace (Commonwealth v. O'Connor, 7 Allen, 583). Compare statutory rights of arrest for drunkenness. G.L. (Terr. Ed.) C. 272, Section 44; Commonwealth v. Cheney, 141 Mass. 102, 6 N.E. 724, 55 Am. Rep. 448; Trebeck v. Croudace, (1918) 1 K.B. 158. On the other hand, *an affray or assault* is a typical breach of the peace. Commonwealth v. Tobin, 108 Mass. 426, 429, 11 Am. Rep. 375; Leddy v. Crossman, 108 Mass. 237. In Ford v. Breen, 173 Mass. 52, 53 N.E. 136, *violent, profane and obscene language used in a dwelling to the annoyance of persons outside was deemed a breach of the peace.* See also Commonwealth v. Foley, 99 Mass. 497; Commonwealth v. Oaks, 113 Mass. 8. This case does not require us to draw the line among conflicting decisions in other jurisdictions for the purpose of classifying offenses as involving a breach of the peace, or not. *It is worth notice, however, that in United States v. Hart,* Fed. Cas. No. 15, 213, Pet. C. C.390 Washington, J., *held that driving a carriage at an immoderate rate of speed through a principal street was a breach of the peace, justifying an arrest by a constable without a warrant.*

If there is a present criminal offense (Quinn v. Heisel, 40 Mich. 576), the breach of the peace that justifies arrest without a warrant may be a prospective or anticipated one. An officer who sees a person committing a misdemeanor of such a sort that a breach of the peace is likely to follow unless the offender be restrained, need not delay an arrest until the harm has been done, nor limit his acts of restraint or detention to those which may be necessary merely to prevent the expected breach (Commonwealth

v. Hastings, 9 Met. Ch. 263, 263). We think that the dictum of Bankes, L.J., in Trebeck v. Croudace, (1918) I. K.B. 158, 166, states the common law. He said: "From the very nature of things the arrest of a drunken person in the street may very frequently be justified on the ground of an anticipated breach of the peace, and *particularly so when the alleged offender is in charge either of a loaded gun, or of a motor vehicle, both dangerous instruments from the point of view of the public safety when in the hands of a drunken person.*" The only difference between the case so stated, and the present defendant was not that he was intoxicated or in a drunken condition, but merely that he was under the influence of intoxicating liquor. Commonwealth v. Lyseth, 250 Mass. 555, 558, 146 N.E. 18; State v. Rodgers, 91 N.J. Law, 212, 215, 102 A. 433. *But even that milder degree of alcoholic effect is likely to make an operator of a motor vehicle a public menace and to induce in him such reckless conduct as may make him criminally responsible for unintended assault and even manslaughter* (Banks v. Braman, 188 Mass. 367, 369, 74 N.E. 594; Commonwealth v. Arone, 265 Mass. 128, 163, N.E. 758). *In our opinion, the offense involves a breach of the peace, and justifies an officer in arresting without a warrant a person whom he sees in the act of committing it.*

Comment

We see in the Carroll v. United States case, certainly not a binding precedent for Massachusetts, that Chief Justice William Howard Taft equates the power of a private person to arrest for a misdemeanor to that of a peace officer. Then the Gorman case sets forth the required elements before a peace officer may arrest without a warrant for a misdemeanor, i.e. (1) committed in his presence, (2) is still continuing, and (3) which amounts to a Breach of Peace. Since the legal issue in the Gorman case was only the question of whether or not the misdemeanor involving the operation of a motor vehicle while under the influence of intoxicating liquor is a BREACH OF THE PEACE, answering that it is and justifies the arrest by a peace officer, if the other two elements are present.

The following case demonstrates a limitation on the power of arrest by a peace officer, but more importantly, for our purposes, the changing nature of the law. It spends time discussing the power of a police officer to arrest without a warrant for a misdemeanor outside his jurisdiction, when not in fresh pursuit, as the same as a private person, but now decides in Grise, as a case of first impressions concerning the power of a private person to arrest for a misdemeanor, that a private person has no right in Massachusetts to arrest for a misdemeanor, but recognizing that Carroll v. United States was the rule at common law in Merry Olde England, allowing such an arrest for a misdemeanor involving a breach of the peace.

Commonwealth v. Grise
Supreme Judicial Court of Massachusetts
398 Mass 247, 496 N.E.2D 162 (1986)

HENNESSEY, Chief Judge.

The question of first impression presented by this case is whether a police officer lawfully may arrest a motorist for operating under the influence of intoxicating liquor, G.L. c. 90, Section 24 (1984 ed.), outside of the officer's territorial jurisdiction, where the arresting officer was not in "fresh and continued pursuit" of the motorist. G.L. c. 41, Section 98A (1984 ed.).

On December 12, 1984, two officers of the Ludlow police department, operating a marked Ludlow police cruiser, were stopped at a traffic light at an intersection in the city of Springfield. One of the officers, Basil Crandell, observed the defendant's motor vehicle traveling through the intersection while the light was red. The officers waited until the traffic light had turned green and then followed the defendant's vehicle. Officer Crandell observed the defendant's vehicle crossing the center line of the roadway repeatedly and weaving back and forth between the two westbound lanes. Believing that the defendant may have been operating under the influence of intoxicating liquor, Officer Crandell put on the overhead blue lights of the police cruiser and stopped the defendant's car within the Springfield city limits. Based upon his observations of the defendant, Officer Crandell arrested him for operating under the influence of intoxicating liquor. He placed the defendant in the Ludlow police cruiser, and called the Springfield police for assistance. Springfield police officers transported the defendant to the Springfield Police Department. He was cited for operating a motor vehicle while under the influence of intoxicating liquor, G.L. c. 90, Section 24.

On May 20, 1985, the defendant filed a motion to dismiss the complaint on the ground that his arrest occurred outside of the territorial jurisdiction of the arresting officer. The judge allowed the defendant's motion to dismiss, ruling that (1) Officer Grandell was outside of his jurisdiction and not in "fresh and continued pursuit" of the defendant at the time of making the arrest, G.L. c. 41, Section 98A, and therefore was acting as a private citizen; and (2) a private citizen has no authority to arrest for traffic violations or for operating under the influence of intoxicating liquor. The Commonwealth appealed this dismissal, Crim. P. 15 (a)(1), 378 Mass. 882 (1979), and we transferred the case here on our own motion. We affirm.

[1] When executing a warrant of arrest, a police officer's power is Statewide. G.L. c. 41, Section 95, 98 (1984 ed.). Commonwealth v. Martin, 98 Mass. 4 (1867). However, the power of a police officer at common law to make an arrest without a warrant is limited to the boundaries of the governmental unit by which he was appointed, unless the police officer is acting in fresh and continued pursuit of a suspected felon who has committed an offense in the officer's presence and within his territorial jurisdiction. Commonwealth v. Harris, 11 Mass.App.Ct. 165, 168, 415 N.E.2d 216 (1981). See K.B. Smith, Criminal Practice and Procedure Section 100 (1983); 5 Am.Jur.2d Arrest Section 50 (Supp. 1985); Rep. A.G.Pub.Doc. No. 12, at 136–137 (1967). In 1967, the Legislature broadened this common law rule by allowing extraterritorial "fresh pursuit" arrests for any offense, felony, or misdemeanor, committed in the arresting officer's presence and within his jurisdiction. G.L. c. 41, Section 98A, inserted by St. 1967, c. 263. This statute empowers a police officer to make a warrantless, extraterritorial arrest of a suspect who is being pursued into a neighboring town. However, G.L. c. 41, Section 98A, does not validate the arrest in this case, since the Ludlow police officer's observation, pursuit and arrest of the defendant all occurred in Springfield.

[2] When a police officer makes a warrantless arrest outside of his jurisdiction and not in "fresh and continued pursuit" of the suspect within the meaning of G.L. c. 41, Section 98A, then he acts as a private citizen, and the arrest will be held valid only if a private citizen would be justified in making the arrest under the same circumstances. Commonwealth v. Gullick, 386 Mass. 278, 282, 435 N.E.2d 348 (1982) (Massachusetts State trooper lawfully arrested felon in New Hampshire). Commonwealth v. Harris, supra, 11 Mass.App.Ct. at 168–170, 415 N.E.2d 216 (Revere police officers lawfully arrested suspected felon in Chelsea). When police officers leave their jurisdiction "they cease[] to be officers but they d[o] not cease to be persons." *Id.* Thus the critical issue is whether a private citizen would have been authorized to arrest the defendant in the circumstances of this case.

[3] In Massachusetts a private citizen may lawfully arrest someone who has in fact committed a felony. Commonwealth v. Lussier, 333 Mass. 83, 92, 128 N.E.2d 569 (1955). Commonwealth v. Colitz, 13 Mass.App.Ct. 215, 220, 431 N.E.2d 600 (1982). However, operating a motor vehicle while under the influence of liquor is a misdemeanor. See G.L. c. 90, Section 24; G.L. c. 274, Section 1 (1984 ed.). This court has never squarely addressed the issue of a private person's power to arrest for a misdemeanor. The Commonwealth urges us to adopt a rule which would allow a private person, like a police officer, to arrest a suspect for a misdemeanor amounting to a breach of the peace which is committed in the arresting person's presence. This was the rule at common law in England. See Timothy v. Simpson, 1 Crompton M. & R 757, 762–763 (1835); 10 Halsbury's Laws of England at 343 (1955); Carroll v. United States, 267 U.S. 132, 157, 45 S.Ct. 280, 286, 69 L.Ed. 543 (1925). Numerous jurisdictions in this country allow for such arrests. See Cal. Penal Code Section 837 (Deering 1983); Me. Rev.Stat.Ann. tit. 17-A, Section 16 (1964); Minn. Stat. Section 629.37 (Supp. 1985); Miss. Code Ann. Section 99-3-7 (1972); S.D. Codified Laws Ann. Section 23A-3-3 (1979). However, other jurisdictions limit a private person's power of arrest to felonies. See Ark. Stat. Ann. Section 43-404 (1977); Mich. Comp.Laws Section 764.16 (1979); Ohio Rev. Code Ann. Section 2935.04 (Baldwin 1979); Schachter v. State, 338 So.2d 269 (Fla. Dist. Ct. App. 1976). In the absence of legislative direction, we believe the latter approach to be more sound. Although the Commonwealth advances strong arguments in favor of allowing a private person to abate or prevent a disruption of the peace, there are equally compelling policy reasons for limiting such powers of arrest to police officers. Since "breach of the peace" may be construed by laymen as a somewhat elastic concept, empowering private persons to arrest for such misdemeanors might only encourage "vigilantism and anarchistic actions." See Commonwealth v. Klein, 372 Mass. 823, 829, 363 N.E.2d 1313 (1977) (discussing citizen's privilege to use deadly force in preventing escape of felons).

[4] In addition, it is clear from the provisions of our statutes relating to motor vehicle offenses that the legislature did not intend to authorize a citizen's arrest for operating under the influence of intoxicating liquor. General Laws c. 90, Section 21 (1984 ed. & Supp. 1985) authorizes police officers to make warrantless arrests for this crime, subject to the specific requirement that "such officer is in uniform or conspicuously displaying his badge of office." *Id.* One of the obvious purposes of requiring a police officer to make known his authority for stopping a vehicle is to reduce

the fear or anxiety which a driver might otherwise experience. This purpose would be defeated if the power to arrest for operating under the influence of intoxicating liquor were bestowed upon private individuals. Also, G.L. c. 90C, Section 4 (1984 ed. & Supp. 1985) allows "a person other than a police officer" to apply "for a criminal complaint for an automobile law violation . . . and such person need not show that the alleged violator has been issued a citation in connection with such violation." *Id.* Although not conclusive, this section suggests that the legislature's preferred method of dealing with personal grievances regarding motor vehicle violations is through application for a criminal complaint, and not through private arrest.

We recognize the strong public policy in this Commonwealth against drunk driving, and the necessity for removing intoxicated motorists from the roads before they harm themselves or other persons. See Commonwealth v. Trumble, 396 Mass. 81, 86–87, 483 N.E.2d 1102 (1985). We also appreciate that these interests might best be served by allowing police officers to apprehend intoxicated motorists outside of the officers' territorial jurisdictions. However, we decline to reach this result through the circuitous route of empowering private persons to arrest for misdemeanors involving a breach of the peace. If the Legislature in its wisdom wishes to broaden the powers of police officers acting outside of their territorial jurisdictions, it may amend G.L. c. 41, Section 98A, to accomplish this purpose.

The judge was correct in ruling that the arrest of the defendant was unlawful. We add a comment as to a point which neither the judge nor the parties addressed: that it does not follow ineluctably from the unlawful arrest of the defendant that the complaint against him must be dismissed. Rather, the inquiry in such a case ordinarily should determine what, if any, evidence should be suppressed as a result of the unlawful arrest. Cf. Wong Sun v. United States, 371 U.S. 471, 488, 83 S.Ct. 407, 417, 9 L.Ed.2d 441 (1963) (evidence excluded under "fruit of poisonous tree" doctrine where arrest violated Fourth Amendment). In this case, however, it is palpably clear that evidence that the defendant was under the influence of intoxicating liquor would not have been obtained but for the arrest, and that the defendant thus was irretrievably prejudiced by the unlawful arrest. See Commonwealth v Andrade, 389 Mass. 874, 879–880, 453 N.E.2d 415 (1983). Therefore, the judge's order of dismissal is affirmed.

So ordered.

B. FELONY

Rohan v. Sawin
Supreme Judicial Court of Massachusetts, 1849
5 Cush. 281, 59 Mass. 281, at page 284

"It has been sometimes contended, that an arrest of this character, without a warrant, was a violation of the great fundamental principles of our national and state constitutions, forbidding unreasonable searches and arrests, except by warrant founded upon a complaint made under oath. Those provisions doubtless had another and different purpose, being in restraint of general warrants to make searches, and requiring warrants to issue only upon a complaint under oath. They do not conflict with the authority of constables or other peace officers, *or private persons under proper limitations, to arrest without warrant those who have committed felonies.* The public safety, and the due apprehension of criminals, charged with heinous offenses, imperiously require that such arrest should be made without warrant by officers of the law. As to the right appertaining to private individuals to arrest without warrant, it is a much more restricting authority, and is confined to cases of the *actual guilt* of the party arrested; and the arrest can only be justified by proving such guilt. But as to constables, and other peace officers, acting officially, the law clothes them with greater authority, and they are held to be justified, if they act, in making the arrest, upon probable and reasonable grounds for believing the party guilty of a felony; and this is all that is necessary for them to show, in order to sustain a justification of an arrest, for the purpose of detaining the party to await further proceedings under a complaint on oath and a warrant thereon. It was not necessary, therefore, in the present case, for the defendant to establish the actual guilt of the plaintiff of the offense imputed to him. It was only necessary to show, that upon the representation made to him of the commission of a felony, and the other circumstances coming to his knowledge, he had reasonable ground to suspect the plaintiff of having committed the crime of receiving stolen goods, knowing them to be stolen."

Commonwealth v. Lussier
Supreme Judicial Court of Massachusetts
333 Mass. 83, 128 N.E. 2d 569 (1955)

"Lussier, after waiting for some customers to leave, entered the store wearing the overcoat and the bandana knotted around his neck. He carried the loaded pistol in his hand. He pulled the bandana up so that it covered the lower part of his face. It was shortly before 9 P.M. and Miss Mary Phelan, the proprietor of the store, was behind the counter. Pointing the pistol in her direction Lussier said, "This is a hold up" and ordered her to open the cash register. One Timothy McCarthy, a relative of Miss Phelan came in at that time and Lussier ordered him to open the register. McCarthy was unable to open it. Lussier then tried himself to open it but without success. Meanwhile Miss Phelan was attempting to use the telephone. Lussier turned and hurried to the front door by which he had entered. The door was three feet wide and opened outwards. As shown on photographs which are in evidence, it was located about four feet in from the sidewalk at the back of a recess or open vestibule formed by the store windows. As Lussier was at or near this door, Miss Phelan saw someone approaching the door from the sidewalk and shouted "Grab him." When Lussier had opened the door about two feet, he was met by Blanchard, the deceased, who had parked his automobile in front of the store and was seeking to enter the store. The men struggled at the door. Two shots were fired in close sequence from the pistol held by Lussier, and Blanchard collapsed on the sidewalk or in the street in front of the store entrance. He had been shot in the back below the left shoulder the bullet penetrating both lungs and lodging in his right chest. He died from the wound before reaching the hospital. It was the second shot which killed him."

"Both defendants were separately arrested within a short time and each admitted to the police that he participated in the homicide substantially in the manner and to the extent stated in the above recital of evidence. At the trial, however, Parks testified that he withdrew from the enterprise after the ineffective approach to the first package store. Lussier testified that each of the shots from his pistol was fired by accident and produced a witness named Samson who testified that the fatal shot was fired when Lussier slipped on the ice while running toward the automobile."

"If the jury found that the shooting of Blanchard was not an incident in the attempted commission of armed robbery it was nevertheless an incident of an effort to escape after the commission of a felony. *A private person may lawfully arrest one who in fact has committed a felony (Rohan v. Sawin, 5 Cush. 281, 285);* (Pilos v. First National Stores Inc. 319 Mass. 475, 478), and to kill in resisting such arrest is murder and not manslaughter. See Commonwealth v. Carey, 12 Cush. 246. Manslaughter is the unlawful killing of another without malice and malice is an unlawful and unjustifiable motive. Commonwealth v. Webster, 5 Cush. 295, 304. Commonwealth v. Demboski, 283 Mass. 315, 322. The motive here was plainly unjustifiable. By shooting Blanchard, Lussier sought to avoid arrest for a crime which admittedly he had committed. There was no evidence of reasonable provocation (see Commonwealth v. Soaris, 275 Mass. 291, 299; Commonwealth v. Young, 326 Mass. 597, 601) or of other extenuating circumstances.

Comment

We can conclude then that the legal power of a private security person to arrest without a warrant for a felony arises only when the person arrested in fact committed a felony. A private security person must be right; must be able to prove the arrestee guilty. If the arrested person is acquitted, the arresting private person, his employer, or both should expect a civil lawsuit against them for damages.

In regard to the Power of arrest for a felony, we conclude this section with the case of Commonwealth v. Harris, a case similar to the Grise Case involving an extraterritorial arrest by police officers for a felony, which fails to follow the reasoning of Grise, i.e., that police acting extraterritorially are acting as private persons, and applies the established standard for police arrests for felony, reasonable grounds, to believe that the arrestee has committed a felony. This could very well be interpreted as saying that a private citizen may arrest for a felony, but at the same risk as in the past, i.e., that the person arrested is found guilty.

Commonwealth v. Harris
Appeals Court of Massachusetts
11 Mass Appeal, 165 N.E.2d, 218 (1981)

Before HALE, C. J., and GOODMAN and GREANEY, JJ.

GREANEY, Justice.

On August 15, 1975, a Superior Court jury convicted the defendant on indictments charging three counts of rape of a child (G.L. c. 265, Section 23), and he was sentenced to concurrent terms at the Massachusetts Correctional Institution at Walpole. No appeal was taken from the judgments of conviction. On August 10, 1977, the defendant filed a writ of error in the Supreme Judicial Court alleging that he had been denied the effective assistance of counsel. That court referred the matter to a special master, and on March 16, 1979, adopted the master's recommendation that the defendant's appellate rights be fully reinstated. On June 27, 1979, the defendant filed a motion for a new trial on the ground of ineffective assistance of counsel. That motion was heard by the trial judge and denied on November 2, 1979. The defendant appeals from errors assigned in connection with the trial and from the denial of the motion for a new trial. These appeals raise the following questions: (1) whether the defendant's warrantless arrest in Chelsea by the Revere police was valid; (2) whether certain incriminating information was obtained from the defendant in violation of his *Miranda* rights; (3) whether an out-of-court identification made by the victim at the police station should have been suppressed; (4) whether a new trial is required because of alleged prejudicial final argument by the prosecutor; and (5) whether the defendant was effectively represented by his trial counsel. We find no error.

The evidence pertinent to a resolution of the questions may be summarized as follows. The rapes occurred on February 26, 1975. The victim, an eleven-year-old girl, had just completed dancing lessons in Chelsea and was on her way home to Revere. She boarded a bus in front of the dance school at 6:50 P.M. There were approximately six to eight people aboard the bus, including the defendant, who continually stared at the victim. She got off the bus about twenty minutes later and started to walk home. The defendant, who had alighted from the bus at the previous stop, was now following her on the opposite side of the street. She started to walk faster and noticed that the defendant was running toward her. To reach home quickly, she cut through a parking lot and a grassy area, but the defendant caught up to her in the back of the lot, grabbed her and threw her down onto the grassy area. There, he forced her to engage in natural and unnatural acts of sexual intercourse. The entire incident lasted approximately one and one half hours. She immediately went home, told her father about the incident, and described her assailant as five feet, eleven inches in height, 150 pounds with long brown hair parted in the middle, two to four upper teeth missing, a black left eye which was bloodshot, and wearing brown corduroy slacks and a jacket. Her father called the Revere Police, who came to the home, at which time she repeated her description. The victim was then taken to the hospital for an examination and later drew a sketch of her attacker before going to bed.

In the meantime, her father had called his brother-in-law, John Parker, about the incident and given him the description. Parker lived in Chelsea. The father spent the next day searching for the assailant but without success. That night, at approximately 11:00 P.M., Parker noticed the defendant waiting for a bus in Chelsea. Upon observing that he met the description, Parker offered the defendant a ride, which the defendant accepted. Parker convinced the defendant to go to Parker's home and invited him in for a beer. There, Parker called the victim's father, who in turn notified the Revere Police. The police quickly picked up the father and proceeded directly to Parker's house in Chelsea. Upon approaching the house, the officers observed the defendant and Parker coming out the front door. Noticing that the defendant fitted the description given by the victim, the officers placed him under arrest and advised him of his *Miranda* rights. The officers then brought the defendant back to the police station in Revere while the victim's father, Parker, and Parker's wife went to pick up the victim. The victim was told that the police had apprehended the man who fit the description. Unknown to the officers who had arrested the defendant and who were questioning him at the station, the victim and her party arrived and were placed in a room by a stairway. The officers, after completing their questioning, proceeded down the stairway in order to take the defendant back to his cell. The victim, who had left the room to get a drink of water, noticed the defendant coming down the stairs and immediately cried out: "Daddy, that's him over there." This identification was introduced at trial and an in-court identification was made. The defense was based on evidence of alibi.

1. *Validity of the Arrest.* The defendant contends that his warrantless

arrest in Chelsea by the Revere Police was effectuated without authority, and, as a consequence, that all statements and evidence obtained pursuant thereto should have been excluded at the trial on an application of the fruit of the poisonous tree doctrine. See Wong Sun v. United States, 371 U.S. 471, 488, 83 S.Ct. 407, 417, 9 L.Ed.2d 441 (1963). See generally, United States v. Crews, 445 U.S. 463, 469–470, 100 S.Ct. 1244, 1249–1250, 63 L.Ed.2d 537 (1980).

[1] In Massachusetts a police officer may make a warrantless arrest of any person who he reasonably believes has committed a felony. Commonwealth v. Holmes, 344 Mass. 524, 525, 183 N.E.2d 279 (1962). The officer's official authority to make such a warrantless arrest, however, is limited to the territorial jurisdiction of his appointment (Report of the Attorney Gen., Pub. Doc.No. 12, at 136 [1967]; Smith, Criminal Practice and Procedure Section 103 [1970]), unless the officer is "on fresh and continued pursuit" of a felon "for any offense committed . . . in his presence within his jurisdiction" (G.L. c. 41, Section 98A, inserted by St. 1967, c. 263)—a situation which has no applicability to this case. Apart from this statutory exception, Massachusetts has yet to determine when a police officer may make a valid warrantless felony arrest outside of his jurisdiction. We now turn to that question.

[2] An extensive line of cases from other states upholds the validity of an extraterritorial arrest made by a police officer who lacked the official authority to arrest where the place of arrest authorizes a private person to make a "citizen's arrest" under the same circumstances. State v. McCullar, 110 Ariz. 427, 428, 520 P.2d 299 (1974). People v. Monson, 28 Cal.App.3d 935, 939–940, 105 Cal.Rptr. 92 (1972). State v. Shipman, 370 So.2d 1195, 1196 (Fla.Dist Ct.App. 1979). State v. O'Kelly, 211 N.W.2d 589, 595 (Iowa 1973), cert. denied, 417 U.S. 936, 94 S.Ct. 2652, 41 L.Ed.2d 240 (1974). State v. Shienle, 218 Kan. 637, 640, 545 P.2d 1129 (1976). State v. Jones, 263 La. 164, 174–175, 267 So.2d 559 (1972). Stevenson v. State, 287 Md. 504, 510, 413 A.2d 1340 (1980). People v. Bashans, 80 Mich.App. 702, 713, 265 N.W.2d 170 (1978). State v. Fritz, 490 S.W.2d 30, 32 (Mo.), cert. denied 411 U.S. 985, 93 S.Ct. 2282, 36 L.Ed.2d 962 (1973). State v. McCarthy, 123 N.J.Super 513, 517, 303 A.2d 626 (1973). State v. MacDonald, 260 N.W.2d 626, 627 (S.D. 1977). State v. Harp, 13 Wash.App. 239, 242, 534 P.2d 842 (1975). To the same effect are several federal cases. As aptly expressed in State v. O'Kelly, supra at 595: "When the . . . officers came to [the adjoining jurisdiction], they ceased to be officers but they did not cease to be persons." In Massachusetts a private person may lawfully arrest someone

who has in fact committed a felony. Commonwealth v. Lussier, 333 Mass. 83, 92, 128 N.E.2d 569 (1955). The stricter requirement for a citizen's arrest—that the person arrested be shown in fact to have committed a felony—is designed to discourage such arrests and to prevent "the dangers of uncontrolled vigilantism and anarchistic actions." Commonwealth v. Klein, 372 Mass. 823, 829, 363 N.E.2d 1313 (1977). Cf. Commonwealth v. Mahnke, 368 Mass. 662, 688–689, 335 N.E.2d 660 (1975), cert. denied, 425 U.S. 959, 96 S.Ct. 1740, 48 L.Ed.2d 204 (1976). See also Rohan v. Sawin, 5 Cush. 281, 285 (1851); Commonwealth v. Carey, 12 Cush. 246, 251 (1853); Commonwealth v. Walden, —Mass.—,— n.2, 405 N.E.2d 939 (1980); Note, Arrest Without a Warrant in New England, 40 B.U.L.Rev. 58, 76 (1960). Generally, the person arrested must be convicted of a felony before the "in fact committed" element is satisfied and the arrest validated. If the citizen is in error in making the arrest, he may be liable in tort for false arrest or false imprisonment. See Rohan v. Sawin, 5 Cush. at 285; Morley v. Chase, 143 Mass. 396, 398, 9 N.E. 767 (1887); Jacques v. Childs Dining Hall Co., 244 Mass. 438, 440–441, 138 N.E.2d 843 (1923); Pilos v. First Natl. Stores, Inc., 319 Mass. 475, 478, 66 N.Ed.2d 576 (1946).

[3, 4] As a practical matter, the "in fact committed" requirement cannot be met when the propriety of a citizen's arrest is questioned on a motion to suppress because there has been no validating conviction. The obvious purpose of that requirement is to deter private citizens from irresponsible action by exposing them to possible civil liability if it turns out later that the arrested party was innocent. Since the requirement is not designed to frustrate legitimate law enforcement activities, insistence on rigid compliance with the rule would be senseless in the circumstances present here. No one can seriously question the fact that the Revere Police acted responsibly and that taking the time to arrange an arrest with the Chelsea Police might have permitted the defendant to escape. "If in cases like this an officer, who must necessarily act with more or less haste in order to prevent a possible felon from making his escape, would have to satisfy himself beyond question that a felony had been committed or must act at his peril, the great public necessity for a prompt . . . enforcement of the law would be largely curtailed." Grau v. Forge, 183 Ky. 521, 528, 209 S.W. 369 (1919). We believe it to be sounder analysis to uphold the arrest, even though technically a citizen's arrest, made by the police officers in this case if the evidence introduced at the motion to suppress establishes that the police had probable cause to believe that a felony had been committed and that the person arrested

had committed it. See People v. Wilkins, 27 Cal.App.3d 763, 770, 104 Cal.Rptr. 89 (1972); People v. Marino, 80 Ill.App.3d 657, 661, 663–665, 400 N.E.2d 491 (1980); Dodson v. State, 381 N.E.2d 90, 92 (Ind. 1978); Stevenson v. State, 287 Md. at 520, 413 A.2d 1340; Nash v. State, 207 So.2d 104, 106–107 (Miss. 1968). Compare State v. Cohen, 73 N.J. 331, 344–345, 375 A.2d 259 (1977). See also Bassiouni, Citizen's Arrest 17–22, 27 (1977). It is clear that these requirements were met in this case.

2. The only recent case concerning an extraterritorial arrest is Commonwealth v. Mottola, —Mass.App.—(1980) (Mass App.Ct.Adv.Sh. [1980] 2095), 412 N.E.2d 1280. This decision held that a police officer of the Massachusetts Bay Transportation Authority (MBTA) had the power to make an arrest outside of MBTA property by virtue of St. 1968, c. 664, which confers on MBTA officers the powers and duties given to police officers of cities and towns under G.L. c, 41, Section 98. *Id.* at—(Mass. App.Ct.Adv.Sh. [1980] at 2099–2101). Since the result depended on a statutory basis for the arrest, it does not apply here.

3. See Ward v. United States, 316 F.2d 113, 116–118 (9th Cir.), cert. denied, 375 U.S. 862, 84 S.Ct. 132, 11 L.Ed.2d 89 (1963) (warrantless arrest by postal inspectors, who lacked power to arrest under Federal law, held valid as an arrest by private persons under California law); United States v. DeCatur, 430 F.2d 365, 367 (9th Cir. 1970) (dicta); United States v Swarovski, 557 F.2d 40, 46–47 (2d Cir. 1977), cert denied, 434 U.S. 1045, 98 S.Ct. 889, 54 L.Ed.2d 796 (1978) (arrest by customs Service agents, who are not empowered to arrest by Federal law, held valid as a citizen's arrest under New York law). a. Mass.Adv.Sh. (1980) 1309, 1313 n.2.

C. SPECIAL LAW FOR MERCHANTS

McDermott v. W.T. Grant Company
Supreme Judicial Court of Massachusetts, 1943
313 Mass. 736, 49 N.E. 2d 115

LUMMER, J. This is an action of tort, with one count for false arrest and another for slander. The plaintiff got a verdict of $1 on the count for slander, and the defendant's exceptions relating to that count are waived. On the count for false arrest the plaintiff got a verdict for $1,425, and the case is here on the defendant's exception to the denial of its motion for a directed verdict.

The following facts could have been found upon the evidence. On October 25, 1940, a woman clerk in the defendant's store in Clinton observed two men acting suspiciously in the store and at the same time she saw the plaintiff across the street. She called the facts to the attention of the store manager. The manager followed the two men down the street, but they disappeared in the crowd. The manager then went to lunch. On his return he saw a police officer, and told him that the plaintiff was standing across the street while the two men were in the store. The officer asked the plaintiff to accompany him to the place where the manager stood on the sidewalk outside the store. The officer asked the manager if the plaintiff was the man he wanted placed under arrest, and the manager said, "I want that man locked up. He's one of the three men who has been in my store and have stolen things." The officer then placed the plaintiff in a "cruising car" and told him he was under arrest and took him to the police station. The manager came to the police station and insisted that the plaintiff be kept under arrest. But the manager testified that he told the chief of police that he had never seen the plaintiff before, had not seen him in the store, and that he did not want to press any charges or have any charges to press against the plaintiff. After being at the police station for about two hours, the plaintiff was released. The plaintiff testified that he had never been in the defendant's store, and the manager testified that "the plaintiff was never in the store, as far as the witness knew." *The burden was upon the defendant to prove justification for any arrest for which it was responsible.* Roseman v. Korb, 311 Nass. 75, 77.

The defendant does not contend that the plaintiff was guilty of any felony, or was suspected of any. Commonwealth v. Phelps, 209 Mass. 396, 404. Shoplifting in a store like that of the defendant would not be likely to involve the felony of stealing property exceeding $100 in value, and there is no suggestion that it would. G.L. (Ter. Ed.) C.266, Section 30. Zinkfein v. W.T. Grant Co., 236 Mass. 228, 233. Neither would it constitute larceny in a building, under G.L. (Ter. Ed.) C.266, Section 20, for the property was the protection of the defendant's servants rather than that of the building. Commonwealth v. Lester, 129 Mass., 101. Commonwealth v. Nott, 135 Mass. 269, 272. Zinkfein v. W.T. Grant Co., 236 Mass. 228, 233. The crime involved, if any there was, was only a misdemeanor. G.L. (Ter. Ed.) C.266, Section 30. *Without going into the refinements of the right of a private person or an officer to arrest without a warrant for a misdemeanor it is enough to say that no such right exists where no offense is committed in the presence of the one who makes the arrest.* Commonwealth v. Gorman, 288 Mass., 294, 297, and cases cited.

It could have been found that the defendant's manager actively instigated the arrest, and that he did not merely report the facts to the officer and leave the result to the officer's judgement. Zinkfein v. W.T. Grant Co., 236 Mass. 228, 232. Compare Burnham v. Collateral Loan Co., 179 Mass. 268, 274; Shea v. Sullivan, 261 Mass. 255, 256, 259.

It could also have been found that the manager was acting within the scope of his employment for the defendant. Fanciullo v. B.G. & S. Theatre Corp., 297 Mass. 44, 47. He testified that he "was general manager of the defendant's store and all other persons in the store were under his supervision and that he had complete charge of the store, including the problem of employing and discharging help"; also that "he was responsible for seeing that no merchandise went out that was not purchased; that if any did get out he was responsible in making every effort he could to recover it; that his instructions with reference to what he was to do if anyone took goods out of the store without paying for them was to apprehend them outside of the store if he saw a person take them himself." In Mason v. Jacot, 235 Mass. 521, evidence not as strong as that in this case was held to warrant a finding that the defendant's manager was authorized to call a police officer to arrest the plaintiff for failing to pay for food eaten.

The defendant cites cases in North Carolina to the effect that the implied authority of a store manager ends as a matter of law when the stolen goods have once been taken from the store. Daniel v. Atlantic Coast Line Railroad, 136 N.C. 517. Lamm v. Charles Stores Co., Inc., 201 M.D. 596. Cases in other jurisdictions appear to be to the contrary. Staples v. Schmid, 18 R.I. 224. Mosley v. J.G. McCrory Co. of West Virginia, 101 W. Va. 480. Pruitt v. Watson, 103 W. Va. 627. McCrory Stores Corp. v. Stachell, 148 Md. 279. We need not discuss these cases, for in the present case there was evidence that the authority of the manager included the attempted recovery of the goods and the apprehension of the suspected thief. Exceptions Overruled.

The following statute is in effect in Massachusetts. It was enacted in 1958 and amended in 1971:

SECTION 94B. False arrest; Shoplifting; Defrauding Inkeepers; Defenses

In an action for false arrest or false imprisonment brought by any person by reason of having been detained for questioning on or in the immediate vicinity of the premises of a merchant or an innkeeper, if such person was detained in a reasonable manner and for not more than a reasonable length of time by a person authorized to make arrests or by the merchant or innkeeper or his agent or servant authorized for such purpose and if there were reasonable grounds to believe that the person so detained was committing or attempting to commit a violation of section thirty A of chapter two hundred and sixty-six, or section twelve of chapter one hundred and forty or was committing or attempting to commit larceny of goods for sale on such premises or larceny of the personal property of employees or customers or others present on such premises, it shall be a defense to such action.

Amended by St.1985, c. 348, Section 2.

Many other states have enacted legislation similar to Massachusetts' General Laws, Chapter 231. Section 94B which excepts merchants and/or innkeepers and provides for a defense against False Arrest or False Imprisonment civil lawsuits.

Coblyn v. Kennedy's Inc.
Supreme Judicial Court of Massachusetts 1971
359 Mass. 319, 268 N.E.2D 860

SPEIGEL, J. This is an action of tort for false imprisonment. At the close of the evidence the defendants filed a motion for directed verdicts which was denied. The jury returned verdicts for the plaintiff in the sum of $12,500. The case is here on the defendant's exceptions to the denial of their motion and to the refusal of the trial judge to give certain requested instructions to the jury.

We state the pertinent evidence most favorable to the plaintiff. On March 5, 1965, the plaintiff went to Kennedy's Inc., (Kennedy's) a store in Boston. He was seventy years of age and about five feet four inches in height. He was wearing a woolen shirt, which was "open at the neck," a topcoat and a hat. "Around his neck" he wore an ascot which he had "purchased . . . previously at Filene's." He proceeded to the second floor of Kennedy's to purchase a sport coat. He removed his hat, topcoat and ascot, putting the ascot in his pocket. After purchasing a sport coat and leaving it for alterations, he put on his hat and coat and walked downstairs. Just prior to exiting through the door of the store, he stopped, took the ascot out of his pocket, put it around his neck, and knotted it. The knot was visible "above the lapels of his shirt". The only stop that the plaintiff made on the first floor was immediately in front of the exit in order to put on his ascot.

Just as the plaintiff stepped out of the door, the defendant Goss, an employee, "loomed up in front of him with his hand up and said: "Stop. Where did you get that scarf?" The plaintiff responded "Why?" Goss firmly grasped the plaintiff's arm and said: "You better go back and see the manager." Another employee was standing next to him. Eight or ten other people were staring at the plaintiff. The plaintiff then said, "Yes, I'll go back in the store" and proceeded to do so. As he and Goss went upstairs to the second floor, the plaintiff paused twice because of chest and back pains. After reaching the second floor, the salesman from whom he had purchased the coat recognized him and asked what the trouble was. The plaintiff then asked: "Why did these two gentlemen stop me?" The salesman confirmed that the plaintiff had purchased a sport coat and that the ascot belonged to him.

The salesman became alarmed by the plaintiff's appearance and the store nurse was called. She brought the plaintiff into the nurse's room and gave him a soda mint tablet. As a direct result of the emotional upset caused by the incident, the plaintiff was hospitalized and treated for a "myocardial infarct."

Initially, the defendants contend that as a matter of law the plaintiff was not falsely imprisoned. They argue that no unlawful restraint was imposed by either force or threat upon the plaintiff's freedom of movement. Wax v. McGrath, 255 Mass. 340, 342. However, "the law is well settled that 'any general restraint is sufficient to constitute an imprisonment . . . ' and 'any demonstration of physical power which, to all appearances, can be avoided only by submission, operates as effectually to constitute an imprisonment, if submitted to, as if any amount of force had to be exercised.' 'If a man is restrained of his personal liberty by fear of a personal difficulty, that amounts to a false imprisonment' within the legal meaning of such term." Jacques v. Childs Dining Hall Co., 244 Mass. 438, 438–439.

We think it is clear that there was sufficient evidence of unlawful restraint to submit this question of the jury. Just as the plaintiff had stepped out of the door of the store, the defendant Goss stopped him, firmly grasped his arm and told him that he had "better go back and see the manager." There was another employee at his side. The plaintiff was an elderly man and there were other people standing around staring at him. Considering the plaintiff's age and his heart condition, it is hardly to be expected that with one employee in front of him firmly grasping his arm and another at his side the plaintiff could do other than comply with Goss's "request" that he go back and see the manager. The physical restraint imposed upon the plaintiff when Goss grasped the plaintiff's arm readily distinguished this case from Sweeney v. F.W. Woolworth Co., 247 Mass. 277, relied upon by the defendants.

In addition, as this court observed in the Jacques case, supra, at p.441 the "honesty and veracity (of the plaintiff) had been openly . . . challenged. If she had gone out before . . . (exonerating herself), her departure well might have been interpreted by the lookers on as an admission of guilt, or of circumstances from which guilt might be inferred. The situation was in the control of the defendant. The restraint or duress imposed by the mode of investigation . . . the jury could say was for the accomplishment of the defendant's purpose, even if no threats of public exposure or of arrest were made, and no physical restraint of . . . (the plaintiff) was attempted." For cases in other jurisdictions, where the evidence tended to support the tort of false imprisonment, see Clark v. Kroger Co., 382 F. 2D 562, 563 (7th Cir.); Patrick v. Esso Standard Oil Co., 156 F. Supp. 336, 340 (D.N.J.); Daniel v. Phillips Petroleum Co., 229 Mo. App. 150, 155; Lukas v. J.C. Penney Co., 233 Ore. 345, 354.

The defendants next contend that the detention of the plaintiff was sanctioned by G.L., C.231 Section 94B, inserted by ST. 1958, C.337. This statute provides as follows: "In an action for false arrest or false imprisonment brought by any person by reason of having been detained for questioning on or in the immediate vicinity of the premises of a merchant, if such person was detained in a reasonable manner and for not more than a reasonable length of time by a person authorized to make arrests or by the merchant or by his agent or servant authorized for such purpose and if there were reasonable grounds to believe that the person so detained was committing or attempting to commit larceny of goods for sale on such premises, it shall be a defense to such action. If such goods had not been purchased and were concealed on or amongst the belongings of a person so detained it shall be presumed that there were reasonable grounds for such belief."

The defendants argue in accordance with the conditions imposed in the statute that the plaintiff was detained in a reasonable manner for a reasonable length of time and that Goss had reasonable grounds for believing that the plaintiff was attempting to commit larceny of goods held for sale.

It is conceded that the detention was for a reasonable length of time. See Proulx v. Pinkerton's National Detective Agency, Inc., 343 Mass. 390, 392–393. We need not decide whether the detention was effected in a reasonable manner for we are aware of opinion that there were no reasonable grounds for believing that the plaintiff was committing larceny and, therefore, he should not have been detained at all. However, we observe that Goss's failure to identify himself as an employee of Kennedy's and to disclose the reasons for his inquiry and actions, coupled with the physical restraint in a public place imposed upon the plaintiff, an elderly man, who had exhibited no aggressive intention to depart, could be said to constitute an unreasonable method by which to effect detention. See Lukas v. J.C. Penney Co., 233 Ore. 345, 352, 360.

The pivotal question before us as in most cases of this character is whether the evidence shows that there were reasonable grounds for the detention. At common law in an action for false imprisonment, the defense of probable cause, as measured by the prudent and cautious man standard, was available to a merchant. Standish v. Narraganset S.S. Co., 111 Mass. 512, 517. Jacques v. Childs Dining Hall Co., 244 Mass. 438, 439. Muniz v. Mehlman, 327 Mass. 353, 358. In enacting G.L., C.231, Section 94B, the legislature inserted the words, "reasonable grounds." Historically, the words "reasonable grounds" and "probable cause" have been given the same meaning by the courts. In the case of United States v. Walker, 246 F. 2D 519, 526 (7th Cir.) it was said: " 'Probable cause' and 'reasonable grounds' are concepts having virtually the same meaning." The following cases have expressly stated that the words may be used interchangeably and without distinction: Draper v. United States, 358 U.S. 307, 310. United States v. Vasquez, 183 F. Supp. 190, 193 (E.D.N.Y.). Smallwood v. Commonwealth, 305 Ky. 520, 524. McKeon v. National Gas, Co., 216 Mo. App. 507–524. Adams v. State, 137 Tex. Cr. 43, 46. Stelloh v. Liban, 21 Wis. 2D 119, 125. In the case of Lukas v. J.C. Penney Co. supra, at p.361, the Oregon Supreme Court construed the meaning of the words "reasonable grounds" in its shoplifting Statute as having the same meaning as they have in a statute authorizing arrest without a warrant and applied the probable cause standard to the facts before it.

The defendants assert that the judge improperly instructed the jury in stating that "grounds are reasonable when there is a basis which would appear to the reasonably prudent, cautious, intelligent person." In their brief, they argue that the "prudent and cautious man rule" is an *objective* standard and required a more rigorous and restrictive standard of conduct than is contemplated by G.L., C.231, Section 94B. The defendants' requests for instructions, in effect, state that proper test is a subjective one, viz., whether the *defendant Goss* had an honest and strong suspicion that the plaintiff was committing or attempting to commit larceny.

We do not agree. As we have attempted to show, the words "reasonable grounds" and "probable cause" have traditionally been accorded the same meaning. In the case of Terry v. Ohio, 392 U.S. 1, involving the question whether a police officer must have probable cause within the Fourth Amendment to "stop and frisk" a suspected individual, the Supreme Court of the United States held that the "probable cause" requirement of the Fourth Amendment applies to a "stop-and-frisk" and that a "stop-and-frisk" must "be judged against an objective standard: would the facts available to the officer at the moment . . . 'warrant a man of reasonable caution in the belief' that the action taken was appropriate? . . . Anything less would invite intrusions upon constitutionally guaranteed rights based on nothing more substantial than inarticulate hunches, a result this Court has consistently refused to sanction." Pp. 21–22.

If we adopt the subjective test as suggested by the defendants, the individual's right to liberty and freedom of movement would become subject to the "honest . . . suspicion" of a shopkeeper based on his own "inarticulate hunches" without regard to any discernable facts. In effect, the result would be to afford the merchant even greater authority than that given to a police officer. In view of the well established meaning of the words "reasonable grounds" we believe that the legislature has permitted an individual to be detained for a "reasonable length of time". This would be at least analogous to a "stop" within the meaning of the Terry case.

We also note that an objective standard is the criterion for determining probable cause or reasonable grounds in malicious prosecution and false arrest cases. Bacon v. Towns, 4 Cush. 217, 238–239, Wax v. McGrath, 255 Mass. 340, 343. We see no valid reason to depart from this precedent in regard to cases involving false imprisonment.

Applying the standard of reasonable grounds as measured by the *reasonably prudent man* test to the evidence in the instant case, we are of the opinion that the evidence warranted the conclusion that Goss was *not* reasonably justified in believing that the plaintiff was engaged in shoplifting. There was no error in denying the motion for directed verdicts and in the refusal to give the requested instructions.

Comment

Note here the development of the law. McDermott v. W.T. Grant Co. demonstrates the difficulty which the law of arrest presented to retail the merchants in their battle against shoplifting in 1943. Fifteen years later the legislature acted, providing a change in the law for retail merchants: they did not have to be right; they could detain on "reasonable grounds" in a reasonable manner.

The legislative relief softened the sanction (i.e., civil liability) imposed on previously overly aggressive merchants, but maintained a sense of "reasonableness." Interestingly, shoplifting continues to grow and has become a "cost-of-doing-business factor" which is added to the price of the goods for all consumers.

Also note that in this "merchant-shoplifting" situation the Court follows precedents of other courts establishing the *objective* test, i.e., whether a reasonably prudent and cautious person (a non-existent person) would act similarly, and scorns the argument of the defense to the Court to accept in this situation a subjective test, i.e., whether *this* person acting in *this* situation had an honest and strong suspicion. Compare this result with the case of Commonwealth vs. Joseph Puleio, Chapter 4 herein, where a court recognized the *subjective* purpose of an officer conducting a search incident to an arrest.

We summarize the power of a private person to arrest as follows:

I. Massachusetts
   A. Misdemeanor: no power whatsoever except under Mass G.L. c.231, Section 94B, where merchants and innskeepers or their agents or servants are given a limited defense. Any other misdemeanor arrest may subject the person or their employer to civil liability.
   B. Felony: A private person may arrest for a felony, but if the arrestee is exonerated, civil liability may attach.

II. For other jurisdiction, the Grise case should be read closely to determine if that court's research indicated any law in those jurisdictions.

Chapter 3

USE OF FORCE TO EFFECT AN ARREST

Since a private security person's legal rights are equated to those of a private citizen, to determine the law relating to the amount of force a private security person may use to make an arrest, we must examine the law as it pertains to a private citizen. As a general rule, one may use as much force as is reasonably necessary to effect a lawful arrest. If the arrest is not lawful, any force is unreasonable.

The most serious question arises when a private security person considers the use of deadly force (likely or intended to cause death or serious bodily harm) to effect a lawful arrest.

Commonwealth v. Klein

Supreme Judicial Court of Massachusetts, 1977
372 Mass. 823, 363 N.E.2d 1313

HENNESSEY, C.J. The defendant, a dentist residing in Springfield, was found guilty by a jury of charges in two indictments. One indictment charged him with assault and battery by means of a dangerous weapon (a firearm) on Napolean J. LaDue; the other indictment charged the same offense against John Savageau (G.L. ch. 265, § 15A). Both offenses were alleged to have occurred on August 1, 1973. It is undisputed that the defendant shot and wounded the two men after they had in the nighttime broken into a drug store across the street from the defendant's home. The defendant telephoned the police, and after a time went outside his home, armed with a pistol, and the confrontation occurred which gave rise to these indictments.

We hold that the judge charged the jury correctly in this case, as judged in light of principles of law which we in this case adopt governing the right of citizens to use deadly force in attempting to effect the arrest of felons. Further, we conclude that the jury were warranted in returning guilty verdicts on the evidence as considered in light of the judge's instructions to them. Nevertheless, since we are now expounding these rules of law for the first time in the Commonwealth, we also hold that the rules should not be applied retroactively against this defendant. Consequently, we are ordering that judgements of not guilty be entered as to both indictments.

1. The central question in this case is whether the defendant was justified in using deadly force. We define deadly force as force intended or likely to cause death or great bodily harm. This tracks with our long-standing definition of a "dangerous weapon", viz.: an instrument that is likely to produce death or serious bodily injury. Commonwealth v. Farrell, 322 Mass. 606, 615 (1948). Clearly the defendant in this case used deadly force in firing shots from a handgun.

The defendant's first contention is that his conduct in shooting the two men was justifiable on the ground of self-defense, and that on this ground he was entitled to directed verdicts of not guilty. The judge properly instructed the jury that, the defendant having introduced evidence that he acted in self-defense, the burden of proving beyond a reasonable doubt that he was not justified in his use of deadly force to defend himself rested on the Commonwealth. Commonwealth v. Rodriguez, Mass. (1976). It is clear to us that the judge correctly ruled that the defendant was not entitled to directed verdicts of not guilty on the ground of self-defense.

The jury were instructed in substance that, in order to create a right to defend oneself with a dangerous weapon likely to cause serious injury or death, it must appear that the person using the weapon had a reasonable apprehension of great bodily harm and a reasonable belief that no other means would suffice to prevent such harm. See Commonwealth v. Kendrick, 351 Mass. 203, 211 (1966); Commonwealth v. Houston, 332 Mass. 687, 690 (1955). Although there was some testimony by the defendant from which the jury could have concluded that the defendant acted reasonably in an attempt to prevent great bodily harm to himself, there was also evidence which warranted the jury in deciding that the defendant did not act in self-defense at all. The testimony of Napolean LaDue tended to negate the claim of self-defense. Also, the defendant himself stated in substance to the police on the night of the incident that he shot the two men, not as they were attacking or threatening him, but as they were escaping from the scene.

Considering the jury's privilege to accept or reject evidence selectively there was ample basis for them to reject (as they obviously did) the defendant's claim of self-defense, either on the basis that the defendant was not under attack at all, or on the ground that he used excessive force to defend himself in the circumstances. There was evidence which, if believed, supported either conclusion.

2. We turn to consideration of the defendant's claim that he was justified in using deadly force to prevent the escape of the two men from his attempt to make a citizen's arrest.

The defendant's arguments as to citizen's arrest are three in number. First, he contends that he was entitled on this ground to directed verdicts of not guilty. Second, he says that he is entitled at least to a new trial because the judge's charge to the jury was in error as too restrictive in its definition of the defendant's rights in the circumstances of this case. The third contention is that the law applicable to the citizen's right to use deadly force in arresting a felon has never been expounded in this Commonwealth. Therefore, the defendant says that, if he acted excessively in light of the applicable law as decided in this case, that law cannot fairly be applied retroactively to his detriment.

In a few instances, this court has considered the broad issue of the use of excessive force in effecting an arrest. Commonwealth v. Lussier, 333 Mass. 83, 92–93 (1955). Commonwealth v. Young, 326 Mass. 597 (1950). Powers v. Sturtevent, 199 Mass. 265 (1908). Commonwealth v. Cheney, 141 Mass. 102 (1886). Commonwealth v. Presby, 14 Gray 65 (1859). Commonwealth v. Goodwin, 3 Cush. 154 (1849). However, it is true as the defendant contends that we have never clearly set the limits of the arresting citizen's right to use deadly force.

Thus, we must consider in this context what rules of law will best serve the public interest in this Commonwealth. Our common law has long recognized a private citizen's right to arrest. Commonwealth v. Lussier, 333 Mass. 83, 92 (1955). Nevertheless, limits must be set as to the use of deadly force against the dangers of uncontrolled vigilantism and anarchistic actions (cf. Commonwealth v. Mahnke, Mass. (1975), *cert. denied,* 425 U.S. 959 (1976), and particularly against the danger of death or injury of innocent persons at the hands of untrained volunteers using firearms. In our view, for example, there would be no wisdom in approving the unqualified right of a private citizen to use deadly force to prevent the escape of one who has committed a crime against property only.

Some jurisdictions have adopted such limiting rules. See 32 A.L.R. 3d 1072–1077, Annot., 1078–1119, (1970). In Commonwealth v. Chermansky, 430 Pa. 170 (1968), for example, it was held that the prerequisites to justify the use of deadly force by a private person in order to effect the arrest or prevent the escape of a felon are that the person must be in fresh pursuit of the felon and that he must give notice of his purpose to make the arrest for the felony if the attendant circumstances are themselves insufficient to warn the felon of the intention of the pursuing party to arrest him; that such felony must actually have been committed by the person against whom the force is used; and the felony must be one which normally causes or threatens death or great bodily harm.

We have examined comparable law elsewhere, and we think the relevant provisions of the Model Penal Code will best serve this Commonwealth. These provisions were adopted after extensive debate among knowledgeable and distinguished contributors. In the past we have relied on portions of the code to clarify vague areas of our criminal law. See Alegata v. Commonwealth, 353 Mass. 287, 304 (1967). Accordingly, we establish as the law of Massachusetts the rules (in so far as they are material to the instant case) as found in § 3.07 of the Model Penal Code (Proposed Official Draft 1962). They are as follows:

> § 3.07. Use Of Force In Law Enforcement.
>
> (1) *Use Of Force Justifiable To Effect An Arrest.* Subject to the provisions of this Section and of § 3.09, the use of force upon or toward the person of another is justifiable when the actor is making or assisting in making an arrest and the actor believed that such force is immediately necessary to effect lawful arrest.
>
> (2) *Limitations On The Use Of Force.*
>
> (a) The use of force is not justifiable under this section unless:
>
> (i)the actor makes known the purpose of the arrest or believes that it is otherwise known by or cannot reasonably be made known to the person to be arrested; and
>
> (ii)when the arrest is made under a warrant, the warrant is valid or believed by the actor to be valid.
>
> (a) The use of deadly force (emphasis supplied) is not justified under this Section unless:
>
> (i)the arrest is for a *felony;* and
>
> (ii)the person effecting the arrest is authorized to act as a peace officer or is assisting a person whom he believes to be authorized to act as a peace officer; and
>
> (iii)the actor believes that the force employed creates no substantial risk or injury to innocent persons; and

(iv)the actor believes that:
  (1) the crime for which the arrest is made involved conduct including the use or threatened use of deadly force; or
  (2) there is a substantial risk that the person to be arrested will cause death or serious bodily harm if his apprehension is delayed.

We further hold that, since the right of the defendant to arrest and prevent the escape of the victims was raised in the evidence, the burden of disproving this defense beyond a reasonable doubt rested on the Commonwealth. See Commonwealth v. Rodriguez, Mass. (1976).

The judge's instructions to the jury in this case were, in most important respects, consistent with the rules of the Model Penal Code quoted above. He charged in substance that deadly force could not be used to effect the arrest or prevent the escape of one who had committed a felony concerned with property only.

As measured by the principles which we have now established and the judge's charge, it is clear that the Commonwealth met its burden of proving beyond a reasonable doubt that the shootings were not justified. There was evidence which tended to show that, even though the victims had been engaged in a serious crime, it was a crime concerned with property only and entailed no threat of death or great bodily harm. Thus, under the rules of law that we have established here, the guilty verdicts were clearly warranted over the defendant's claim of justification.

We conclude that, in the circumstances of this case, the standards we have now established should not be applied retroactively. We reach this conclusion through considerations of fairness; it cannot fairly be said that the defendant was on notice of the possible criminality of his conduct. We need not consider whether, additionally, a retroactive application of the law to the defendant might be violative of his constitutional right to due process of the law.

The defendant was aware that he had a citizen's right of arrest; the felony was committed in his presence; it could fairly be said that there was evidence that he gave notice to the two men that he intended their arrest and that he was assisting the police (whom the defendant had called) by attempting to prevent the escape of the men. He met the standards for justification of his use of the firearm (as we not for the first time establish them) in all respects except that the felons were not themselves engaged in a crime which threatened death or great bodily harm.

In these circumstances the defendant should not be held to have the knowledge of the "possible criminality" of his conduct (see Mullaney v. Wilbur, supra), and the law should not be applied retroactively against him. His judgement was undoubtedly poor; his conduct could justly be called rash. Nevertheless his intent was to assist the cause of law enforcement; on the evidence, no lawless motive or malicious spirit can be attributed to him.

In the interest of curbing the promiscuous use of firearms, and the unnecessary and dangerous use of deadly force in the community, we have now set limits applicable to arrests by private persons. The defendant can be held to have used excessive force only in the light of the fact that the felons here were not themselves engaged in the use or threatened use of deadly force in their crimes directed against the drug store. Public knowledge of this somewhat subtle requirement of the law, a requirement which we shall apply in the future, should not be charged against the defendant retroactively.

3. Since the Commonwealth had the burden of disproving, by proof beyond a reasonable doubt, the defendant's assertion of justification, and, since we have concluded that he is not to be charged retroactively with the rules we have established in this opinion, it follows that in the circumstances of this case, as a matter of law, the Commonwealth has not met its burden. The judgements are reversed and the verdicts set aside. Judgements of not guilty shall be entered as to both indictments.

Comment

A large portion of this case is reproduced herein because it included a repetition of the law on the issue of self-defense, the defendant's first contention. The second contention raises the issue of a citizen's right to use deadly force to effect an arrest.

The readers should note in the Klein case that the court admits that the law of Massachusetts had been silent on the issue raised by the defendant's second contention; that the court established as the law of Massachusetts material provisions of the Model Penal Code (Proposed Official Draft *1962*) adopted "after extensive debate among knowledgeable and distinguished contributors." Further note that the court decided this case in 1977, after the legislature of Massachusetts chose not to act on this question of law for fifteen years. Could it not be reasonably argued that the members of the legislature did not act because they did not wish to establish the Model Penal Code or its material provision as the law of the Commonwealth? Is this judicial legislation?

Finally, this case established the legal principle that deadly force may *not* be used to arrest a felon fleeing from a crime involving only property.

Tennessee v. Garner
471 U.S. 23, 105 S.CT. 1694 (1985)

Household Burglary 4 (1985). See also T. Reppetto, Residential Crime 17, 105 (1974); Conklin & Bittner, Burglary in a Suburb, 11 Criminology 208. 214 (1973).

We wish to make clear what our holding means in the context of this case. The complaint has been dismissed as to all the individual defendants. The State is a party only by virtue of 28 U.S.C. section 2403(b) and is not subject to liability. The possible liability of the remaining defendants—the Police Department and the city of Memphis—hinges on Monell v. New York City Dept. of Social Services, 436 U.S. 658, 98 S.Ct. 2018, 56 L.Ed.2d 611 (1978), and is left for remand. We hold that the statute is invalid insofar as it purported to give Hymon the authority to act as he did. As for the policy of the Police Department, the absence of any discussion of this issue by the courts below, and the uncertain state of the record, preclude any consideration of its validity.

The judgement of the Court of Appeals is affirmed, and the case is remanded for further proceedings consistent with this opinion.

So ordered.

Justice O'CONNOR, with whom THE CHIEF JUSTICE and Justice REHNQUIST join, dissenting.

The Court today holds that the Fourth Amendment prohibits a police officer from using deadly force as a last resort to apprehend a criminal suspect who refuses to halt when fleeing the scene of a nighttime burglary. This conclusion rests on the majority's balancing of the interests of the suspect and the public interest in effective law enforcement. Ante, at 1699. Notwithstanding the venerable commonlaw rule authorizing the use of deadly force if necessary to apprehend a fleeing felon, and continued acceptance of this rule by nearly half the States, ante, at 1703–1704, the majority concludes that Tennessee's statute is unconstitutional inasmuch as it allows the use of such force to apprehend a burglary suspect who is not obviously armed or otherwise dangerous. Although the circumstances of this case are unquestionably tragic and unfortunate, our constitutional holdings must be sensitive both to the history of the Fourth Amendment and to the general implications of the Court's reasoning. By disregarding the serious and dangerous nature of residential burglaries and the long-standing practice of many states, the Court effectively creates a Fourth Amendment right allowing a burglary suspect to flee unimpeded from a police officer who has probable cause to arrest, who has ordered the suspect to halt and who has no means short of firing his weapon to prevent escape. I do not believe that the Fourth Amendment supports such a right, and I accordingly dissent.

The facts below warrant brief review because they highlight the difficult, split-second decisions police officers must make in these circumstances. Memphis Police Officers Elton Hymon and Leslie Wright responded to a late-night call that a burglary was in progress at a private residence. When the officers arrived at the scene, the caller said that "they" were breaking into the house next door. App. in No. 81-5605 (CA6), p. 207. The officers found the residence had been forcibly entered through a window and saw lights on inside the house. Officer Hymon testified that when he saw the broken window he realized "that something was wrong inside," Id., at 656, but that he could not determine whether anyone—either a burglar or a member of the household—was within the residence. Id., at 209. As Officer Hymon walked behind the house, he heard a door slam. He saw Edward Eugene Garner run away from the house through the dark and cluttered backyard. Garner crouched next to a 6-foot-high fence. Officer Hymon thought Garner was an adult and was unsure whether Garner was armed because Hymon "had no idea what was in the hand [that he could not see] or what he might have had on his person." Id., at 658–659. In fact, Garner was 15 years old and unarmed. Hymon also did not know whether accomplices remained inside the house. Id., at 657. The officer identified himself as a police officer and ordered Garner to halt. Garner paused briefly and then sprang to the top of the fence. Believing that Garner would escape if he climbed over the fence, Hymon fired his revolver and mortally wounded the suspected burglar.

Appellee-respondent, the deceased's father, filed a 42 U.S.C. section 1983 action in federal court against Hymon, the city of Memphis, and other defendants, for asserted violations of Garner's constitutional rights. The District Court for the Western District of Tennessee held that Officer Hymon's actions were justified by a Tennessee statue that authorizes a police officer to "use all the necessary means to effect the arrest," if "after notice of the intention to arrest the defendant, he either flee or forcibly resist." Tenn.Code Ann. section 40-7-108 (1982). As construed by the Tennessee courts, this statute allows the use of deadly force only if a police officer has probable cause to believe that a person has committed a felony, the officer warns the person that he intends to arrest him, and the officer reasonably believes that no means less than such force will prevent the escape. See, e.r., Johnson v. State, 173 Tenn. 134, 114 S.W.2d 819 (1938). The District Court held that the Tennessee statute is constitutional and that Hymon's actions as authorized by that statute did not violate Garner's constitutional rights. The Court of Appeals for the Sixth Circuit reversed on the grounds that the Tennessee statute "authorizing the killing of an unarmed, nonviolent fleeing felon by police in order to prevent escape" violates the Fourth Amendment and the Due Process Clause of the Fourteenth Amendment. 710 F.2d 240, 244 (1983).

The Court affirms on the ground that application of the Tennessee statute to authorize Officer Hymon's use of deadly force constituted an unreasonable seizure in violation of the Fourth Amendment. The precise issue before the Court deserves emphasis, because both the decision below and the majority obscure what must be decided in this case. The issue is not the constitutional validity of the Tennessee statute on its face or as applied to some hypothetical set of facts. Instead, the issue is whether the use of deadly force by Officer Hymon under the circumstances of this case violated Garner's constitutional rights. Thus, the majority's assertion that a police officer who has probable cause to seize a suspect "may not always do so by killing him," ante, at 1700, is unexceptionable but also of little relevance to the question presented here. The same is true of the rhetorically stirring statement that "[t]he use of deadly force to prevent the escape of all felony suspects, whatever the circumstances, is constitutionally unreasonable." Ante, at 1701. The question we must address is whether the Constitution allows the use of such force to apprehend a suspect who resists arrest by attempting to flee the scene of a nighttime burglary of a residence.

For purposes of Fourth Amendment analysis, I agree with the Court that Officer Hymon "seized" Garner by shooting him. Whether that seizure was reasonable and therefore permitted by the Fourth Amendment requires a careful balancing of the important public interest in crime prevention and detection and the nature and quality of the intrusion upon legitimate interests of the individual. United States v. Place,

462 U.S. 696, 703, 103 S.Ct. 2637, 2642, 77 L.Ed.2d 110 (1983). In striking this balance here, it is crucial to acknowledge that police use of deadly force to apprehend a fleeing criminal suspect falls within the "rubric of police conduct . . . necessarily [involving] swift action predicated upon the on-the-spot observations of the officer on the beat." Terry v. Ohio, 392 U.S. 1, 20, 88 S.Ct. 1868, 1879, 20 L.Ed.2d 889 (1968). The clarity of hindsight cannot provide the standard for judging the reasonableness of police decisions made in uncertain and often dangerous circumstances. Moreover, I am far more reluctant than is the Court to conclude that the Fourth Amendment proscribes a police practice that was accepted at the time of the adoption of the Bill of Rights and has continued to receive the support of many state legislatures. Although the Court has recognized that the requirements of the Fourth Amendment must respond to the reality of social and technological change, fidelity to the notion of constitutional—as opposed to purely judicial—limits on governmental action requires us to impose a heavy burden on those who claim that practices accepted when the Fourth Amendment was adopted are now constitutionally impermissible. See, e.g., United States v. Watson, 423 U.S. 411, 416–421, 96 S.Ct. 820, 824–827, 46 L.Ed.2d 598 (1976); Carroll v. United States, 267 U.S. 132, 149–153, 45 S.Ct. 280, 283–285, 69 L.Ed. 543 (1925). Cf. United States v. Villamonte-Marquez, 462 U.S. 579, 585, 103 S.Ct. 2573, 2582, 77 L.Ed.2d 22 (1983) (noting "impressive historical pedigree" of statute challenged under Fourth Amendment).

The public interest involved in the use of deadly force as a last resort to apprehend a fleeing burglary suspect relates primarily to the serious nature of the crime. Household burglaries not only represent the illegal entry into a person's home, but also "pose real risk of serious harm to others." Solem v. Helm, 463 U.Z. 277, 315–316, 103 S.Ct. 3001, 3023, 77 L.Ed.2d 637 (1983) (BURGER, C.J., dissenting). According to recent Department of Justice statistics, "[t]hree-fifths of all rapes in the home, three-fifths of all home robberies, and about a third of home aggravated and simple assaults are committed by burglars." Bureau of Justice Statistics Bulletin, Household Burglary 1 (January 1985). During the period 1973–1982, 2.8 million such violent crimes were committed in the course of burglaries. Ibid. Victims of a forcible intrusion into their home by a nighttime prowler will find little consolation in the majority's confident assertion that "burglaries only rarely involve physical violence." Ante, at 1707. Moreover, even if a particular burglary, when viewed in retrospect, does not involve physical harm to others, the "harsh potentialities for violence" inherent in the forced entry into a home preclude characterization of the crime as "innocuous, inconsequential, minor, or 'nonviolent.'" Solem v. Helm, supra, at 316, 103 S.Ct., at 3023 (BURGER, C.J., dissenting). See also Restatement of Torts section 131, Comment g (1934) (burglary is among felonies that normally cause or among felonies that normally cause or threaten death or serious bodily harm); R. Perkins & R. Boyce, Criminal Law 1110 (3d ed. 1982) (burglary is dangerous felony that creates unreasonable risk of great personal harm).

Because burglary is a serious and dangerous felony, the public interest in the prevention and detection of the crime is of compelling importance. Where a police officer has probable cause to arrest a suspected burglar, the use of deadly force as a last resort might well be the only means of apprehending the suspect. With respect to a particular burglary, subsequent investigation simply cannot represent a substitute for immediate apprehension of the criminal suspect at the scene. See President's Commission on Law Enforcement and Administration of Justice, Task Force Report: The Challenge of Crime in a Free Society 97 (1967). Indeed, the Captain of the Memphis Police Department testified that in his city, if apprehension is not immediate, it is likely that the suspect will not be caught. App. in No. 81-5605 (CA6), p. 334. Although some law enforcement agencies may choose to assume the risk that a criminal will remain at large, the Tennessee statute reflects a legislative determination that the use of deadly force in prescribed circumstances will serve generally to protect the public. Such statutes assist the police in apprehending suspected perpetrators of serious crimes and provide notice that a lawful police order to stop and submit to arrest may not be ignored with impunity. See, e.g., Wiley v. Memphis Police Department, 548 F.2d 1247, 1252–1253 (CA6), cert. denied, 434 U.S. 822, 98 S.Ct. 65, 54 L.Ed.2d 78 (1977); Jones v. Marshall, 528 F.2d 132, 142 (CA2 1975).

The Court unconvincingly dismisses the general deterrence effects by stating that "the presently available evidence does not support [the] thesis" that the threat of force discourages escape and that "there is a substantial basis for doubting that the use of such force is an essential attribute to the arrest power in all felony cases." Ante, at 1701. There is no question that the effectiveness of police use of deadly force is arguable and that many states or individual police departments have decided to those presented here. But it should go without saying that the effectiveness or popularity of a particular police practice does not determine its constitutionality. Cf. Spaziano v. Florida, 468 U.S. 447, 464, 104 S.Ct.

3154, 3164, 82 L.Ed.2d 340 (1984) ("The Eighth Amendment is not violated every time a state reaches a conclusion different from a majority of its sisters over how best to administer its criminal laws"). Moreover, the fact that police conduct pursuant to a state statute is challenged on constitutional grounds does not impose a burden on the state to produce social science statistics or to dispel any possible doubts about the necessity of the conduct. This observation, I believe, has particular force where the challenged practice both predates enactment of the Bill of Rights and continues to be accepted by a substantial number of the states.

Against the strong public interests justifying the conduct at issue here must be weighed the individual interests implicated in the use of deadly force by police officers. The majority declares that "[t]he suspect's fundamental interest in his own life need not be elaborated upon." Ante, at 1700. This blithe assertion hardly provides an adequate substitute for the majority's failure to acknowledge the distinctive manner in which the suspect's interest in his life is even exposed to risk. For purposes of this case, we must recall that the police officer, in the course of investigating a nighttime burglary, had reasonable cause to arrest the suspect and ordered him to halt. The officer's use of force resulted because the suspected burglar refused to heed this command and the officer reasonably believed that there was no means short of firing his weapon to apprehend the suspect. Without questioning the importance of a person's interest encompasses a right to flee unimpeded from the scene of a burglary. Cf. Payton v. New York, 445 U.S. 573, 617, n. 14, 100 S.Ct. 1371, 1395, n. 14, 63 L.Ed.2d 639 (1980) (WHITE, J., dissenting) ("[T]he policeman's hands should not be tied merely because of the possibility that the suspect will fail to cooperate with legitimate actions by law enforcement personnel"). The legitimate interests of the suspect in these circumstances are adequately accommodated by the Tennessee statute: to avoid the use of deadly force and the consequent risk to his life, the suspect need merely obey the valid order to halt.

A proper balancing of the interests involved suggests that use of deadly force as a last resort to apprehend a criminal suspect fleeing from the scene of a nighttime burglary is not unreasonable within the meaning of the Fourth Amendment. Admittedly, the events giving rise to this case are in retrospect deeply regrettable. No one can view the death of an unarmed and apparently nonviolent 15-year-old without sorrow, much less disapproval. Nonetheless, the reasonableness of Officer Hymon's conduct for purposes of the Fourth Amendment cannot be evaluated by what later appears to have been a preferable course of police action. The officer pursued a suspect in the darkened backyard of a house that from all indications had just been burglarized. The police officer was not certain whether the suspect was alone or unarmed; nor did he know what had transpired inside the house. He ordered the suspect to halt, and when the suspect refused to obey and attempted to flee into the night, the officer fired his weapon to prevent escape. The reasonableness of this action for purposes of the Fourth Amendment is not determined by the unfortunate nature of this particular case; instead, the question is whether it is constitutionally impermissible for police officers, as a last resort, to shoot a burglary suspect fleeing the scene of the crime.

Because I reject the Fourth Amendment reasoning of the majority and the Court of Appeals, I briefly note that no other constitutional provision supports the decision below. In addition to his Fourth Amendment claim, appellee-respondent also alleged violations of due process, the Sixth Amendment right to trial by jury, and the Eighth Amendment proscription of cruel and unusual punishment. These arguments were rejected by the District Court and, except for the due process claim, not addressed by the Court of Appeals. With respect to due process, the Court of Appeals reasoned that statutes affecting the fundamental interest in life must be "narrowly drawn to express only the legitimate state interests at stake." 710 F.2d, at 245. The Court of Appeals concluded that a statute allowing police use of deadly force is narrowly drawn and therefore constitutional only if the use of such force is limited to situations in which the suspect poses an immediate threat to others. Id, at 246–247. Whatever the validity of Tennessee's statute in other contexts, I cannot agree that its application in this case resulted in a deprivation "without due process of law." Cf. Baker v. McCollan, 443 U.S. 137, 144–145, 99 S.Ct. 2689, 2694–2695, 61 L.Ed.2d 433 (1979). Nor do I believe that a criminal suspect who is shot while trying to avoid apprehension has a cognizable claim of a deprivation of his Sixth Amendment right to trial by jury. See Cunningham v. Ellington, 323 F.Supp. 1072, 1075–1076 (WD Tenn.1971) (three-judge court). Finally, because there is no indication that the use of deadly force was intended to punish rather than to capture the suspect, there is no valid claim under the Eighth Amendment. See Bell v. Wolfish, 441 U.S. 520, 538–539, 99 S.Ct. 1861, 1873–1874, 60 L.Ed.2d 447 (1979). Accordingly, I conclude that the District Court properly entered judgment against appellee-respondent, and I would reverse the decision of the Court of Appeals.

Even if I agreed that the Fourth Amendment was violated under the circumstances of this case, I would be unable to join the Court's opinion. The Court holds that deadly force may be used only if the suspect "threatens the officer with a weapon or there is probably cause to believe that he has committed a crime involving the infliction or threatened infliction of serious physical harm." Ante, at 1701. The Court ignores the more general implications of its reasoning. Relying on the Fourth Amendment, the majority asserts that it is constitutionally unreasonable to use deadly force against fleeing criminal suspects who do not appear to pose a threat of serious physical harm to others. *Ibid.* By declining to limit its holding to the use of firearms, the Court unnecessarily implies that the Fourth Amendment constrains the use of any police practice that is potentially lethal, no matter how remote the risk. Cf. Los Angeles v. Lyons, 461 U.S. 95, 103 S.Ct. 1660, 75 L.Ed.2d 675 (1983).

Although it is unclear from the language of opinion, I assume that the majority intends the word "use" to include only those circumstances in which the suspect is actually apprehended. Absent apprehension of the suspect, there is no "seizure" for Fourth Amendment purposes. I doubt that the Court intends to allow criminal suspects who successfully escape to return later with section 1983 claims against officers who used, albeit unsuccessfully, deadly force in their futile attempt to capture the fleeing suspect. The Court's opinion despite its broad language, actually decides only that the shooting of the fleeing burglary suspect who was in fact neither armed nor dangerous can support a section 1983 action.

The Court's silence on critical factors in the decision to use deadly force simply invites second-guessing of difficult police decisions that must be made quickly in the most trying of circumstances. Cf. Payton v. New York, 445 U.S., at 619, 100 S.Ct., at 1396 (WHITE, J., dissenting). Police are given no guidance for determining which objects, among an array of potentially lethal weapons ranging from guns to knives to baseball bats to rope, will justify the use of deadly force. The Court also declines to outline the additional factors necessary to provide "probably cause" for believing that a suspect "poses a significant threat of death or serious injury," ante, at 1697, when the officer has probable cause to arrest and the suspect refuses to obey an order to halt. But even if it were appropriate in this case to limit the use of deadly force to that ambiguous class of suspects, I believe the class should include nighttime residential burglars who resist arrest by attempting to flee the scene of the crime. We can expect an escalating volume of litigation as the lower courts struggle to determine if a police officer's split-second decision to shoot was justified by the danger posed by a particular object and other facts related to the crime. Thus, the majority opinion portends a burgeoning area of Fourth Amendment doctrine concerning the circumstances in which police officers can reasonably employ deadly force.

The Court's opinion sweeps broadly to adopt an entirely new standard for the constitutionality of the use of deadly force to apprehend fleeing felons. Thus, the Court "lightly brushe[s] aside," Payton v. New York, supra, at 600, 100 S.Ct., at 1387, a long-standing police practice that predates the Fourth Amendment and continues to receive the approval of nearly half of the state legislatures. I cannot accept the majority's creation of a constitutional right to flight for burglary suspects seeking to avoid capture at the scene of the crime. Whatever the constitutional limits on police use of deadly force in order to apprehend a fleeing felon, I do not believe they are exceeded in a case in which a police officer has probable cause to arrest a suspect at the scene of a residential burglary, orders the suspect to halt, and then fires his weapon as a last resort to prevent the suspect's escape into the night. I respectfully dissent. O'CONNOR.

Comment

Although this case deals solely with law enforcement, it presents several valuable insights:

It confirms the position of the Klein Case insofar as demonstrating the judicial abhorence to the use of deadly force by police. This should act as a strong guide to the private security industry that the courts which do not look favorably of the use of deadly force by police are hardly going to allow the use of deadly force by private citizens, and are apt to come down very heavily on such a person. Of course, one can argue, as the law indicates, that the Fourth Amendment was not intended to protect society from private persons, only governmental action; to follow that logic would recreate the Wild West! Therefore, I would not recommend the widespread use of armed private security persons.

I would be remiss if I did not highlight the statement of the Court as follows on page 1709; "the Court has recognized that the requirements of the Fourth Amendment must respond to the reality of social and technological CHANGE," another way of stating judicial supremacy, and judicial legislation, let alone the amending of the U.S. Constitution. It strikes me as more of the kind of judicial activism that has resulted in the increase of violence and crime.

Lastly, I highly recommend a close reading again of the dissent by Justice O'Connor.

Chapter 4

SEARCH AND SEIZURE

CONSTITUTIONAL APPLICATION OF FOURTH AMENDMENT TO U.S. CONSTITUTION

"The right of the people to be secure in their persons, houses, papers, and effects, against unreasonable searches and seizures, shall not be violated, and no warrants shall issue, but upon probable cause supported by oath or affirmation, and particularly describing the place to be searched, and the persons or things to be seized." After many years, the United States Supreme Court developed its own sanction, a rule of evidence known as the Exclusionary Rule, which prohibits the introduction in evidence at a trial of any evidence, or the fruits thereof, which has been obtained by government agents in violation of the U.S. Constitution. The two basic reasons usually stated for this rule are: (1) To maintain the integrity of the judiciary by refusing to allow itself to "dirty its hands," by handling tainted evidence; and, (2) to deter overzealous law enforcement officers.

Note that the constitutional prohibition against unreasonable searches and seizures includes no sanction, no statement as to how the Amendment (see also the Fifth and Sixth Amendments) is to be enforced. At least, if the person who violated the Fourth Amendment committed a criminal act while so doing, or facts give rise to a civil cause of action, then the violator would be subject to criminal prosecution or a civil law suit, or both. These sanctions have always existed, and may have been deemed sufficient by the authors of our Bill of Rights, but the judiciary has legislated a sanction; more correctly amended the U.S. Constitution by addition. For our purpose, the basic question arises whether evidence obtained by a private security person under circumstances which would render such search or seizure by governmental agents a violation of the Fourth Amendment will also be excluded as evidence in a subsequent trial.

Burdeau v. McDowell
United States Supreme Court, 1920
256 U.S. 465, 41 S. Ct. 574

The Fourth Amendment gives protection against unlawful searches and seizures, and as shown in the previous cases, its protection applies to governmental action. Its origin and history clearly show that it was intended as a restraint upon the activities of sovereign authority, and was not intended to be a limitation upon other than governmental agencies; as against such authority it was the purpose of the Fourth Amendment to secure the citizen in the right of unmolested occupation of his dwelling and the possession of his property, subject to the right of seizure by process duly issued.

In the present case the record clearly shows that no official of the federal government had anything to do with the wrongful seizure of the petitioner's property, or any knowledge thereof until several months after the property had been taken from him and was in the possession of the Cities Service Company. It is manifest that there was no invasion of the security afforded by the Fourth Amendment against unreasonable search and seizure, as whatever wrong was done was the act of individuals in taking the property of another. A portion of the property so taken and held was turned over to the prosecuting officers of the federal government. *We assume that petitioner has an unquestionable right of redress against those who illegally and wrongfully took his private property under the circumstance herein disclosed, but with such remedies we are not now concerned.*

The Fifth Amendment, as its terms import, is intended to secure the citizen from compulsory testimony against himself. It protects from extorted confessions, or examinations in court proceedings by compulsory methods.

The exact question to be decided here is: may the government retain incriminating papers, coming to it in the manner described, with a view to their use in a subsequent investigation by a grand jury where such papers will be part of the evidence against the accused, and may be used against him upon trial should an indictment be returned?

We know of no constitutional principle which requires the government to surrender the papers under such circumstances. Had it learned that such incriminatory papers, tending to show a violation of federal law, were in the hands of a person other than the accused, it having had no part in wrongfully obtaining them, we know of no reason why a subpoena might not issue for the production of the papers as evidence. Such production would require no unreasonable search and seizure nor would it amount to compelling the accused to testify against himself.

The papers having come into the possession of the government without a violation of petitioner's rights by the governmental authority, we see no reason why the fact that individuals, unconnected with the government, may have wrongfully taken them, should prevent them from being held for use in prosecuting an offense where the documents are of an incriminatory character.

It follows that the District Court erred in making the order appealed from, and the same is reversed.

Mr. Justice Brandeis dissenting, with whom Mr. Justice Holmes concurs.

Plaintiff's private papers were stolen. The thief, to further his own ends, delivered them to the law officer of the United States. He, knowing them to have been stolen, retains them for use against the plaintiff. Should the court permit him to do so?

That the court would restore the papers to plaintiff if they were still in the thief's possession is not questioned. That it has power to control the disposition of these stolen papers, although they have passed into the possession of the law officer, is also not questioned. But it is said that no provision of the Constitution requires their surrender and that the papers could have been subpoenaed. This may be true. Still I cannot believe that action of a public official is necessarily lawful, because it does not violate constitutional prohibitions and because the same result might have been attained by other and proper means. At the foundation of our civil liberty lies the principle which denied to government officials an exceptional position before the law and which subjects them to the same rules of conduct that are commands to the citizen. And in the development of our liberty insistence upon procedural regularity has been a large factor. Respect for law will not be advanced by resort, in its enforcement, to means which shock the common man's sense of decency and fair play.

United States v. Harding
Circuit Court of Appeals (Cir.), 1973
475 F.2d 480

WHETHER There Was Invalidity in Connection with the Seizure of the Materials by the Government

Defendant contends that there was no lawful authority for the procedure used, that the search was illegal and that the obscene matter was seized without prior adversary hearing on obscenity. There is no showing whatever that the employees of Emery were working in conjunction with the FBI. Moreover, Emery had a valid interest in checking the contents of the package and so this particular search was not carried out pursuant to any direction by the government.

A search and seizure by a private person not acting in collusion with federal officers does not render the subsequently seized material inadmissible in evidence. See Burdeau v. McDowell, 256 U.S. 465, 474, 41 S.Ct. 574, 65 L.Ed. 1048 (1921), an early Supreme Court decision wherein business associates of the accused actually stole certain incriminating documents. Notwithstanding the theft aspect, a majority of the Supreme Court held that it was valid for the government to introduce this illegally obtained evidence. Other decisions have gone a long way, perhaps too far, in allowing the government to use evidence obtained by private individuals. Thus, in Cohen v. United States, 36 F.2d 461, 462 (3d Cir. 1929), cert denied, 281 U.S. 742, 50 S.Ct. 348, 74 L.Ed. 1156 (1930), it was held that notwithstanding the existence of an illegal search and seizure, the testimony of a stranger entering the premises during the search at the invitation of the occupant was admissible.

In United States v. Ashby, 245 F.2d 684, 686 (5th Cir. 1957), joint income tax returns voluntarily turned over by a wife were admitted over the objection of the husband, the spouse being separated. See United States v. Winfree, 170 F.Supp. 659 (E.D.Pa. 1959).

In United States v. Goldberg, 330 F.2d 30 (3d Cir. 1964), cert, denied, 377 U.S. 953, 84 S.Ct. 1630, 12 L.Ed. 2d 497 (1964), documents and records of a corporation of which the taxpayer was president were taken without his knowledge by former employees, but were nevertheless held to be admissible.

It has been argued that Elkins v. United States, 364 U.S. 206, 80 S.Ct. 1437, 4 L.Ed. 2d 1669 (1960) has generally condemned receipt of tainted evidence and has thus undermined the authority of the cases holding the evidence obtained by private persons is admissible. However, the tendencies have been to narrowly construe Elkins and to limit its effect to seizures by state officers.

Appellant placed reliance on Corngold v. United States, 367 F.2d 1 (9th Cir. 1966). It is true that in the Corngold case the airline transportation agent participated in the search and was advancing the interests of his employer in doing so. The court held that the evidence was in admissible, but carefully pointed out that the search was a joint operation of the customs agent and the TWA employee. The court said:

> When a federal agent participates in such a joint endeavor, "the effect is the same as though he had engaged in the undertaking as one exclusively his own." Byars v. United States, supra, 273 U.S. 28, at 33, 47 S.Ct. 248 at 250, 71 L.Ed. 520, 367 F.2d at 6 (footnote omitted). The court went on to quote Justice Frankfurter in Lustig v. United States, 338 U.S. 74, 78–79, 69 S.Ct. 1372, 1374, 93 L.Ed. 1819 (1949) as follows:
>
> (A) search is a search by a federal official if he had a hand in it***. The decisive factor in determining the applicability of the Byars case is the actuality of a share by a federal official in the total enterprise of securing and selecting evidence by other than sanctioned means.

No such federal participation, direct or indirect, in the initial search is present in our case. Consequently, the initial search was a private one and therefore there is no room for a claim that the evidence here was inadmissible. It is true that following the encounter with Mrs. Stewart at the airport the officers had a practical control over the material. At that point, however, the court had issued its initial orders, and there was probable cause growing out of the search in Los Angeles for the issuance of the search warrant and the order to show cause. The officers promptly caused the carton to be taken before the United States District Court Judge and an adversary hearing followed. After hearing the evidence that judge made extensive findings and conclusions that the material was obscene.

While it is true that expert testimony was not presented, the judge did not believe that this was necessary. He concluded that the material spoke for itself. We see no merit in the defendant's contentions as to the manner of obtaining possession of the material and validity of the procedure followed.

Surgical Search and Seizure
Commonwealth v. Storella
Appeals Court of Massachusetts, 1978
1978 Mass. App. Adv. Shts. 499, 375 N.E. 2d 348

ARMSTRONG, Justice. On May 2, 1974, defendant, giving a false name and address, walked into the emergency room of the Bon Secours Hospital in Methuen with a bullet wound. The bullet had entered through his neck and had lodged itself behind his left ear, near the mastoid process. The defendant was not in acute distress, though he had some pain.

The hospital notified the Methuen Police Department, as required by G.L., C.112, Section 12A, and Captain DeSantis went to the hospital on May 3rd to question the defendant. The latter gave his correct name and false address different from the one given earlier. He said that he had been involved with a married woman and had been beaten and shot by her irate husband on April 29, but he refused to divulge their names. He said he had given a false name because he was married and did not want his own wife to learn about the affair which had led to his being shot.

Dr. Dragone, a surgical resident who undertook care of the defendant, advised him that the bullet was not an immediate danger to his health but that it should be removed and could lead to serious complications if it were not. The defendant postponed surgery for two days and then left the hospital on May 5. He telephoned Captain DeSantis on May 7, and informed DeSantis that he had decided not to have the bullet removed.

Meanwhile, the May 4 edition of the *Lawrence Eagle Tribune* had carried a story about the defendant's admission to the hospital and the amorous explanation he had given for the gunshot wound. The story was seen by Sergeant Willcox of the Malden police, who had been investigating an armed robbery of a Malden liquor store on the evening of April 29. One of three robbers had been shot by the proprietor during their getaway. Sergeant Willcox contacted Captain DeSantis and the hospital and arrangements were made for him to be notified if the defendant showed up again at the hospital.

On May 7, and again on May 14, the defendant appeared at the hospital to have his wound examined (he was being treated with antibiotics) and was advised again, on each occasion, to have the operation performed. On the latter date, Dr. Dragone told the defendant that the police would get the bullet eventually, apparently explaining to the defendant what the judge found to be the normal hospital procedure, to turn bullets over to the police for ballistics examination after they were removed surgically. On May 14, the defendant signed a consent form for an operation, and the operation was scheduled to be performed on May 17.

That morning, Captain DeSantis, who had been notified by either Dr. Dragone or by a Dr. McCarthy, a staff surgeon, in turn notified Sergeant Willcox of the Malden police. Willcox received two calls: the first, at 9:00 A.M., indicating that the operation would take place at 1:30 P.M., and the second, about an hour after the first, indicating that the time of the operation was to be advanced to 11:00 A.M. Willcox called one Windisch, a State ballistician, and both went to the hospital, joining Captain DeSantis. None had obtained a search warrant.

DeSantis was given permission, either by Dr. McCarthy or by a head nurse, to be present in the operating room, according to the defendant's allegations (the judge's findings are silent on the subject), after the defendant was anesthetized and without any prior knowledge by the defendant that he was to be there. The operation began at 11:29 A.M. At 11:46 A.M., Dr. Dragone removed the bullet, washed it, and handed it to DeSantis. The latter gave it directly to Windisch, the ballistics expert, who was waiting outside the operating room. By 2:30 P.M., Windisch reported to Willcox that he had identified the bullet as having come from the gun used by the proprietor of the liquor store on the evening of April 29.

Through the use of the bullet and the ballistics report, the Commonwealth secured the indictment and conviction of the defendant for robbery while masked and armed with a dangerous weapon. The sole questions presented in this appeal are whether the judge who denied the defendant's pretrial motion to suppress that evidence erred in so doing and whether he erred in denying the defendant's motion (also pretrial) to reopen and reconsider his earlier action on the basis of "newly available" testimony.

One of the factual conclusions on which the judge predicated his denial of the motion to suppress was that the doctor who removed the bullet and turned it over to the police was not acting as an agent of the police but merely as a private citizen cooperating with the police by turning evidence of crime over to them. It has long been settled that the Fourth Amendment to the United States Constitution applies only to searches and seizures taken by or at the direction of the State and, consequently, evidence obtained illegally by private parties and turned over to the police is not obtained in violation of the Fourth Amendment. Burdeau v. McDowell, 256 U.S. 465, 475, 41 S.Ct. 574, 65 L.Ed. 1048 (1921). The judge's finding concerning lack of agency is therefore dispositive of the case, assuming that it was warranted by the evidence and involved no misapplication of constitutional principles.

On the first score, the evidence adduced at the hearing on the motion to suppress fully supported the finding. In particular, there was ample evidence that the operation was necessitated by good medical practice, was advised as necessary (though not on an emergency basis) from the outset, was performed for medical reasons only and only incidentally resulted in the recovery of evidence for police use. There was no evidence suggesting that the police played a role in the decision whether to operate. They merely asked to be advised when an operation was to be performed, if the defendant and doctors made the decision to take that route. The doctor's acts in keeping the police notified and in turning the bullet over to them were not the result of official pressure or duress. They were merely praiseworthy acts of citizen cooperations. "It is no part of the policy underlying the Fourth and Fourteenth Amendments to discourage citizens from aiding to the utmost of their ability in the apprehension of criminals." Coolidge v. New Hampshire, 403, U.S. 443, 488, 91 S.Ct. 2022, 2049, 29 L.Ed. 2d 564 (1971).

The defendant cites several cases in which unlawful searches by private individuals have been held to constitute State action because of a degree of involvement, sometimes slight, by police: State v. Becich, 13 Or. App. 415, 509 P.2d 1332 (1973); Williams v. State, 501 P.2d 841 (Okl. Crim. 1972); Stapleton v. Superior Court, 70 Cal. 2d 97, 73 Cal. Rptr 575, 447 P.2d 967 (1986); and, in a different (but arguably related) context, United States v. Price, 383 U.S. 787, 794, 86 S.Ct. 1152, 16 L.Ed.2d 267 (1966). See also Byars v. United States, 338 U.S. 74, 78–79, 69 S.Ct. 1372, 93 L.Ed. 1819 (1949); People v. Tarantino, 45 Cal. 2d 590, 595, 290 P.2d 505 (1955). *A crucial element in all those cases was a finding that police participated in or directed the challenged search or seizure. In this case, by contrast, the spent bullet came into the hands of the doctors with no element of participation by or direction from the police. A second crucial distinction between the cases relied on by the defendant and this one is that in those cases the purpose of the challenged search was investigatory.* The purpose of the operation in this case, by contrast, was medical; the fact that the doctors knew that the police wanted the bullet was not the reason the operation took place. More in point, therefore, are cases such as Commonwealth v. Tanchyn, 200 Pa.

Super. 148, 150–154, 188 A.2d 824, cert. denied, 375 U.S. 866, 84 S.Ct. 138, 11 L.Ed. 2d 92 (1963), and Commonwealth v. Gordon, 431 Pa. 512, 517, 246 A.2d 325 (1968), cert. denied, 394 U.S. 937, 89 S.Ct. 1215, 22 L.Ed. 2d 269 (1969), in each of which the police were permitted to use evidence derived from a blood sample given them by hospital authorities, the said sample being part of a larger sample extracted from the defendant earlier for purely medical purposes and with no police involvement; and Webb, State, 467 S.W. 2d 449, 450–451 (Tex. Crim. App. 1971), a case, like this, where doctors operated for purely medical reasons to remove a bullet and then turned it over to the police. In all these cases the evidence was held to have been obtained without violation of the Fourth Amendment because the doctors did not act as agents of the State in acquiring or "seizing" the evidence.

The defendant suggests that the doctor's actions were State actions because G.L., C.112, Section 12A, required that they notify the police forth with that they were treating a bullet wound. But the notification required by Section 12A was not the "search" and "seizure" complained of; the statute imposes no duty on the doctor beyond notification. Even if the statute went further and mandated, for example, that the hospital retain the bullet, when extracted, for use as evidence, it would not follow that the doctor's removal of the bullet and transmission of it to the police would be deemed State action. The point is governed in principle by United States v. Miller, 425 U.S. 435, 96 S.Ct. 1619, 48 L.Ed. 2d (1976), which held that no Fourth Amendment rights of depositors are infringed by statutes requiring banks to keep copies of all checks, deposit slips, and statements and to turn them over to the State for use as evidence in criminal proceedings. "The depositor takes the risk, in revealing his affairs to another, that the information will be conveyed by that person to the Government." Id. at 443, 96 S.Ct. at 1624. The defendant in the case before us knew the risk. He had been told, specifically, that the bullet, if removed, would be turned over to the police. These considerations indicate that the judge was probably correct in his further conclusions that, even if the doctors had been acting as agents of the police, the evidence was admissible because (1) the defendant had no reasonable expectation of privacy in the context for the operating room (see Venner v. State, 279 Md. 47, 367 A2d 949 (1977), and (2) the defendant had, in effect, consented to the removal of the bullet and its transmission to the police (compare Lewis v. United States, 385 U.S. 206, 211–212, 87 S.Ct. 424, 17 L.Ed. 2d 312 (1966); Hoffa v. United States, 385 U.S. 293, 300–303,

87 S.Ct. 408, 17 L.Ed. 2d 374 (1966)). But as we have concluded that the judge did not err in finding that the doctors were acting as private citizens merely and not as agents for the police in retrieving the bullet, it is unnecessary for us to consider the judge's alternate basis for his denial of the defendant's motion to suppress.

The defendant, relying on Commonwealth v. Antobenedetto 366, Mass. 51, 57, 315 N.E. 2d 530 (1974), contends that the judge erred by refusing to rule that the Commonwealth had the burden of proving a justification for the warrantless search for and seizure of the bullet. The difficulty with the contention is that the defendant failed to sustain his preliminary burden of showing that the police executed a search or seizure. On the judge's findings, the "search and seizure," which in this context can only mean the surgical removal of the bullet, was not done by or for the "seizure." "If a transfer is voluntary, then it is not a seizure and the Fourth Amendment's reasonableness standard is simply inapplicable." United States v. Sherwin, 539 F.2d 1, 8 (9th Cir. 1976).

After the adverse ruling on the motion to suppress, the defendant filed a motion asking for a rehearing in order that the testimony of D. McCarthy might be considered. The motion for rehearing was supported by an affidavit of defendant's counsel which was uninformative as to the content of Dr. McCarthy's expected testimony. At the hearing on the motion the defendant's counsel indicated that he hoped to show by Dr. McCarthy's testimony that he had been in charge or control of the operating room and had not given his consent to the presence of Captain DeSantis therein at the time of the operation. Such a showing would have done more to undercut the defendant's agency theory than to support the defendant's contention that the evidence was obtained by illegal police methods, as it is clear that the presence of DeSantis within the operating room, rather than in the corridor outside, was an immaterial factor in the judge's discretion to deny the motion.

Judgement affirmed.

Comment

In the Storella case the Massachusetts Appeals Court, an intermediate appellate court, distinguished prior cases cited by the defendant as precedents to render unlawful certain searches by private persons as constituting state action because of (1) the degree of involvement by police, and (2) that the search was investigatory. This Court proceeded to decide that the search was not state action, and therefore that Fourth Amendment did not apply.

Seven years later the United States Supreme Court established as a nationwide rule as when and when not surgical intrusions to recover evidence violate the Fourth Amendment on a basis of balancing the community's interest in fairly accurately determining guilt or innocence against the extent of the surgical intrusion. And finally hangs its hat on a failure of the prosecution to demonstrate a reasonable search!

Winston v. Lee
470 U.S. 753, 105 S.Ct. 1611 (1985)
Syllabus*

A shopkeeper was wounded by gunshot during an attempted robbery but, also being armed with a gun, apparently wounded his assailant in his left side, and the assailant then ran from the scene. Shortly after the victim was taken to a hospital, police officers found respondent, who was suffering from a gunshot wound to his left chest area, eight blocks away from the shooting. He was also taken to the hospital, where the victim identified him as the assailant. After an investigation, the police charged respondent with, *inter alia,* attempted robbery and malicious wounding. Thereafter the Commonwealth of Virginia moved in state court for an order directing respondent to undergo surgery to remove a bullet lodged under his left collarbone, asserting that the bullet would provide evidence of respondent's guilt or innocence. On the basis of expert testimony that the surgery would require an incision of only about one-half inch, could be performed under local anesthesia, and would result in "no danger on the basis that there's no general anesthesia employed," the court granted the motion, and the Virginia Supreme Court denied respondent's petition for a writ of prohibition and/or a writ of habeas corpus. Respondent then brought an action in Federal District Court to enjoin the pending operation on Fourth Amendment grounds, but the court refused to issue a preliminary injunction. *Subsequently,* X rays taken just before surgery was scheduled showed that the bullet was lodged substantially deeper than had been thought when the state court granted the motion to compel surgery, and the *surgeon concluded that a general anesthetic would be desirable.* Respondent unsuccessfully sought a rehearing in the state trial court, and the Virginia Supreme Court affirmed. However, respondent then returned to the Federal District Court, which, after an evidentiary hearing, *enjoined the threatened* surgery. The Court of Appeals affirmed.

Justice BRENNAN delivered the opinion of the Court.

Schmerber v. California, 384 U.S. 757, 86 S.Ct. 1826, 16 L.Ed.2d 908 (1966), held, *inter alia,* that a state may, over the suspect's protest, have a physician extract blood from a person suspected of drunken driving without violation of the suspect's right secured by the Fourth Amendment not to be subjected to unreasonable searches and seizures. However, Schmerber cautioned: "That we today hold that the Constitution does not forbid the States['] minor intrusions into an individual's body under stringently limited conditions in no way indicates that it permits more substantial intrusions, or intrusions under other conditions." *Id.,* at 772, 86 S.Ct., at 1836. In this case, the Commonwealth of Virginia seeks to compel the respondent Rudolph Lee, who is suspected of attempting to commit armed robbery, to undergo a surgical procedure under a general anesthetic for removal of a bullet lodged in his chest. Petitioners allege that the bullet will provide evidence of respondent's guilt or innocence. We conclude that the procedure sought here is an example of the "more substantial intrusion" cautioned against in Schmerber, and hold that to permit the procedure would violate respondent's right to be secure in his person guaranteed by the Fourth Amendment.

I

(A) At approximately 1:00 A.M. on July 18, 1982, Ralph E. Watkinson was closing his shop for the night. As he was locking the door, he observed someone armed with a gun coming toward him from across the street. Watkinson was also armed and when he drew his gun, the other person told him to freeze. Watkinson then fired at the other person, who returned fire. Watkinson was hit in the legs, while the other individual, who appeared to be wounded in his left side, ran from the scene. The police arrived on the scene shortly thereafter, and Watkinson was taken by ambulance to the emergency room of the Medical College of Virginia (MCV) Hospital.

Approximately 20 minutes later, police officers responding to another call found respondent eight blocks from where the earlier shooting occurred. Respondent was suffering from a gunshot wound to his left chest area and told the police that he had been shot when two individuals attempted to rob him. An ambulance took respondent to the MCV

Hospital. Watkinson was still in the MCV emergency room and, when respondent entered that room, said "[t]hat's the man that shot me." App 14. After an investigation, the police decided that respondent's story of having been himself the victim of a robbery was untrue and charged respondent with attempted robbery, malicious wounding, and two counts of using a firearm in the commission of a felony.

(B) The Commonwealth shortly thereafter moved in state court for an order directing respondent to undergo surgery to remove an object thought to be a bullet lodged under his left collarbone. The court conducted several evidentiary hearings on the motion. At the first hearing, the Commonwealth's expert testified that the surgical procedure would take 45 minutes and would involve a 3 to 4 percent chance of temporary nerve damage, a 1 percent chance of permanent nerve damage, and a one-tenth of 1 percent chance of death. At the second hearing, the expert testified that on reexamination of respondent, he discovered that the bullet was not "back inside close to the nerves and arteries," *Id.,* at 52, as he originally had thought. Instead, he now believed the bullet to be located "just beneath the skin." *Id.,* at 57. He testified that the surgery would require an incision of only one and one-half centimeters (slightly more than one-half inch), could be performed under local anesthesia, and would result in "no danger on the basis that there's no general anesthesia employed." *Id.,* at 51.

The state trial judge granted the motion to compel surgery. Respondent petitioned the Virginia Supreme Court for a writ of prohibition and/or a writ of habeas corpus, both of which were denied. Respondent then brought an action in the United States District Court for the Eastern District of Virginia to enjoin the pending operation of Fourth Amendment grounds. The court refused to issue a preliminary injunction, holding that respondent's cause had little likelihood of success on the merits. 551 F.Supp. 247, 247–253 (1982).

On October 18, 1982, just before the surgery was scheduled, the surgeon ordered that X rays be taken of respondent's chest. The X rays revealed that the bullet was in fact lodged two and one-half to three centimeters (approximately one inch) deep in muscular tissue in respondent's chest, substantially deeper than had been thought when the state court granted the motion to compel surgery. The surgeon now believed that a general anesthetic would be desirable for medical reasons.

Respondent moved the state trial court for rehearing based on the new evidence. After holding an evidentiary hearing, the state trial court denied the rehearing, and the Virginia Supreme Court affirmed. Respondent then returned to federal court, where he moved to alter or amend the judgment previously entered against him. After an evidentiary hearing, the District Court enjoined the threatened surgery. 551 F.Supp., at 253–261 (supplemental opinion). A divided panel of the Court of Appeals for the Fourth Circuit affirmed. 717 F.2d 888 (1983). We granted certiorari, 466 U.S. 942, 104 S.Ct. 1906, 80 L.Ed.2d 455 (1984), to consider whether a state may consistently with the Fourth Amendment compel a suspect to undergo surgery of this kind in a search for evidence of a crime.

II

[1,2] The Fourth Amendment protects "expectations of privacy," see Katz v. United States, 389 U.S. 347, 88 S.Ct. 507, 19 L.Ed.2d 576 (1967)—the individual's legitimate expectations that in certain places and at certain times he had "the right to be let alone—the most comprehensive of rights and the right most valued by civilized men." Olmstead v. United States, 277 U.S. 438, 478, 48 S.Ct. 564, 572, 72 L.Ed. 944 (1928) (Brandeis, J., dissenting). Putting to one side the procedural protections of the warrant requirement, the Fourth Amendment generally protects the "security" of "persons, houses, papers, and effects" against official intrusions up to the point where the community's need for evidence surmounts a specified standard, ordinarily "probable cause." Beyond this point, it is ordinarily justifiable for the community to demand that the individual give some part of his interest in privacy and security to advance the community's vital interests in law enforcement; such a search is generally "reasonable" in the Amendment's terms.

A compelled surgical intrusion into an individual's body for evidence, however, implicates expectations of privacy and security of such magnitude that the intrusion may be "unreasonable" even if likely to produce evidence of a crime. In Schmerber v. California, 384 U.S. 757, 86 S.Ct. 1826, 16 L.Ed.2d 908 (1966), we addressed a claim that the State had breached the Fourth Amendment's protection of the "right of the people to be secure in their *persons* . . . against unreasonable searches and seizures" (emphasis added) when it compelled an individual suspected of drunken driving to undergo a blood test. Schmerber had been arrested at a hospital while receiving treatment for injuries suffered when the automobile he was driving struck a tree. *Id.,* at 758, 86 S.Ct., at 1829. Despite Schmerber's objection, a police officer at the hospital had directed a physician to take a blood sample from him. Schmerber subsequently objected to the introduction at trial of evidence obtained as a result of the blood test.

The authorities in Schmerber clearly had probable cause to believe that he had been driving while intoxicated, *Id.*, at 768, 86 S.Ct., at 1834, and to believe that a blood test would provide evidence that was exceptionally probative in confirming this belief. *Id.*, at 770, 86 S.Ct., at 1835. Because the case fell within the exigent-circumstances exception to the warrant requirement, no warrant was necessary. *Ibid.* The search was not more intrusive than reasonably necessary to accomplish its goals. Nonetheless, Schmerber argued that the Fourth Amendment prohibited the authorities from intruding into his body to extract the blood that was needed as evidence.

[3] Schmerber noted that "[t]he overriding function of the Fourth Amendment is to protect personal privacy and dignity against unwarranted intrusion by the State." Id., at 767, 86 S.Ct., at 1834. Citing Wolf v. Colorado, 338 U.S. 25, 27, 69 S.Ct. 1359, 1361, 93 L.Ed. 1782 (1949), and Mapp v. Ohio, 367 U.S. 643, 81 S.Ct. 1684, 6 L.Ed.2d 1081 (1961), we observed that these values were "basic to free society." We also noted that "[b]ecause we are dealing with intrusions into the human body rather than with state interferences with property relationships or private papers— 'houses, papers, and effects'—we write on a clean slate." 384 U.S., at 767–768, 86 S.Ct., at 1833–1835. The intrusion perhaps implicated Schmerber's most personal and deep-rooted expectations of privacy, and the Court recognized that Fourth Amendment analysis thus required a discerning inquiry into the facts and circumstances to determine whether the intrusion was justifiable. The Fourth Amendment neither forbids nor permits all such intrusions; rather, the Amendment's "proper function is to constrain, not against all intrusions as such, but against intrusions which are not justified in the circumstances, or which are made in an improper manner." *Id.*, at 768, 86 S.Ct., at 1834.

[4] The reasonableness of surgical intrusions beneath the skin depends on a case-by-case approach, in which the individual's interests in privacy and security are weighed against society's interests in conducting the procedure. In a given case, the question whether the community's need for evidence outweighs the substantial privacy interests at stake is a delicate one admitting of few categorical answers. We believe that Schmerber, however, provides the appropriate framework of analysis for such cases.

Schmerber recognized that the ordinary requirements of the Fourth Amendment would be the threshold requirements for conducting this kind of surgical search and seizure. We noted the importance of probable cause. *Id.,* at 768–769, 86 S.Ct., at 1834–1835. And we pointed out: "Search warrants are ordinarily required for searches of dwellings, and absent an emergency, no less could be required where intrusions into the human body are concerned. . . . The importance of informed, detached and deliberate determinations of the issue whether or not to invade another's body in search of evidence of guilt is indisputable and great." *Id.,* at 770, 86 S.Ct., at 1835.

[5] Beyond these standards, Schmerber's inquiry considered a number of other factors in determining the "reasonableness" of the blood test. A crucial factor in analyzing the magnitude of the intrusion in Schmerber is the extent to which the procedure may threaten the safety or health of the individual. "[F]or most people [a blood test] involves virtually no risk, trauma, or pain." *Id.,* at 771, 86 S.Ct., at 1836. Moreover, all reasonable medical precautions were taken and no unusual or untested procedures were employed in Schmerber; the procedure was performed "by a physician in a hospital environment according to accepted medical practices." *Ibid.* Notwithstanding the existence of probable cause, a search for evidence of a crime may be unjustifiable if it endangers the life or health of the suspect.

Another factor is the extent of intrusion upon the individual's dignitary interests in personal privacy and bodily integrity. Intruding into an individual's living room, see Payton v. New York, 445 U.S. 573, 100 S.Ct. 1371, 63 L.Ed.2d 639 (1980), eavesdropping upon an individual's telephone conversations, see Katz v. United States, 389 U.S., at 361, 88 S.Ct., at 516, or forcing an individual to accompany police officers to the police station, see Dunaway v. New York, 442 U.S. 200, 99 S.Ct. 2248, 60 L.Ed.2d 824 (1979), typically do not injure the physical person of the individual. Such intrusions do, however, damage the individual's sense of personal privacy and security and are thus subject to the Fourth Amendment's dictates. In noting that a blood test was "a commonplace in these days of periodic physical examinations," 384 U.S., at 771, 86 S.Ct., at 1836, Schmerber recognized society's judgment that blood tests do not constitute an unduly extensive imposition on an individual's personal privacy and bodily integrity.

Weighed against these individual interests is the community's interest in fairly and accurately determining guilt or innocence. This interest is, of course, of great importance. We noted in Schmerber that a blood test is "a highly effective means of determining the degree to which a person is under the influence of alcohol." *Id.,* at 771, 86 S.Ct., at 1836. Moreover, there was "a clear indication that in fact [desired] evidence [would] be found: if the blood test were undertaken. *Id.,* at 770, 86 S.Ct., at 1835. Especially given the difficulty of proving drunkenness by other means, these considerations showed that results of the blood test were of vital importance if the State were to enforce its drunken driving laws. In Schmerber, we concluded that this state interest was sufficient to justify the intrusion, and the compelled blood test was thus "reasonable" for Fourth Amendment purposes.

Applying the Schmerber balancing test in this case, we believe that the Court of Appeals reached the correct result. The Commonwealth plainly had probable cause to conduct the search. In addition, all parties apparently agree that respondent has had a full measure of procedural protections and has been able fully to litigate the difficult medical and legal questions necessarily involved in analyzing the reasonableness of a surgical incision of this magnitude. Our inquiry therefore must focus on the extent of the intrusion on respondent's privacy interests and on the State's need for the evidence.

The threats to the health or safety of respondent posed by the surgery are the subject of sharp dispute between the parties. Before the new revelations of October 18, the District Court found that the procedure could be carried out "with virtually no risk to [respondent]." 551 F.Supp., at 252. On rehearing, however, with new evidence before it, the District Court held that "the risks previously involved have increased in magnitude even as new risks are being added." *Id.,* at 260.

[6] The Court of Appeals examined the medical evidence in the record and found that respondent would suffer some risks associated with the surgical procedure. One surgeon had testified that the difficulty of discovering the exact location of the bullet "could require extensive probing and retracting of muscle tissue," carrying with it "the concomitant risks of injury to the muscle as well as injury to the nerves, blood vessels and other tissue in the chest and pleural cavity." 717 F.2d, at 900. The court further noted that "the greater intrusion and the larger incisions increase the risks of infection." *Ibid.* Moreover, there was conflict in the testimony concerning the nature and the scope of the operation. One surgeon stated that it would take 15 to 20 minutes, while another predicted the procedure could take up to two and one-half hours. *Ibid.* The court

properly took the resulting uncertainty about the medical risks into account.

Both lower courts in this case believed that the proposed surgery, which for purely medical reasons required the use of a general anesthetic, would be an "extensive" intrusion on respondent's personal privacy and bodily integrity. *Ibid.* When conducted with the consent of the patient, surgery requiring general anesthesia is not necessarily demeaning or intrusive. In such a case, the surgeon is carrying out the patient's own will concerning the patient's body and the patient's right to privacy is therefore preserved. In this case, however, the Court of Appeals noted that the Commonwealth proposes to take control of respondent's body, to "drug this citizen—not yet convicted of a criminal offense—with narcotics and barbiturates into a state of unconsciousness," *Id.,* at 901, and then to search beneath his skin for evidence of a crime. This kind of surgery involves a virtually total divestment of respondent's ordinary control over surgical probing beneath his skin.

The other part of the balance concerns the Commonwealth's need to intrude into respondent's body to retrieve the bullet. The Commonwealth claims to need the bullet to demonstrate that it was fired from Watkinson's gun, which in turn would show that respondent was the robber who confronted Watkinson. However, although we recognize the difficulty of making determinations in advance as to the strength of the case against respondent, petitioners' assertions of a compelling need for the bullet are hardly persuasive. The very circumstances relied on in this case to demonstrate probable cause to believe that evidence will be found tend to vitiate the Commonwealth's need to compel respondent to undergo surgery. The Commonwealth has available substantial additional evidence that respondent was the individual who accosted Watkinson on the night of the robbery. No party in this case suggests that Watkinson's entirely spontaneous identification of respondent at the hospital would be inadmissible. In addition, petitioners can no doubt prove that Watkinson was found a few blocks from Watkinson's store shortly after the incident took place. And petitioners can certainly show that the location of the bullet (under respondent's left collarbone) seems to correlate with Watkinson's report that the robber "jerked" to the left. App. 13. The fact that the Commonwealth had available such substantial evidence of the origin of the bullet restricts the need for the Commonwealth to compel respondent to undergo the contemplated surgery.

[7] In weighing the various factors in this case, we therefore reach the

same conclusion as the courts below. The operation sought will intrude substantially on respondent's protected interests. The medical risks of the operation, although apparently not extremely severe, are a subject of considerable dispute; the very uncertainty militates against finding the operation to be "reasonable." In addition, the intrusion on respondent's privacy interests entailed by the operation can only be characterized as severe. On the other hand, although the bullet may turn out to be useful to the Commonwealth in prosecuting respondent, the Commonwealth has failed to demonstrate a compelling need for it. We believe that in these circumstances the Commonwealth has failed to demonstrate that it would be "reasonable" under the terms of the Fourth Amendment to search for evidence of this crime by means of the contemplated surgery.

III

The Fourth Amendment is a vital safeguard of the right of the citizen to be free from unreasonable governmental intrusions into any area in which he has a reasonable expectation of privacy. Where the Court had found a lesser expectation of privacy, see, e.g., Rakas v. Illinois, 439 U.S. 128, 99 S.Ct. 421, 58 L.Ed.2d 387 (1978); South Dakota v. Opperman, 428 U.S. 364, 96 S.Ct. 3092, 49 L.Ed.2d 1000 (1976), or where the search involves a minimal intrusion on privacy interests, see, e.g., United States v. Hensley, 469 U.S. 221, 105 S.Ct. 675, 83 L.Ed.2d 604 (1985); Dunaway v. New York, 442 U.S., at 210–211, 99 S.Ct., at 2255–2256; United States v. Brignoni-Ponce, 422 U.S. 873, 880, 95 S.Ct. 2574, 2579, 45 L.Ed.2d 607 (1975); Adams v. Williams, 407 U.S. 143, 92 S.Ct. 1921, 32 L.Ed.2d 612 (1972); Terry v. Ohio, 392 U.S. 1, 88 S.Ct. 1868, 20 L.Ed.2d 889 (1968), the Court had held that the Fourth Amendment's protections are correspondingly less stringent. Conversely, however, the Fourth Amendment's command that searches be "reasonable" requires that when the State seeks to intrude upon an area in which our society recognizes a significantly heightened privacy interest, a more substantial justification is required to make the search "reasonable." Applying these principles, we hold that the proposed search in this case would be "unreasonable" under the Fourth Amendment.

Affirmed.

Justice Blackmun and Justice Rehnquist concur in the judgment.

Chief Justice Burger, concurring.

I join because I read the Court's opinion as not preventing detention of an individual if there are reasonable grounds to believe that natural bodily functions will disclose the presence of contraband materials secreted internally.

Comment

In Winston v. Lee, the United States Supreme Court, speaking through Mr. Justice Brennan, held that "the Fourth Amendment neither forbids nor permits all such intrusion, rather the Amendment's proper function is to constrain, not against all intrusions as such, but against intrusions which are not justified in the circumstances, or which are made *in an improper manner.*" This court then went on to mention factors of importance in weighing the community's interest in fairly and accurately determining guilt or innocence:

(A) Was there probable cause?
(B) The extent to which the medical procedure may threaten the safety or health of the individual?
(C) The extent of intrusion upon the individual's dignitary interests in personal privacy and bodily integrity.

The Court then held that in *this* case the intrusion would be unreasonable and, therefore in violation of the Fourth Amendment.

Search By Special Police Officer
Commonwealth v. Leone
Supreme Judicial Court of Massachusetts
386 Mass. 329, N.E. 2d 1036 (1982)

HENNESSEY, Chief Justice. This is an interlocutory appeal by the Commonwealth which objects to the suppression of certain evidence in a criminal proceeding in a District Court. The issues posed are whether the Fourth Amendment to the United States Constitution affects the admissibility of evidence discovered by special police officer privately employed as a plant security guard, and if so, whether the officer's conduct constituted an unreasonable search and seizure. We conclude that the Fourth Amendment does apply, but that the officer's private function may affect the constitutionality of his conduct. Further, because of the incomplete record before us, we vacate the judge's ruling suppressing the evidence, and we direct that further proceedings be held.

The defendant is charged with possession of a firearm and receipt of stolen goods (the firearm). At the time of his arrest, he was employed as a truck driver by an independent contractor which leased his services to General Electric Company. He drove exclusively for General Electric, and regularly traveled between General Electric plants in Lynn, Massachusetts, and Durham, North Carolina. On these trips the defendant used a truck bearing General Electric insignia and leased by General Electric from a truck rental company. Inside the cab of the truck was a sleeping compartment, which the defendant used as his personal living quarters while driving between Lynn and Durham.

On January 29, 1981, John Vousboukis, a General Electric security guard, stopped the defendant at the gate of General Electric's Lynn plant to determine whether the defendant's cargo was properly authorized to leave the plant. Vousboukis first inspected the cargo section of the truck, checking the cargo against a description on the defendant's gate pass. Then, over the defendant's objection, he entered the cab of the truck. On the bed in the defendant's sleeping quarters was a travel bag. It appears that the bag was closed, but not secured. Vousboukis picked up the bag, and discovered a gun within.

After questioning the defendant concerning firearms identification (the defendant stated that he had no Massachusetts identification card but had a North Carolina card at his home), Vousboukis took custody of the gun. He then contacted another security officer, who came to the gate and questioned the defendant further. The second officer contacted the Lynn police, and learned that the gun had been stolen from a Lynn police officer. Vousboukis turned over the gun to the police when they arrived.

The defendant moved to suppress the gun on the ground that Vousboukis had conducted an unreasonable search and seizure in violation of the United States and Massachusetts constitutions. At a hearing on the defendant's motion, Vousboukis testified that he was a "special police officer" for the city of Lynn, employed by General Electric to patrol its Lynn plant. His duties at General Electric included checking persons entering or leaving the plant to determine whether they were company personnel and inspecting vehicles to ensure that any "company materials" leaving the property were authorized to leave. There was no evidence explaining his status and duties as a special police officer.

Vousboukis stated that gate inspections of vehicles and their contents, including the drivers' personal bags, were routine practice. He also mentioned a company regulation providing that security plant guards could inspect any items brought onto or taken away from company property. According to Vousboukis, all employees and contractors were provided with a copy of the company regulations. The defendant testified that security guards had never inspected his truck or belongings during the eight years in which he had driven to and from the Lynn plant. He also stated that he had not received a copy of the company regulations, and had no knowledge of the provision for inspections.

The judge assumed that the Fourth Amendment governed the admissibility of the gun. He found that Vousboukis had acted in accordance with plant custom in stopping the defendant at the gate, but did not state whether he believed that further inspection was customary. He rules that Vousboukis "had the right and duty to inspect the cargo, and the inside of the cab, but had no right to handle the travel bag," and that Vousboukis' conduct had violated the reasonable expectation of privacy held by the defendant." On this ground, he suppressed the evidence.

There is no suggestion that, before stopping the defendant's truck, Vousboukis had probable cause to search the truck, or even reason to suspect that the defendant was involved in crime. Under the standards applied to ordinary police officers, he was not entitled to conduct even a cursory search. See, e.g., Commonwealth v. Loughlin, 385 Mass. 60, 62, 430 N.E.2d 823 (1982); Commonwealth v. Silva, 366 Mass. 402, 404–407, 318 N.E.2d 895 (1974); Robbins v. California, 453 U.S. 420, 101 S.Ct. 2841, 2844–2847, 69 L.Ed.2d 744 (1981); Carroll v. United States, 267 U.S. 132, 155–156, 45 S.Ct. 280, 285–286, 69 L.Ed. 543 (1925). Therefore, the admissibility of the evidence he discovered depends on whether and in what manner the Fourth Amendment applies to privately employed special police officers such as Officer Vousboukis.

(1) The Fourth Amendment, and the accompanying rule of exclusion, apply only to government action. Evidence discovered and seized by private parties is admissible without regard to the methods used, unless State officials have instigated or participated in the search. Commonwealth v. Richmond, 379 Mass. 557,____, Mass. Adv.Sh. (1980) 167, 171, 399 N.E.2d 1069; Commonwealth v. Weiss, 370 Mass. 416, 419–420, 348 N.E.2d 787 (1976); Walter v. United States, 447 U.S. 649, 656, 100 S.Ct. 2395, 2401–2402, 65 L.Ed.2d 410 (1980); Burdeau v. McDowell, 256 U.S. 465, 475, 41 S.Ct. 574, 576, 65 L.Ed. 1048 (1921). See generally, 1 W. LaFave, Search and Seizure Section 1.6 (1978); Annot., 36 A.L.R. 3d 553 (1971). This rule follows from the origins and design of the Fourth

Amendment as a restraint against arbitrary or lawless use of sovereign power, with its great potential for intrusion upon the privacy of individuals. See, Burdeau v. McDowell, supra at 475, 41 S.Ct. at 576; 1 W. LaFave, supra Section 1.1(a)I Limitation of Fourth Amendment sanctions to government action is also consistent with a major objective of the rule of exclusion—deterrence of unreasonable searches and seizures. Private persons are not regularly involved in law enforcement, and those who undertake searches generally do so for reasons other than to secure criminal conviction. Therefore, exclusion of the fruits of their activities will not have a significant deterrent effect. See 1 W. LaFave, supra Section 1.6, at 112–113; Annot., 36 A.L.R. 3d 553, 558 (1971).

Privately employed security forces pose a difficult problem of a distinction between State and private action. Most courts have held that the Fourth Amendment does not apply to private security personnel who hold no special authority under State Law. In reaching this conclusion, they have reasoned that the primary function and concern of privately employed security officers is protection of their employer's property, rather than conviction of wrongdoers. See, e.g., United States v. Francoeur, 547 F2d 891, 893–894 (5th Cir.), cert. denied, 431 U.S. 918, 923, 97 S.Ct. 2182, 2197, 53 L.Ed.2d 228, 238 (1977); United States v. Lima, 424 A.2d 113, 118, 121 (D.C. 1980); State v. McDaniel, 44 Ohio App. 2d 163, 170–174, 337 N.E. 2d 173 (1975); State v. Robinson, 86 N.J. Super. 308, 318, 206 A.2d 779 (1965). Several courts and commentators have taken a different view, pointing out that private security forces have come into increasing use as supplements to police protection, and perform functions much like those of ordinary police. Private security personnel investigate criminal activity on a regular basis, and may well have an interest in the outcome of criminal actions against persons who pose a threat to the employer's property. See People v. Zelinski, 24 Cal.3d 357, 365–368, 155 Cal Rptr. 575, 594 P.2d 1000 (1979); People v. Holloway, 82 Mich. App. 629, 639–641, 267 N.W.2d 454 (1978) (Kaufman, J., concurring); People v. Eastway, 67 Mich. App. 464, 467–468, 241 N.W.2d 249 (1976); 1 W. LaFave, supra Section 1.6(d), at 128–129; Note, Seizures by Private Parties: Exclusion in Criminal Cases, 19 Stan.L. Rev. 608, 614–617 (1967). See also District Attorney v. Coffey, 386 Mass. 218, 434 N.E.2d 1276 (1982) (Liacos, J., concurring). Cf. Marsh v. Alabama, 326 U.S. 501, 505–510, 66 S.Ct. 276, 278–280, 90 L.Ed. 265 (1946) (conduct of private entity exercising "public function" may be treated as State action). Nevertheless, the majority continue to view purely private security officers as private actors. See 1 W. LaFave, supra Section 1.6(d), at 126–127.

A different rule prevails when an officer possesses additional status as a special or deputy officer. Specially commissioned officers are formally affiliated with the sovereign and generally possess authority beyond that of an ordinary citizen in matters such as arrest and the use of weapons. Therefore, they are treated as agents of the State, subject to the constraints of the Fourth Amendment. See, e.g., United States v. Lima, supra at 118–119; People v. Smith, 82 Misc. 2d 204, 206–208, 368 N.Y. S.2d 954 (N.Y. 1975). See State v. Wilkerson, 367 So.2d 319, 321 (La. 1979) (off-duty police officer); Pratt v. State, 9 Md. App. 220, 224–225, 263 A.2d 247 (1970) (Miranda warnings). Cf. Griffin v. Maryland, 378 U.S. 130, 135–137, 84 S.Ct. 1770, 1772–1773, 12 L.Ed. 2d 754 (1964) (action of amusement park guard who asserted his authority as deputy sheriff in excluding and arresting black patrons was State action); Williams v. United States, 341 U.S. 97, 99–100, 71 S.Ct. 576, 578–579, 95 L.Ed. 774 (1951) (beating of suspects by private detective commissioned as special policeman and acting in company of regular policeman, was action "under color of state law," for purpose of criminal action against him). But see State v. McDaniel, supra 44 Ohio App.2d at 174–175, 337 N.E. 2d 173.

(2) We agree that a *State officer privately employed* as a security guard is bound to comply with the Fourth Amendment when performing investigatory duties, and that evidence he discovers through methods in violation of the Fourth Amendment is subject to the rule of exclusion. But this does not mean that the bounds of permissible conduct are the same for the privately employed special officer as they would be for an ordinary police officer. The guard's private function adds a new aspect to his activities, which we believe is relevant to the proper application of the Fourth Amendment. The action he takes on behalf of his employer may be a lawful and necessary means of protecting the employer's property although it would be impermissible if taken on behalf of the State in pursuit of evidence. Cf. Restatement (Second) of Torts Section 260 (1965) (privilege to interfere with another's property in defense of actor's property). When the guard's conduct is justified by his legitimate private duties, it should not be treated as lawless, or "unreasonable," search and seizure.

Established principles support the conclusion that the existence of a lawful private purpose should be taken into account in applying the Fourth Amendment. The guard's position is similar to that of a police officer who intrudes by lawful means upon an individual's privacy, and then discovers unanticipated evidence. See, e.g., Commonwealth v. Cefalo, 381 Mass. 719, ——, Mass, Adv.Sh. (1980) 1877, 1888–1889, 409 N.E. 2d 719; Coolidge v. New Hampshire, 403 U.S. 443, 464–471, 91 S.Ct. 2022, 2037–2040, 29 L.Ed. 2d 564 (1971). The subject of the search, for his part, has reason to expect some scrutiny or interference by the agents of the private party whose property he uses or handles. Cf. Katz v. United States, 389 U.S. 347, 351–353, 88 S.Ct. 507, 511–512, 19 L.Ed. 2d 576 (1967). Moreover, when the guard takes legitimate steps for the protection of his employer's property, there is no cause for the deterrent sanction of the exclusionary rules. Cf. Terry v. Ohio, 392 U.S. 1, 12–15, 88 S.Ct. 1868, 1875–1876, 20 L.Ed. 2d 889 (1968). Exclusion would serve only to frustrate prosecution of those whose crimes happen to come to light in the course of a routine inspection by a security guard.

(3) For these reasons, we conclude that an investigation by a special officer privately employed as a security guard does not violate the Fourth Amendment when it is conducted on behalf of the private employer's property. If, on the other hand, the officer steps outside this sphere of legitimate private action, the exclusionary rule applies as it would to any State officer. The burden of establishing the constitutionality of the officer's conduct rests with the Commonwealth. See Commonwealth v. Antobenedetto, 366 Mass, 51, 56–58, 315 N.E. 2d 530 (1974).

(4) The present record does not afford sufficient basis for applying the principle we have outlined. We have no information concerning Vousboukis' duties as a special police officer in the city of Lynn. Nor does the record reveal the nature of the private property he purported to protect. Neither the judge nor the parties could have anticipated the requirements of our decision, and a new hearing is necessary.

(5) At the new hearing, the propriety of the guard's action should be determined in light of the reasons for special treatment of a privately employed special police officer acting on his employer's behalf. These reasons are the private nature and purpose of his conduct, the legitimacy of the specification he takes as a means of protecting private property, and the diminished expectations of privacy of the subject of the investigation. Several definite requirements follow from these foundations.

(6) First, the guard must have acted under the control of his private employer. See State v. McDaniel, 44 Ohio App. 2d 163, 174–175, 337 N.E.2d 173 (1975). If the investigation exceeded his private duties or authorization, he must be considered to have acted in his official capacity.

Similarly, if the guard has received instructions from State authorities, on a regular basis or in regard to the particular investigation at issue, his conduct is not protected by his private role.

(7) Second, the guard's actions must be clearly related to his employer's private purposes. An investigation that goes beyond the employer's needs cannot be justified as an incident of the guard's private function. If, for example, none of the General Electric property to which the defendant had access could have been concealed in travel bag or sleeping compartment, Vousboukis was not entitled to search these areas.

(8) Third, the investigation must be a legitimate means of protecting the employer's property, and so must be reasonable in light of the circumstances surrounding it. Cf. Restatement (Second) of Torts Section 278 (1965). Reasonableness depends in part on the expectations engendered by the particular setting. If the employer has maintained the private character of his property, those who use it must anticipate and accept supervision. But if the employer has exposed his premises and chattels to semipublic use, the sense of private prerogative to control its users is much diminished. Custom or advance warning may bear upon the propriety of an investigation, but should not be determinative. See Commonwealth v. Storella, 6 Mass. App. 310, 315–316, 375 N.E. 2d 348 (1978); Gillett v. State, 588 S.W. 2d 361, 366 (Tex. Cr. App. 1979) (Roberts, J., dissenting); 2 W. LaFave, supra Section 8.2(1) (1978). Finally, the judge should consider the methods chosen and the manner in which they are carried out. Failure to employ available, less intrusive alternatives may suggest that the methods employed were unwarranted, and an offense to individual dignity is impermissible in almost any circumstances. See Gillett v. State, supra.

Accordingly, we vacate the judge's decision. Further evidence on the motion to suppress the gun from evidence is to be received in the judge's discretion, and further proceedings shall be in accord with this opinion.

So ordered.

Comment Outline

Although the opinion in the Leone case contains some dicta indicating that a few states may look differently at the relationship of the Fourth Amendment to private security persons, this case as a matter of law deals with the issue as it applies to private security persons who may be "Specially commissioned officers***formally affiliated with the sovereign and generally possess authority beyond that of an *ordinary citizen* in matters such as arrest and the use of weapons.

This case established the law that a special or ordinary police officer *privately employed as a security guard acting on behalf of the private employer* does not violate the Fourth Amendment as long as this person acts "in a manner that is reasonable and necessary for protection of the employer's property."

The Court then goes on to state several reasons for special treatment of such a person, and then sets three definite requirements which must be found:

(1) the guard must have acted under the control of his private employer;

(2) the guard's actions must be clearly related to his employer's private purposes;

(3) the investigation must be a legitimate means of protecting the employee's property and so must be reasonable in light of circumstances surrounding it.

The cases in the Chapter hopefully demonstrate the law as it develops, but most significantly the quiet battle of change vs. continuity. Briefly, the early cases simply talk about private persons not subject to the exclusionary rule sanction of the Fourth Amendment. Shortly, we see some qualifications as to the permissible relationships between the private person and the state in connection with the questioned search or seizure, to wit, the police cannot be found to have participated in or directed it and its purpose must not be investigatory. Next, we see special requirements detailed for special police officers acting as private security guards. As mentioned earlier several states have had courts indicate total erosions of the basic doctrine as enunciated in the Burdeau v. McDowell case although these decisions do not appear to be very strong. However, one might also discern a glimmer of future changes. Many states are experiencing heavy fiscal restrictions on police activities; many police departments are curtailing patrols and limiting their accent, when necessary, to violent crimes. These circumstances, perceived by other citizens as a curtailment of police services, give rise to the growth and proliferation of private security industry, which in turn shall probably cause more cases to arrive in our judicial systems where these kinds of legal issues will be heard and decided giving rise to further changes, perhaps continuity to our laws as they are now. Certainly as the private industry grows and abuses occur and increase, the cries for increased state control and regulation of the private security industry will grow.

One can see the development of the concept that when private security persons are recruited, trained, and/or licensed by the state, they should be considered formally affiliated with the state, or are quasi-police, and therefore constitutional limitations on police action apply equally to them.

Public School Searches
Commonwealth v. Snyder
413 Mass. 521, 597 N.E.2d 1363 (1992)
Supreme Judicial Court of Massachusetts

WILKINS, Justice.

This appeal concerns Jeffrey Snyder, who, at the time of the events involved here, was an eighteen-year-old high school senior in a Berkshire county regional high school. Snyder challenges the admission of certain evidence in his trial on charges of violation of the drug laws. School administrators obtained some of that evidence during a warrantless search of the defendant's school locker and the valance of it during a subsequent interrogation of the defendant, before which the administrators did not warn Snyder of his rights, including his right to remain silent.

Snyder argues that, when the school administrators looked for and took marihuana found in his locker, they violated his constitutional rights against unreasonable searches and seizures. He also contends that the school administrators violated his rights by not giving him Miranda warnings before questioning him. During that questioning, the defendant confessed to having sold a bag of marihuana to a fellow student and to owning the three other bags of marihuana found in his locker.

We conclude that the defendant's arguments lack merit. We, therefore, need not consider the separate question whether, if one or more of his contentions were valid, the evidence obtained in violation of his rights should not have been admitted in evidence at his trial.

We recite facts that were found by the judge who denied the defendant's motion to suppress the evidence. We supplement them with details from the uncontroverted testimony of the school administrators and a Great Barrington police officer.

Linda Day, the principal of Monument Mountain Regional High School in Great Barrington, testified that about 12:45 p.m. on December 21, 1989, a faculty member came to see her. The faculty member reported that a student had said that the defendant had approached the student and had asked if the student wanted to buy some marihuana for twenty-five dollars. The faculty member had worked at the school for approximately fifteen years, had extensive contact with students, and had many times provided reliable information to school administrators. Principal Day asked John F. Canning, the assistant principal, to join them in her office, and the faculty member repeated the information. The faculty member added that the student had reported the attempted sale about 10:30 a.m. The student said that Snyder had showed the student a video cassette case that contained three bags of marihuana and that Snyder had then put the video cassette case in his book bag.

The school administrators decided to locate Snyder. Canning found Snyder in the student center, which was crowded with students. From a distance Canning could not see Snyder's book bag. Canning and Day then consulted. They did not know if other students were involved. Nor did they know the full extent of the marihuana. They did not want to arouse suspicion. The administrators decided not to approach Snyder in the student center but rather to wait until the beginning of the next school period (about 1:20 P.M.), when Snyder was scheduled to be in a class, and then search Snyder's locker for the book bag. At that time, Canning and Day, using the combination to the locker that was available at the school's main office, opened the locker. They found the book bag, the video cassette case, and three bags containing marihuana. They took these items to Day's office and concealed them behind her desk.

Day then located Snyder and brought him to her office. There, in Canning's presence, Day asked Snyder if it was true, as reported to her, that he had offered to sell marihuana in the school. Snyder admitted that he had. Snyder, who was upset, said that he could not believe this was happening and that he had never done this before. He said that a friend had given him the marihuana to sell, that he had become troubled about doing it, and that he had called his friend to come to the school at two o'clock to take back what he had not sold. Snyder admitted that the book bag, the video cassette, and the bags of marihuana were his. Snyder said that there had been four bags of marihuana but he had sold one for twenty-five dollars to a student. Day called Snyder's mother, who came to the school. Canning called the police. Snyder was allowed to meet with his girl friend alone in Day's office before the police came.

Shortly before two o'clock, Officer Beckwith of the Great Barrington police department arrived at the school. Day recited what Snyder had said; Beckwith gave Snyder his Miranda warnings; and Snyder confirmed that Day's recitation was true. Not long after that, the person who had provided Snyder with the marihuana, a graduate of the school, was located in the school. Officer Beckwith took Snyder to the police station shortly before 2:30 p.m. where the officer again warned Snyder of his rights. Snyder signed a rights waiver and gave a written statement, the substance of which Officer Beckwith testified to at Snyder's trial.

The motion judge denied Snyder's motion to suppress the evidence found in Snyder's locker and the admissions that Snyder made to Day, Canning, and Beckwith. The argument that the statements made to Beckwith should be suppressed, even though Beckwith had given the defendant Miranda warnings, was based on the theory that this evidence would not have been obtained if Day and Conning had not already violated Snyder's rights by failing to advise him of those rights. The motion judge concluded that, because Snyder had no reasonable expectation of privacy in his locker, the locker search did not violate Snyder's constitutional rights. He concluded alternatively that the school authorities had reasonable suspicion that a crime had been committed and that the search of Snyder's locker was, therefore, reasonable. He further concluded that the defendant's admissions were made in circumstances that were fair and proper.

[1] Snyder waived a jury trial, and on April 8, 1991, a judge in the Pittsfield District Court found Snyder guilty of (1) illegal possession of a class D substance, (2) possession of a class D substance with intent to distribute it, and (3) possession of a class D substance with intent to distribute it in a school. The judge sentenced Snyder to one day in a house of correction of the charge of possession of a class D substance with intent to distribute it (G.L. c. 94C, Section 32C [1990 ed.]), and two years in a house of correction, following service of the first sentence, on the charge of possession of a class D substance with intent to distribute it in a public high school (G.L. c. 94C, Section 32J [1990 ed.]). The charge of simple possession was placed on file with the defendant's consent. The trial judge stayed execution of the sentence pending Snyder's appeal, which we transferred to this court.

We consider first the question whether the search of Snyder's locker violated Snyder's rights.

[2] The motion judge's conclusion that Snyder had no legitimate expectation of privacy in his school locker was wrong. Recent decisions elsewhere have recognized that, barring some express understanding to

the contrary, students have a reasonable and protected expectation of privacy in their school lockers. See State v. Engerud, 94 N.J. 331, 348, 463 A.2d 934 (1983); State v. Michael G., 106 N.M. 644, 646, 748 P.2d 17 (Ct.App.1987); In re Durmas, 357 Pa. Super. 294, 297, 515 A.2d 984 (1986); State v. Joseph T., 175 W.Va. 598, 606, 336 S.E.2d 728 (1985). In this case, the school administration explicitly acknowledged in the students' rights and responsibility code that each student had the right "[n]ot to have his/her locker subjected to unreasonable search." In light of this assurance from the school administration, it is especially clear that Snyder had a reasonable expectation of privacy in his locker that was entitled to constitutional protection. See New Jersey v. T.L.O., 469 U.S. 325, 338, 105 S.Ct. 733, 741, 83 L.Ed.2d 720 (1985); Commonwealth v. Panetti, 406 Mass. 230, 231, 547 N.E.2d 46 (1989). Because Snyder had such a reasonable expectation of privacy in his locker, he was entitled to argue that his Fourth Amendment right to be free from unreasonable searches and seizures was violated by the search of his locker and the seizure of the marihuana and to argue, therefore, that the evidence seized (and all evidence subsequently obtained as fruits of the unlawful seizure) must be suppressed. He was entitled to make a similar argument under art. 14 of the Massachusetts Declaration of Rights, both because he had a reasonable expectation of privacy in his locker and because he had automatic standing to challenge the lawfulness of the seizure of the marihuana (see Commonwealth v. Frazier, 410 Mass. 235, 242–244, 571 N.E.2d 1356 [1991]), possession of which was an element of each crime with which he was charged.

[3] We have little difficulty in concluding that the search conducted without the authority of a search warrant did not violate Snyder's rights under the Fourth Amendment to the United States Constitution. The test under the Fourth Amendment for school administrators is whether the search of the locker was reasonable in all the circumstances. See New Jersey v. T.L.O., supra 469 U.S. at 341, 105 S.Ct. at 742; Commonwealth v. Carey, 407 Mass. 528, 533, 554 N.E.2d 1199 (1990) (upholding warrantless search of student locker as not violation Fourth Amendment; defendant makes no proper claim that search violated his parallel right under Constitution of Commonwealth). This Fourth Amendment test is a lower standard than the traditional one, which requires that there be a search warrant (barring circumstances excusing the use of a search warrant) and that there be probable cause to conduct the search. Because, as we shall subsequently explain, there was probable cause to conduct the search, it

follows logically that the lower federal standard applicable here is satisfied. See New Jersey. T.L.O., supra 469 U.S. at 341, 105 S.Ct at 742 ("reasonableness, under all the circumstances, of the search."

[4] The more substantial issue in this case is whether the search and seizure was unreasonable under art. 14 of the Declaration of Rights of the Constitution of the Commonwealth. In construing the Constitution of the Commonwealth, we are not bound to follow the standards that the Supreme Court of the United States has adopted in applying provisions of the Constitution of the United States that are similar or even identical to provisions in the Commonwealth's Constitution. Commonwealth v. Upton, 394 Mass. 363, 372–373, 476 N.E.2d 548 (1985).

We agree with the Supreme Court of the United States that no search warrant was required. It is consistent with the requirements of art.14, except where a school employee is explicitly acting on behalf of law enforcement officials, for a school employee to conduct a search and seize drugs (guns and other contraband) in a school without first obtaining a search warrant. See New Jersey v. T.L.O., supra 469 U.S. at 340, 105 S.Ct. at 742 ("The warrant requirement, in particular, is unsuited to the school environment: requiring a teacher to obtain a warrant before searching a child suspected of an infraction of school rules (or of the criminal law) would unduly interfere with the maintenance of the swift and informal disciplinary procedures needed in the schools"). See also *Id.* at 351, 353, 105 S.Ct at 747, 748 (Blackman, J., concurring). There may be a question, as to a particular search, whether a school employee had a constitutionally adequate basis to conduct the search, and there may be a question about the scope of the search, but the absence of a search warrant will not be a disputable factor.

In deciding whether the search of the locker and the seizure of the marihuana was constitutionally unreasonable, we need not determine whether the requirements of art. 14 of the Declaration of Rights impose a stricter standard than does the Fourth Amendment. The uncontroverted evidence at the hearing on the defendant's motion to suppress shows that the school officials had probable cause to search the defendant's locker and, once they found the book bag, to search the bag and the video cassette holder. Certainly, art. 14 imposes no higher standard than probable cause. Cf. Commonwealth v. Upton, 394 Mass. 363, 370, 476 N.E.2d 548 (1985). Thus, if there was probable cause to search the locker when it was searched, the requirements of art. 14 were met.

We are not dealing here with an anonymous informant but rather with a known student who reported that he or she was an eyewitness to a crime. The faculty member to whom the student reported the defendant's attempt to sell marihuana had a well-established reputation for reliability. The school principal was justified in relying on the faculty member's report of what the student had said. The situation is similar to a known private citizen's eyewitness report to the police of a crime or an attempted crime, on which the authorities are entitled to rely. See Commonwealth v. Carey, 407 Mass. 528, 534 n. 4, 554 N.E.2d 1199 (1990); 4 W.R. LaFave, Search & Seizure Section 10.11(b), at 170 (2d ed. 1987).

The remaining question is whether Principal Day and Assistant Principal Canning, armed with reliable information that Snyder had marihuana in his book bag, were unreasonable in searching the locker without first obtaining more information as to the whereabouts of the book bag. They made an attempt to do so. They discovered where Snyder was but concluded that they should not confront him in the student center. Their judgment that others might be involved and that they should avoid arousing the suspicion of others was reasonable. Prompt action was needed to reduce the chance of further sales and removal of the marihuana from the school.

The school officials were justified in concluding that there was probable cause (1) to believe that marihuana was in Snyder's book bag and (2) to search the defendant and his locker because that book bag was probably either in the locker or with the defendant. Their decision to search the locker first, the less intrusive search, rather than to search the defendant first, was a reasonable judgment. The school officials complied with traditional search and seizure requirements. Consequently, the judge was correct in ruling that the evidence found during the locker search need not be suppressed.

2. Snyder argues next that the statements he made to the principal and assistant principal of his high school and to Officer Beckwith should have been suppressed. He contends that he was entitled to Miranda warnings before the principal and assistant principal interrogated him and that the taint of this improper questioning infected his admissions to Officer Beckwith, even though the officer had promptly given him Miranda warnings.

[5] Without advancing any separate reasoning, Snyder also contends that the questioning in the principal's office without the furnishing of Miranda warnings violated his privilege against self-incrimination stated in art. 12 of the Massachusetts Declaration of Rights ("No subject

shall . . . be compelled to accuse, or furnish evidence against himself"). We have not adopted Miranda or some similar warnings as a means of protecting State constitutional rights. There has been no need to consider the question because Miranda warnings furnish information about State constitutional rights as well as rights contained in the Constitution of the United States. This court, however, as an adjunct to Miranda warnings, has provided additional protections under the common law, protections that go beyond what the Supreme Court would require in similar circumstances as a matter of constitutional imperative. See Commonwealth v. Smith, 412 Mass. 823, 837, 593 N.E.2d 1288 (1992); Commonwealth v. A Juvenile, 402 Mass. 275, 279, 521 N.E.2d 1368 (1988), and cases cited. Snyder makes no argument, however, that we should apply different principles and reasoning under our law from those that the Supreme Court has applied in its *Miranda* opinion and subsequently.

There is no authority requiring a school administrator not acting on behalf of law enforcement officials to furnish Miranda warnings. Even if we were to assume that, during the questioning in the principal's office, the environment was coercive because Snyder was in custody (or because his freedom was significantly restricted) and that, therefore, Miranda warnings would be required if the questioning had been by the police) see Commonwealth v. Bryant, 390 Mass. 729, 737, 459 N.E.2d 792 [1984]), Principal Day and Assistant Principal Canning were not law enforcement officials or agents of such officials. The Miranda rule does not apply to a private citizen or school administrator who is acting neither as an instrument of the police nor as an agent of the police pursuant to a scheme to elicit statements from the defendant by coercion or guile. See Commonwealth v. Allen, 395 Mass. 448, 453–454, 480 N.E.2d 630 (1985); Commonwealth v. A Juvenile, supra 402 Mass. at 278–279, 521 N.E.2d 1368. The fact that the school administrators had every intention of turning the marihuana over to the police does not make then agents or instrumentalities of the police in questioning Snyder.

The motion judge was correct in denying the motion to suppress the defendant's statements to the school administrators and Officer Beckwith.

3. The defendant raises one further point to which we have not yet adverted. He argues that the motion judge erred in refusing to direct the prosecution to disclose the name of the informants, the faculty member, and the student. The judge ruled that disclosure of the identity of the faculty member and the student would discourage others from making similar disclosures. He concluded that they should be protected "from

being bothered, harassed, and probably confronted publicly by unthinking individuals." He also concluded that the defense provided no compelling reason for disclosure. The defendant moved for disclosure on the sole ground that the informants' identities would bear on the question whether the school administrators had probable cause to conduct the search.

[7,8] The judge did not abuse his discretion in denying the request for disclosure. Generally, nondisclosure of a source of information, which, as here, bears on a preliminary question, such as the suppression of evidence, is more readily tolerated than the nondisclosure at trial of a source of evidence, where guilt or innocence is directly involved. See Commonwealth v. Amral, 407 Mass. 511, 518, 554 N.E.2d 1189 (1990); Commonwealth v. Lugo, 406 Mass. 565, 571, 548 N.E.2d 1263 (1990). The government's privilege not to disclose the identity of an informant, which is not absolute, should be respected as far as reasonably possible consistent with fairness to a defendant. Commonwealth v. Douzanis, 384 Mass. 434, 441, 425 N.E.2d 326 (1981). In the circumstances, the defendant's argument for disclosure is not based on any demonstration that the identity of these informants would have been helpful to him or even might have been helpful to him, beyond the speculation that something beneficial might have been discovered. That mere possibility has not been enough to require disclosure of informants in circumstances like those of this case.

Judgments affirmed.

New Jersey v. T.L.O.
United States Supreme Court
469 U.S. 325, 83 L.Ed.2d 720
105 S.Ct. 733 (1985)

Justice WHITE delivered the opinion of the Court.

We granted certiorari in this case to examine the appropriateness of the exclusionary rule as a remedy for searches carried out in violation of the Fourth Amendment by public school authorities. Our consideration of the proper application of the Fourth Amendment to the public schools, however, has led us to conclude that the search that gave rise to the case now before us did not violate the Fourth Amendment. Accordingly, we here address only the questions of the proper standard for assessing the legality of searches conducted by public school officials and the application of that standard to the facts of this case.

On March 7, 1980, a teacher at Piscataway High School in Middlesex County, N.J., discovered two girls smoking in a lavatory. One of the two girls was the respondent T.L.O., who at that time was a 14-year-old high school freshman. Because smoking in the lavatory was a violation of a school rule, the teacher took the two girls to the principal's office, where they met with Assistant Vice Principal Theodore Choplick. In response to questioning by Mr. Choplick, T.L.O.'s companion admitted that she had violated the rule. T.L.O., however, denied that she had been smoking in the lavatory and claimed that she did not smoke at all.

Mr. Choplick asked T.L.O. to come into his private office and demanded to see her purse. Opening the purse, he found a pack of cigarettes, which he removed from the purse and held before T.L.O. as he accused her of having lied to him. As he reached into the purse for the cigarettes, Mr. Choplick also noticed a package of cigarette rolling papers. In his experience, possession of rolling papers by high school students was closely associated with the use of marihuana. Suspecting that a closer examination of the purse might yield further evidence of drug use, Mr. Choplick proceeded to search the purse thoroughly. The search revealed a small amount of marihuana, a pipe, a number of empty plastic bags, a substantial quantity of money in one-dollar bills, an index card that appeared to be a list of students who owed T.L.O. money, and two letters that implicated T.L.O. in marihuana dealing.

Mr. Choplick notified T.L.O.'s mother and the police, and turned the evidence of drug dealing over to the police. At the request of the police, T.L.O.'s mother took her daughter to police headquarters, where T.L.O. confessed that she had been selling marihuana at the high school. On the basis of the confession and the evidence seized by Mr. Choplick, the State brought delinquency charges against T.L.O. in the Juvenile and Domestic Relations Court of Middlesex County. Contending that Mr. Choplick's search of her purse violated the Fourth Amendment, T.L.O. moved to suppress the evidence found in her purse as well as her confession, which, she argued, was tainted by the allegedly unlawful search. The Juvenile Court denied the motion to suppress. State ex rel. T.L.O., 178 N.J.Super. 329, 428 A.2d 1327 (1980). Although the court concluded that the Fourth Amendment did apply to searches carried out by school officials, it held that

> A school official may properly conduct a search of a student's person if the official has a reasonable suspicion that a crime has been or is in the process of being committed, or reasonable cause to believe that the search is necessary to maintain school discipline or enforce school policies. *Id.*, 178 N.J.Super., at 341, 428 A.2d, at 1333 (emphasis in original).

Applying this standard, the court concluded that the search conducted by Mr. Choplick was a reasonable one. The initial decision to open the purse was justified by Mr. Choplick's well-founded suspicion that T.L.O. had violated the rule forbidding smoking in the lavatory. Once the purse was open, evidence of marihuana violations was in plain view, and Mr. Choplick was entitled to conduct a thorough search to determine the nature and extent of T.L.O.'s drug-related activities. *Id.*, 178 N.J.Super., at 343, 428 A.2d, at 1334. Having denied the motion to suppress, the court on March 23, 1981, found T.L.O. to be a delinquent and on January 8, 1982, sentenced her to a year's probation.

On appeal from the final judgment of the Juvenile Court, a divided Appellate Division affirmed the trial court's finding that there had been no Fourth Amendment violation, but vacated the adjudication of delinquency and remanded for a determination whether T.L.O. had knowingly and voluntarily waived her Fifth Amendment rights before confessing. State ex rel. T.L.O., 185 N.J.Super. 279, 448 A.2d 493 (1982). T.L.O. appealed the Fourth Amendment ruling, and the Supreme Court of New Jersey reversed the judgment of the Appellate Division and ordered the suppression of the evidence found in T.L.O.'s purse.

The New Jersey Supreme Court agreed with the lower courts that the Fourth Amendment applies to searches conducted by school officials. The court also rejected the State of New Jersey's argument that the exclusionary rule should not be employed to prevent the use in juvenile proceedings of evidence unlawfully seized by school officials. Declining to consider whether applying the rule to the fruits of searches by school officials would have any deterrent value, the court held simply that the precedents of this Court establish that "if an official search violates constitutional rights, the evidence is not admissible in criminal proceedings." *Id.*, 94 N.J., at 341, 463 A.2d, at 939 (footnote omitted).

With respect to the question of the legality of the search before it, the court agreed with the Juvenile Court that a warrantless search by a school official does not violate the Fourth Amendment so long as the official "has reasonable grounds to believe that a student possesses evidence of illegal activity or activity that would interfere with school discipline and order." *Id.,* 94 N.J., at 346, 463 A.2d, at 941–942. However, the court, with two justices dissenting, sharply disagreed with the Juvenile Court's conclusion that the search of the purse was reasonable. According to the majority, the contents of T.L.O.'s purse had no bearing on the accusation against T.L.O., for possession of cigarettes (as opposed to smoking them in the lavatory) did not violate school rules, and a mere desire for evidence that would impeach T.L.O.'s claim that she did not smoke cigarettes could not justify the search. Moreover, even if a reasonable suspicion that T.L.O. had cigarettes in her purse would justify a search, Mr. Choplick had no such suspicion, as no one had furnished him with any specific information that there were cigarettes in the purse. Finally, leaving aside the question whether Mr. Choplick was justified in opening the purse, the court held that the evidence of drug use that he saw inside did not justify the extensive "rummaging" through T.L.O.'s papers and effects that followed. *Id.,* 94 N.J., at 347, 463 A.2d, at 942–943.

We granted the State of New Jersey's petition for certiorari. 464 U.S. 991, 104 S.Ct. 480, 78 L.Ed.2d 678 (1983). Although the State had argued in the Supreme Court of New Jersey that the search of T.L.O.'s purse did not violate the Fourth Amendment, the petition for certiorari raised only the question whether the exclusionary rule should operate to bar consideration in juvenile delinquency proceedings of evidence unlawfully seized by a school official without the involvement of law enforcement officers. When this case was first argued last term, the State conceded for the purpose of argument that the standard devised by the New Jersey Supreme Court for determining the legality of school searches was appropriate and that the court had correctly applied that standard; the State contended only that the remedial purposes of the exclusionary rule were not well served by applying it to searches conducted by public authorities not primarily engaged in law enforcement.

Although we originally granted certiorari to decide the issue of the appropriate remedy in juvenile court proceedings for unlawful school searches, our doubts regarding the wisdom of deciding that question of what limits, if any, the Fourth Amendment places on the activities of school authorities prompted us to order reargument on that question. Having heard argument on the legality of the search of T.L.O.'s purse, we are satisfied that the search did not violate the Fourth Amendment.

I

[1] In determining whether the search at issue in this case violated the Fourth Amendment, we are faced initially with the question whether that Amendment's prohibition on unreasonable searches and seizures applies to searches conducted by public school officials. We hold that it does.

[2] It is now beyond dispute that "the Federal Constitution, by virtue of the Fourteenth Amendment, prohibits, unreasonable searches and seizures by state officers." Elkins v. United States, 364 U.S. 206, 213, 80 S.Ct. 1437, 1442, 4 L.Ed.2d 1669 (1960); accord, Mapp v. Ohio, 367 U.S. 643, 81 S.Ct. 1684, 6 L.Ed.2d 1081 (1961); Wolf v. Colorado, 338 U.S. 25, 69 S.Ct. 1359, 93 L.Ed. 1782 (1949). Equally indisputable is the proposition that the Fourteenth Amendment protects the rights of students against encroachment by public school officials:

> The Fourteenth Amendment, as now applied to the States, protects the citizen against the State itself and all of its creatures—Boards of Education not excepted. These have, of course, important, delicate, and highly discretionary functions, but none that they may not perform within the limits of the Bill of Rights. That they are educating the young for citizenship is reason for scrupulous protection of Constitutional freedoms of the individual, if we are not to strangle the free mind at its source and teach youth to discount important principles of our government as mere platitudes." West Virginia State Bd. of Ed. v. Barnette, 319 U.S. 624, 637, 63 S.Ct. 1178, 1185, 87 L.Ed. 1628 (1943).

These two propositions—that the Fourth Amendment applies to the States through the Fourteenth Amendment, and that the actions of public school officials are subject to the limits placed on state action by the Fourteenth Amendment—might appear sufficient to answer the suggestion that the Fourth Amendment does not proscribe unreasonable searches by school officials. On reargument, however, the State of New Jersey has argued that the history of the Fourth Amendment indicates that the Amendment was intended to regulate only searches and seizures carried out by law enforcement officers; accordingly, although public school officials are concededly state agents for purposes of the Fourteenth Amendment, the Fourth Amendment creates no rights enforceable against them.

It may well be true that the evil toward which the Fourth Amendment was primarily directed was the resurrection of the pre-Revolutionary practice of using general warrants of "writs of assistance" to authorize searches for contraband by officers of the Crown. See United States v. Chadwick, 433 U.S. 1, 7–8, 97 S.Ct. 2476, 2481, 53 L.Ed.2d 538 (1977); Boyd v. United States, 116 U.S. 616, 624–629, 6 S.Ct. 524, 528–531, 29 L.Ed. 746 (1886). But this Court has never limited the Amendment's prohibition on unreasonable searches and seizures to operations conducted by the police. Rather, the Court has long spoken of the Fourth Amendment's strictures as restraints imposed upon "governmental action"—that is, "upon the activities of sovereign authority." Burdeau v. McDowell, 256 U.S. 465, 475, 41 S.Ct. 574, 576, 65 L.Ed. 1048 (1921). Accordingly, we have held the Fourth Amendment applicable to the activities of civil as well as criminal authorities: building inspectors, see Camara v. Municipal Court, 387 U.S. 523, 528, 87 S.Ct. 1727, 1730, 18 L.Ed.2d 930 (1967), Occupational Safety and Health Act inspectors, see Marshall v. Barlow's Inc., 436 U.S. 307, 312–313, 98 S.Ct. 1816, 1820, 56 L.Ed.2d 305 (1978), and even fireman entering privately owned premises to battle a fire, see Michigan v. Tyler, 436 U.S. 499, 506, 98 S.Ct. 1942, 1948, 56 L.Ed.2d 486 (1978), are all subject to the restraints imposed by the Fourth Amendment. As we observed in Camara v. Municipal Court, supra, "[t]he basic purpose of this Amendment, as recognized in countless decisions of this Court, is to safeguard the privacy and security of individuals against arbitrary invasions by governmental officials." 387 U.S., at 528, 87 S.Ct., at 1730. Because the individual's interest in privacy and personal security "suffers whether the government's motivation is to investigate violations of criminal laws or breaches of other statutory or regulatory standards," Marshal v. Barlow's, Inc., supra, 436 U.S., at 312–313, 98 S.Ct., at 1820, it would be "anomalous to say that the individual and his private property are fully protected by the Fourth Amendment only when the individual is suspected of criminal behavior." Camara v. Municipal Court, supra, 387 U.S., at 530, 87 S.Ct., at 1732.

Notwithstanding the general applicability of Fourth Amendment to the activities of civil authorities, a few courts have concluded that school officials are exempt from the dictates of the Fourth Amendment by virtue of the special nature of their authority over schoolchildren. See, e.g., R.C.M. v. State, 660 S.W.2d 552 (Tex.App. 1983). Teachers and school administrators, it is said, act *in loco parentis* in their dealings with students: their authority is that of the parent, not the State, and is therefore not subject to the limits of the Fourth Amendment. *Ibid.*

Such reasoning is in tension with contemporary reality and the teachings of this Court. We have held school officials subject to the commands of the First Amendment, see Tinker v. Des Moines Independent Community School District, 393 U.S. 503, 89 S.Ct. 733, 21 L.Ed.2d 731 (1969), and the Due Process Clause of the Fourteenth Amendment, see Goss v. Lopez, 419 U.S. 565, 95 S.Ct. 729, 42 L.Ed.2d 725 (1975). If school authorities are state actors for purposes of the constitutional guarantees of freedom of expression and due process, it is difficult to understand why they should be deemed to be exercising parental rather than public authority when conducting searches of their students. More generally, the Court has recognized that "the concept of parental delegation" as a source of school authority is not entirely "consonant with compulsory education laws." Ingraham v. Wright, 430 U.S. 651, 662, 97 S.Ct. 1401, 1407, 51 L.Ed.2d 711 (1977). Today's public school officials do not merely exercise authority voluntarily conferred on them by individual parents; rather, they act in furtherance of publicly mandated educational and disciplinary policies. Se e.g., the opinion in State ex rel. T.L.O., 94 N.J., at 343, 463 A.2d, at 934, 940, describing the new jersey statutes regulating school disciplinary policies and establishing the authority of school officials over their students. In carrying out searches and other disciplinary functions pursuant to such policies, school officials act as representatives of the State, not merely as surrogates for the parents, and they cannot claim the parents' immunity from the strictures of the Fourth Amendment.

II

[3] To hold that the Fourth Amendment applies to searches conducted by school authorities is only to begin the inquiry into the standards governing such searches. Although the underlying command of the Fourth Amendment is always that searches and seizures be reasonable, what is reasonable depends on the context within which a search takes place. The determination of the standard of reasonableness governing any specific class of searches requires "balancing the need to search against the invasion which the search entails." Camara v. Municipal Court, supra, 387 U.S., at 536–537, 87 S.Ct., at 1735. On one side of the balance are arrayed the individual's legitimate expectations of privacy and personal security; on the other, the government's need for effective methods to deal with breaches of public order.

We have recognized that even a limited search of the person is a substantial invasion of privacy. Terry v. Ohio, 392 U.S. 1, 24–25, 88 S.Ct.

1868, 1881–1882, 20 L.Ed.2d 889 (1967). We have also recognized that searches of closed items of personal luggage are intrusions on protected privacy interests, for "the Fourth Amendment provides protection to the owner of every container that conceals its contents from plain view." United States v. Ross, 456 U.S. 798, 822–823, 102 S.Ct. 2157, 2171, 72 L.Ed.2d 572 (1982). A search of a child's person or of a closed purse or other bag carried on her person, no less than a similar search carried out on an adult, is undoubtedly a severe violation of subjective expectations of privacy.

[4] Of course, the Fourth Amendment does not protect subjective expectations of privacy that are unreasonable or otherwise "illegitimate." See, e.g., Hudson v. Palmer, 468 U.S. 517, 104 S.Ct. 3194, 82 L.Ed.2d 393 (1984); Rawlings v. Kentucky, 448 U.S. 98, 100 S.Ct. 2556, 65 L.Ed.2d 633 (1980). To receive the protection of the Fourth Amendment, an expectation of privacy must be one that society is "prepared to recognize as legitimate." Hudson v. Palmer, supra, 468 U.S., at 526, 104 S.Ct., at 3200. The State of New Jersey has argued that because of the pervasive supervision to which children in the schools are necessarily subject, a child has virtually no legitimate expectation of privacy in articles of personal property "unnecessarily" carried into a school. This argument has two factual premises: (1) the fundamental incompatibility of expectations of privacy with the maintenance of a sound educational environment, and (2) the minimal interest of the child in bringing any items of personal property into the school. Both premises are severely flawed.

Although this Court may take notice of the difficulty of maintaining discipline in the public schools today, the situation is not so dire that students in the schools may claim no legitimate expectations of privacy. We have recently recognized that the need to maintain order in a prison is such that prisoners retain no legitimate expectations of privacy in their cells, but it goes almost without saying the "[t]he prisoner and the schoolchild stand in wholly different circumstances, separated by the harsh facts of criminal conviction and incarceration." Ingraham v. Wright, supra, 430 U.S., at 669, 97 S.Ct., at 1411. We are not yet ready to hold that the schools and the prisons need be equated for some purposes of the Fourth Amendment.

Nor does the State's suggestion that children have no legitimate need to bring personal property into the schools seem well anchored in reality. Students at a minimum must bring to school not only the supplies needed for their studies, but also keys, money, and the necessaries of personal hygiene and grooming. In addition, students may carry on their persons or in purses or wallets such nondisruptive yet highly personal items as photographs, letters, and diaries. Finally, students may have perfectly legitimate reasons to carry with them articles of property needed in connection with extracurricular or recreational activities. In short, schoolchildren may find it necessary to carry with them a variety of legitimate, noncontraband items, and there is no reason to conclude that they have necessarily waived all rights to privacy in such items merely by bringing them onto school grounds.

Against the child's interest in privacy must be set the substantial interest of teachers and administrators in maintaining discipline in the classroom and on school grounds. Maintaining order in the classroom has never been easy, but in recent years, school disorder has often taken particularly ugly forms; drug use and violent crime in the schools have become major social problems. See generally 1 NIE, U.S. Dept. of Health, Education and Welfare, Vilent Schools—Safe Schools: The Safe School Study Report to the Congress (1978). Even in schools that have been spared the most severe disciplinary problems, the preservation of order and a proper educational environment requires close supervision of schoolchildren, as well as the enforcement of rules against conduct that would be perfectly permissible if undertaken by an adult. "Events calling for discipline are frequent occurrences and sometimes require immediate, effective action." Goss v. Lopez, 419 U.S., at 580, 95 S.Ct., at 739. Accordingly, we have recognized that maintaining security and order in the schools requires a certain degree of flexibility in school disciplinary procedures, and we have respected the value of preserving the informality of the student-teacher relationship. See *Id.,* at 582–583, 95 S.Ct., at 740; Ingraham v. Wright, 430 U.S., at 680–682, 97 S.Ct., at 1417–1418.

How, then, should we strike the balance between the schoolchild's legitimate expectations of privacy and the school's equally legitimate need to maintain an environment in which learning can take place? It is evident that the school setting requires some easing of the restrictions to which searches by public authorities are ordinarily subject. The warrant requirement, in particular, is unsuited to the school environment: requiring a teacher to obtain a warrant before searching a child suspected of an infraction of school rules (or of the criminal law) would unduly interfere with the maintenance of the swift and informal disciplinary procedures needed in the schools. Just as we have in other cases dispensed with the warrant requirement when "the burden of obtaining a warrant is likely to frustrate the governmental purpose behind the search," Camara v. Municipal Court, 387 U.S., at 532–533, 87 S.Ct., at 1733, we hold today that school officials need not obtain a warrant before searching a student who is under their authority.

The school setting also requires some modification of the level of suspicion of illicit activity needed to justify a search. Ordinarily, a search—even one that may permissibly be carried out without a warrant—must be based upon "probable cause" to believe that a violation of the law has occurred. See, e.g., Almeida-Sanchez v. United States, 413 U.S. 266, 273, 93 S.Ct. 2535, 2540, 37 L.Ed.2d 596 (1973); Sibron v. New York, 392 U.S. 40, 62–66, 88 S.Ct. 1889, 1902–1904, 20 L.Ed.2d 917 (1968). However, "probable cause" is not an irreducible requirement of a valid search. The fundamental command of the Fourth Amendment is that searches and seizures be reasonable, and although "both the concept of probable cause and the requirement of a warrant bear on the reasonableness of a search, . . . in certain limited circumstances neither is required." Almeida-Sanchez v. United States, supra, 413 U.S., at 277, 93 S.Ct., at 2541 (POWELL, J., concurring). Thus, we have a number of cases recognized the legality of searches and seizures based on suspicions that, although "reasonable," do not rise to the level of probable cause. See, e.g., Terry v. Ohio, 392 U.S. 1, 88 S.Ct. 1868, 20 L.Ed.2d 889 (1968); United States v. Brignoni-Ponce, 422 U.S. 873, 881, 95 S.Ct. 2574, 2580, 45 L.Ed.2d 607 (1975); Delaware v. Prouse, 440 U.S. 648, 654–655, 99 S.Ct. 1391, 1396, 59 L.Ed.2d 660 (1979); United States v. Martinez-Fuerte, 428 U.S. 543, 96 S.Ct. 3074, 49 L.Ed.2d 1116 (1976); cf. Camara v. Municipal Court, supra, 387 U.S., at 534–539, 87 S.Ct., at 1733–1736. Where a careful balancing of governmental and private interests suggests that the public interest is best served by a Fourth Amendment standard of reasonableness that stops short of probable cause, we have not hesitated to adopt such a standard.

[5–8] We join the majority of courts that have examined this issue in concluding that the accommodation of the privacy interests of schoolchildren with the substantial need of teachers and administrators for freedom to maintain order in the schools does not require strict adherence to the requirement that searches be based on probable cause to believe that the subject of the search has violated or is violating the law. Rather, the legality of a search of a student should depend simply on the reasonableness, under all the circumstances, of the search. Determining the reasonableness of any search involves a twofold inquiry: first, one must consider "whether the ... action was justified at its inception," Terry v. Ohio, 392 U.S., at 20, 88 S.Ct., at 1879; second, one must determine whether the search as actually conducted "was reasonable related in scope to the circumstances which justified the interference in the first place," *Ibid.* Under ordinary circumstances, a search of a student by a teacher or other school official will be "justified at its inception" when there are reasonable grounds for suspecting that the search will turn up evidence that the student has violated or is violating either the law or the rules of the school. Such a search will be permissible in its scope when the measures adopted are reasonably related to the objectives of the search and not excessively intrusive in light of the age and sex of the student and the nature of the infraction.

This standard will, we trust, neither unduly burden the efforts of school authorities to maintain order in their schools nor authorize unrestrained intrusions upon the privacy of schoolchildren. By focusing attention on the question of reasonableness, the standard will spare teachers and school administrators the necessity of schooling themselves in the niceties of probable cause and permit them to regulate their conduct according to the dictates of reason and common sense. At the same time, the reasonableness standard should ensure that the interests of students will be invaded no more than is necessary to achieve the legitimate end of preserving order in the schools.

III

[9] There remains the question of the legality of the search in this case. We recognize that the "reasonable grounds" standard applied by the New Jersey Supreme Court in its consideration of this question is not substantially different from the standard that we have adopted today. Nonetheless, we believe that the New Jersey court's application of the standard to strike down the search of T.L.O.'s purse reflects a somewhat crabbed notion of reasonableness. Our review of the facts surrounding the search leads us to conclude that the search was in no sense unreasonable for Fourth Amendment purposes.

The incident that gave rise to this case actually involved two separate searches, with the first—the search for cigarettes—providing the suspicion that gave rise to the second—the search for marihuana. Although it is the fruits of the second search that are at issue here, the validity of the search for marihuana must depend on the reasonableness of the initial search for cigarettes, as there would have been no reason to suspect that T.L.O. possessed marihuana had the first search not taken place. Accordingly, it is to the search for cigarettes that we first turn our attention.

The New Jersey Supreme Court pointed to two grounds for its holding that the search for cigarettes was unreasonable. First, the court observed that possession of cigarettes was not in itself illegal or a violation of school rules. Because the contents of T.L.O.'s purse would therefore have "no direct bearing on the infraction" of which she was accused (smoking in a lavatory where smoking was prohibited), there was no reason to search her purse. Second, even assuming that a search of T.L.O.'s purse might under some circumstances be reasonable in light of the accusation made against T.L.O., the New Jersey court concluded that Mr. Choplick in this particular case had no reasonable grounds to suspect that T.L.O. had cigarettes in her purse. At best, according to the court, Mr. Choplick had "a good hunch." 94 N.J., at 347, 463 A.2d, at 942.

[10] Both these conclusions are implausible. T.L.O. had been accused of smoking, and had denied the accusation in the strongest possible terms when she stated that she did not smoke at all. Surely it cannot be said that under these circumstances, T.L.O.'s possession of cigarettes would be irrelevant to the charges against her or to her response to those charges. T.L.O.'s possession of cigarettes, once it was discovered, would both corroborate the report that she had been smoking and undermine the credibility of her defense to the charge of smoking. To be sure, the discovery of the cigarettes would not prove that T.L.O. had been smoking in the lavatory; nor would it, strictly speaking, necessarily be inconsistent with her claim that she did not smoke at all. But it is universally recognized that evidence, to be relevant to an inquiry, need not conclusively prove the ultimate fact in issue, but only have "any tendency to make the existence of any fact that is of consequence to the determination of the action more probable or less probable than it would be without the evidence." Fed.Rule Evid. 401. The relevance of T.L.O.'s possession of cigarettes to the question whether she had been smoking and to the credibility of her denial that she smoked supplied the necessary "nexus" between the item searched for and the infraction under investigation. See Warden v. Hayden, 387 U.S. 294, 306–307, 87 S.Ct. 1642, 1649–1650, 18 L.Ed.2d 782 (1967). Thus, if Mr. Choplick in fact had a reasonable suspicion that T.L.O. had cigarettes in her purse, the search was justified despite the fact that the cigarettes, if found, would constitute "mere evidence" of a violation. *Ibid.*

[11] Of course, the New Jersey Supreme Court also held that Mr. Choplick had no reasonable suspicion that the purse would contain cigarettes. This conclusion is puzzling. A teacher had reported that T.L.O. was smoking in the lavatory. Certainly this report gave Mr. Choplick reason to suspect that T.L.O. was carrying cigarettes with her; and if she did have cigarettes, her purse was the obvious place in which to find them. Mr. Choplick's suspicion that there were cigarettes in the purse was not an "inchoate and unparticularized suspicion or 'hunch,'" Terry v. Ohio, 392 U.S., at 27, 88 S.Ct., at 1883; rather, it was the sort of "common-sense conclusio[n] about human behavior" upon which "practical people"—including government officials—are entitled to rely. United States v. Cortez, 449 U.S. 411, 418, 101 S.Ct. 690, 695, 66 L.Ed.2d 621 (1981). Of course, even if the teacher's report were true, T.L.O. *might* not have had a pack of cigarettes with her; she might have borrowed a cigarette from someone else or have been sharing a cigarette with another student. But the requirement of reasonable suspicion is not a requirement of absolute certainty: "sufficient probability, not certainty, is the touchstone of reasonableness under the Fourth Amendment . . . " Hill v. California, 401 U.S. 797, 804, 91 S.Ct. 1106, 1111, 28 L.Ed.2d 484 (1971). Because the hypothesis that T.L.O. was carrying cigarettes in her purse was itself not unreasonable, it is irrelevant that other hypotheses were also consistent with the teacher's accusation. Accordingly, it cannot be said that Mr. Choplick acted unreasonably when he examined T.L.O.'s purse to see if it contained cigarettes.

[12] Our conclusion that Mr. Choplick's decision to open T.L.O.'s purse was reasonable brings us to the question of the further search for marihuana once the pack of cigarettes was located. The suspicion upon which the search for marihuana was founded was provided when Mr. Choplick observed a package of rolling papers in the purse as he removed the pack of cigarettes. Although T.L.O. does not dispute the reasonableness of Mr. Choplick's belief that the rolling papers indicated the presence of marihuana, she does contend that the scope of the search Mr. Choplick conducted exceeded permissible bounds when he seized and read certain letters that implicated T.L.O. in drug dealing. This argument, too, is unpersuasive. The discovery of the rolling papers concededly gave rise to a reasonable suspicion that T.L.O. was carrying marihuana as well as cigarettes in her purse. This suspicion justified further exploration of T.L.O.'s purse, which turned up more evidence of drug-related activities: a pipe, a number of plastic bags of the type commonly used to store

marihuana, a small quantity of marihuana, and a fairly substantial amount of money. Under these circumstances, it was not unreasonable to extend the search to a separate zippered compartment of the purse; and when a search of that compartment revealed an index card containing a list of "people who owe me money" as well as two letters, the inference that T.L.O. was involved in marihuana trafficking was substantial enough to justify Mr. Choplick in examining the letters to determine whether they contained any further evidence. In short, we cannot conclude that the search for marihuana was unreasonable in any respect.

Because the search resulting in the discovery of the evidence of marihuana dealing by T.L.O. was reasonable, the New Jersey Supreme Court's decision to exclude that evidence from T.L.O.'s juvenile delinquency proceedings on Fourth Amendment grounds was erroneous. Accordingly, the judgment of the Supreme Court of New Jersey is

Reversed.

Justice POWELL, with whom Justice O'CONNOR joins, concurring.

24 Cal.3d 357
The People, Plaintiff and Respondent v. Virginia Alvinia ZELINSKI, Defendant and Appellant.
Cr. 20284.
Supreme Court of California,
In Bank.
May 24, 1979.
Rehearing Denied June 27, 1979

MANUEL, Justice.

Virginia Zelinski was charged with unlawful possession of a controlled substance, heroin (Health & Saf.Code, SECTION 11350). A motion to suppress evidence pursuant to Penal code section 1538.5 was denied. She entered a plea of guilty and appeals. (Pen. Code, SECTION 1538.5, subd. (m).) We reverse.

On March 21, 1976, Bruce Moore, a store detective employed by Zody's Department Store, observed defendant place a blouse into her purse. Moore alerted Ann O'Connor, another Zody detective, and the two thereafter observed defendant select a pair of sandals, which she put on her feet, and a hat, which she put on her head. Defendant also took a straw bag into which she placed her purse. Defendant then selected and paid for a pair of blue shoes and left the store.

Detectives Moore and O'Connor stopped defendant outside the store. Moore placed defendant under arrest for violation of Penal Code section 484 (theft) and asked her to accompany him and detective O'Connor into the store. Defendant was taken by O'Connor to the security office where Pat Forrest, another female store detective, conducted a routine "cursory search in case of weapons" on the person of defendant.

Moore testified that he reentered the security office when the search of defendant's person was completed, opened defendant's purse to retrieve the blouse taken from Zody's, and removed the blouse and a pill vial that lay on top of the blouse. Moore examined the vial, removed a balloon from the bottle, examined the fine powdery substance contained in the balloon and set the vial and balloon on the security office desk to await the police who had been called.

Detective O'Connor, who testified to the search of defendant's person by Forrest was initially confused as to whether the pill vial containing the balloon had been taken from the defendant's purse or from her brassiere. On cross-examination, O'Connor was certain that she saw Forrest taking it from defendant's brassiere. According to O'Connor, the pill bottle was placed on the security office desk where detective Moore shortly thereafter opened it and examined the powdery substance in the balloon. Later the police took custody of the vial and defendant was thereafter charged with unlawful possession of heroin.

Defendant's appeal involves two questions: (1) whether store detectives Moore, O'Connor, and Forrest exceeded the permissible scope of search incident to the arrest, and (2) if they did, whether the evidence thus obtained should be excluded as violation of defendant's rights under federal or state constitutions. We have concluded that the narcotics evidence was obtained by unlawful search and that the constitutional prohibition against unreasonable search and seizure affords protection against the unlawful intrusive conduct of these private security personnel.

[1,2] Store detectives and security guards are retained primarily to protect their employer's interest in property. They have no more powers to enforce the law than other private persons. See Private Police in California: A Legislative Proposal (1975) 5 Golden Gate L.Rev. 115, 129–134; cf. Stapleton v. Superior Court (1968) 70 Cal.2d 97, 100–101, fn. 3, 73 Cal.Rptr. 575, 447 P.2d 967. Like all private persons, security employees can arrest or detain an offender (Pen.Code, SECTION 837) and search for weapons (Pen.Code, SECTION 846) before taking the

offender to a magistrate or delivering him to a peace officer (Pen.Code, SECTION 847, 849). Store personnel Moore and O'Connor were acting under this statutory authority when they arrested defendant and took her into custody for leaving the store with stolen merchandise.

[3] Merchants have traditionally had the right to restrain and detain shoplifters. At the time of the incident at Zody's, merchants were protected from civil liability for false arrest or false imprisonment in their reasonable efforts to detain shoplifters by a common law privilege that permitted detention for a reasonable time for investigation in a reasonable manner of any person whom the merchant had probable cause to believe had unlawfully taken or attempted to take merchandise from the premises. Collyer v. S.H. Kress Co. (1936) 5 Cal.2d 175, 54 P.2d 20. That privilege has since been enacted into state as subdivision (e) of Penal Code section 490.5.

Thus, pursuant to the Penal Code or the civil common law privilege, store personnel Moore and O'Connor had authority to arrest or detain defendant. The question remains, however, whether they exceeded their authority in their subsequent search for and seizure of evidence.

[4,5] The permissible scope of search incident to a citizen's arrest is set out in People v. Sandoval (1966) 65 Cal.2d 303, 311, fn. 5, 54 Cal.Rptr. 123, 128, 419 P.2d 187, 192.5: "A citizen effecting such an arrest is authorized only to 'take from the person arrested all offensive weapons which he may have about his person' (Pen.Code, SECTION 846), not to conduct a search for contraband 'incidental' to the arrest, or to seize such contraband upon recovering it. [Citation.] We reject the suggestion of People v. Alvarado (1962) 208 Cal.App.2d 629, 631, 25 Cal.Rptr. 437, that the search of one private individual or his premises by another is lawful simply because 'incidental' to a lawful citizen's arrest." (See also People v. Cheatham (1968) 263 Cal.App.2d 458, 462, fn. 2, 69 Cal.Rptr. 679; People v. Sjosten (1968) 262 Cal.App.2d 539, 68 Cal.Rptr. 832; People v. Martin (1964) 225 Cal.App.2d 91, 94, 36 Cal.Rptr. 924.) The rationale behind the rule is that, absent statutory authorization, private citizens are not and should not be permitted to take property from other private citizens.

The limits of the merchant's authority to search is now expressly stated in Penal Code section 490.5 Paragraph (3) of subdivision (e) provides that "During the period of detention any items which a merchant has reasonable cause to believe are unlawfully taken from his premises and which are in plain view may be examined by the merchant for the purposes of ascertaining the ownership thereof." Neither the statute nor the privilege which it codified purport to give to the merchant or his employees the authority to search.

[6] In the present case, instead of holding defendant and her handbag until the arrival of a peace officer who may have been authorized to search, the employees instituted a search to recover goods that were not in plain view. Such intrusion into defendant's person and effects was not authorized as incident to a citizen's arrest pursuant to section 837 of the Penal Code (Sandoval, supra, 65 Cal. fn. 5, at p. 311, 54 Cal.Rptr. 123, 419 P.2d 187), or pursuant to the merchant's privilege subsequently codified in subdivision (e) of section 490.5. It was unnecessary to achieve the employees' reasonable concerns of assuming that defendant carried no weapons and of preventing loss of store property. As a matter of law, therefore, the fruits of that search were illegally obtained.

The People contend that the evidence is nevertheless admissible because the search and seizure were made by private persons. They urge that Burdeau v. McDowell (1921) 256 U.S. 465, 41 S.Ct. 574, 65 L.Ed. 1048 holding that Fourth Amendment proscriptions against unreasonable searches and seizures do not apply to private conduct, is still good law and controlling. (See People v. Randazzo (1963) 220 Cal.App2d 768, 770–775, 34 Cal.Rptr. 65; People v. Superior Court (Smith) (1969) 70 Cal.2d 123, 128–129, 74 Cal.Rptr. 294, 298, 449 P.2d 230, 234, ["... acquisition of property by a private citizen from another person cannot be deemed reasonable or unreasonable"]; cf. Stapleton v. Superior Court, supra, 70 Cal.2d at p. 100, fn. 2, 73 Cal.Rptr. 575, 447 P.2d 967.)

Defendant contends, on the other hand, that only by applying the exclusionary rule to all searches conducted by store detectives and other private security personnel can freedoms embodied in the Fourth Amendment of the U.S. Constitution and article i, section 13 of the state Constitution be protected from the abuses and dangers inherent in the growth of private security activities.

More than a decade ago we expressed concern that searches by private security forces can involve a "particularly serious threat to privacy" (Stapleton, supra, 70 Cal.2d at pp. 100–101, fn. 3, 73 Cal.Rptr. at pp. 577 n. 3, 447 P.2d at pp. 969 n. 3); in Stapleton and later in Dyas v. Superior Court (1974) 11 Cal.3d 628, 633, 114 Cal. Rptr. 114, 522 P.2d 674, we left open the question whether searches by such private individuals should be held subject to the constitutional proscriptions. We now address the problem.

Article I, section 13 of the California Constitution provides in part that: "The right of the people to be secure in their persons, houses, papers and effects against unreasonable seizures and searches may not be violated. . . . " Although the constitutional provision contains no language indicating that the "security" protected by the provision is limited to security from governmental searches or seizures, California cases have generally interpreted this provision as primarily intended as a protection of the people against such governmentally initiated or governmentally-directed intrusions. The exclusionary rule, fashioned to implement the rights secured by the constitutional provision, has therefore been applied to exclude evidence illegally obtained by private citizens only where it served the purpose of the exclusionary rule in restraining abuses by the police of their statutory powers. (Stapleton v. Superior Court, supra, 70 Cal.2d 97, 73 Cal.Rptr. 575, 447 P.2d 967; People v. Cahan, 44 Cal.2d 434, 282 P.2d 905; Mapp v. Ohio (1961) 367 U.S. 643, 81 S.Ct. 1684, 6 L.Ed.2d 1081; cf. People v. Payne (1969) 1 Cal.App.3d 361, 81 Cal.Rptr. 635; People v. Randazzo, supra, 220 Cal.App.2d 768, 34 Cal.Rptr. 65; People v. Cheatham, supra, 263 Cal.App.3d 458, 461–462, 69 Cal.Rptr. 679; cf. People v. Mollard (1971) 15 Cal.App.3d 759, 761–762, 93 Cal.Rptr. 402; People v. Superior Court (Smith), supra, 70 Cal.2d 123, 74 Cal.Rptr. 294, 449 P.2d 230; People v. Mangiefico (1972) 25 Cal.App.3d 1041, 1047–1048, 102 Cal.Rptr. 449.)

We have recognized that private security personnel, like police, have the authority to detain suspects, conduct investigations, and make arrests. They are not police, however, and we have refused to accord them the special privileges and protections enjoyed by official police officers. (See People v. Corey (1978) 21 Cal.3d 738, 147 Cal.Rptr. 639, 581 P.2d 644.) We have excluded the fruits of their illegal investigations only when they were acting in concert with the police or when the police were standing silently by. (Stapleton, supra, 70 Cal.2d at p. 103, 73 Cal.Rptr. 575, 447 P.2d 967.) We are mindful, however, of the increasing reliance placed upon private security personnel by local law enforcement authorities for the prevention of crime and enforcement of the criminal law and the increasing threat to privacy rights posed thereby. Since Stapleton was decided, the private security industry has grown tremendously, and, from all indications, the number of private security personnel continues to increase today. A recent report prepared by the Private Security Advisory Council to the United States Department of Justice describes this phenomenon in the following terms: "A vast army of workers are employed in local, state, and federal government to prevent crime and to deal with criminal activity. Generally thought of as the country's major crime prevention force are the more than 40,000 public law enforcement agencies with their 475,000 employees. While they constitute the . . . most visible component of the criminal justice system, another group has been fast rising in both numbers and responsibility in the area of crime prevention. With a rate of increase exceeding even that of the public police, the private security sector has become the largest single group in the country engaged in the prevention of crime." (Private Security Adv. Coun. to U.S. Dept. of Justice, LEAA, Report on the Regulation of Private Security Services (1976), p. 1.)

Realistically, therefore, we recognize that in our state today illegal conduct of privately employed security personnel poses a threat to privacy rights of Californians that is comparable to that which may be posed by the unlawful conduct of police officers. (See generally, Private Police in California—A Legislative Proposal, supra, 5 Golden Gate L.Rev. 115; Bassiouni, Citizen's Arrest: The Law of Arrest, Search and Seizure for Private Citizens and Private Police (1977), p. 72.) Moreover, the application of the exclusionary rule can be expected to have a deterrent effect on such unlawful search and seizure practices since private security personnel, unlike ordinary private citizens, may regularly perform such quasi-law enforcement activities in the course of their employment. (See Seizures by Private Parties: Exclusion in Criminal Cases (1967) 19 Stan.L.Rev. 608, 614 615.)

[7] In the instant case, however, we need not, and do not, decide whether the constitutional constraints of article 1, section 13, apply to all of the varied activities of private security personnel, for here the store security forces did not act in a purely private capacity but rather were fulfilling a public function in bringing violators of the law to public justice. *For reasons hereinafter expressed, we conclude that under* such circumstances, i.e., when private security *personnel conduct an illegal search or seizure while engaged in a statutorily-authorized citizen's arrest and detention of a person in aid of law enforcement authorities, the constitutional proscriptions of article 1, section 13 are applicable.*

[8] *Although past cases have not applied the constitutional restrictions to purely private searches, we have recognized that some minimal official participation or encouragement may bring private action within the constitutional constraints of state action.* (Stapleton v. Superior Court, supra, 70 Cal.2d 97, 101, 73 Cal.Rptr. 575, 447 P.2d 967.) As noted by the United States Supreme Court in United States v. Price (1965) 383 U.S. 787, 86 S.Ct.

1152, 16 L.Ed.2d 267, a person does not need to be an officer of the state to act under color of law and therefore be responsible, along with such officers, for actions prohibited to state officials when such actions are engaged in under color of law. (*Id.*, p. 794, and fn. 7, 86 S.Ct. 1152 thereunder; cf. Burton v. Wilminton Pkg Auth. (1961) 365 U.S. 715, 725, 81 S.Ct. 856, 6 L.Ed.2d 45; Weeks v. U.S. (1914) 232 U.S. 383, 398, 34 S.Ct. 341, 58 L.Ed 652; Marsh v. Alabama (1946) 326 U.S. 501, 66 S.Ct. 276, 90 L.Ed. 265.)

In the instant case, the store employees arrested defendant pursuant to the authorization contained in Penal Code section 837, and the search which yielded the narcotics was conducted incident to that arrest. Their acts, engaged in pursuant to the statute, were not those of a private citizen acting in a purely private capacity. Although the search exceeded lawful authority, it was nevertheless an integral part of the exercise of sovereignty allowed by the state to private citizens. In arresting the offender, the store employees were utilizing the coercive powers of the state to further a state interest. Had the security guards sought only the vindication of the merchant's private interests they would have simply exercised self-help and demanded the return of the stolen merchandise. Upon satisfaction of the merchant's interests, the offender would have been released. By holding defendant for criminal process and searching her, they went beyond their employer's private interests.

[9] *Persons so acting should be subject to the constitutional proscriptions that secure an individual's right to privacy, for their actions are taken pursuant to statutory authority to promote a state interest in bringing offenders to public accounting. Unrestrained, such action would subvert state authority in defiance of its established limits. It would destroy the protection those carefully defined limits were intended to afford to everyone, the guilty and innocent alike. It would afford defacto authorizations for searches and seizures incident to arrests or detentions made by private individuals that even peace officers are not authorized to make. Accordingly, we hold that in any case where private security personnel assert the power of the state to make an arrest or to detain another person for transfer to custody of the state, the state involvement is sufficient for the court to enforce the proper exercise of that power (cf. People v. Haydel (1974) 12 Cal.3d 190, 194, 115 Cal.Rptr. 394, 524 P.2d 866) by excluding the fruits of illegal abuse thereof. We hold that exclusion of the illegally seized evidence is required by article I, section 13 of the California Constitution.*

The judgment (order granting probation) is reversed.

TOBRINER, MOSK, RICHARDSON and NEWMAN, JJ., concur.

BIRD, C. J., concurs in the result.

CLARK, Justice, dissenting.

I dissent for the reason expressed in my dissenting opinion in Dyas v. Superior Court (1974) 11 Cal.3d 628, 637 638, 114 Cal.Rptr. 114, 522 P.2d 674. The judgment should be affirmed.

Rehearing denied; CLARK, J., dissenting.

Zelinski Comment

The Zelinski Case cited earlier is included herein for several reasons: (1) It caused some debate in the private security field by some commentators who immediately were calling wolf and suggesting that private security professionals change their procedures; and "Like it or not, the Zelinski rule is coming."

The March 1980 issue of *Security Management* contained an article which headlined:

PRIVATE SECURITY IN THE COURTROOM: THE EXCLUSIONARY RULE APPLIES

As you note, this California case really indicated that Security Personnel violated the Penal Code by searching for and seizing contraband, a controlled substance, which was not in "plain view." From this condition, the Court reasoned that the *California* Constitution was violated and *evidence* obtained in violation of this California Constitution was inadmissible. The case was certainly not a binding precedent on the courts of states other than California, and as we see in the next case, People v. Adam Jason Taylor, was not long an authority in California, where there was a change to the California Constitution (Proposition 8) and the court stated that Zelinski was abrogated and superseded by a federal case, a prime example of the point which I have tried to demonstrate, i.e., that the law is a dynamic, constantly changing field of study.

222 Cal.App.3d 612
The PEOPLE, Plaintiff and Respondent v. Adam Jason TAYLOR, Defendant and Appellant.
No. H006114.
Court of Appeal, Sixth District.
July 26, 1990.
Review Denied Oct. 11, 1990.

On April 10, 1989, at 9:25 P.M., two security guards employed by the Seaside Security Company, the corporate security department of the Seaside Land Company, owner of the Santa Cruz Beach Boardwalk, encountered appellant and three others on a small path under the boardwalk leading from a parking lot to the beach. The four had open containers of beer. One, a Mr. Light, was smoking a marihuana cigarette. Appellant had a baggie containing a green substance on his lap.

Officer Kerr asked appellant for the baggie and identification. Appellant handed him the baggie, but said he had no identification. Kerr then asked Light, who had turned over both his cigarette and identification, if he had more drugs or contraband on his person. Light said that he did not, and agreed to a search which yielded no additional drugs.

Kerr then asked appellant if he had more drugs on his person and if he could search him. Appellant began to tremble and shake. He denied he had drugs, agreed to a search, and opened and handed over his pouch, known as a "fannypack." After finding no contraband in it, Kerr patted down appellant's pants. As his hand touched appellant's left pocket, he felt a baggie and heard a rustling or crumpling sound. He partially removed four similar baggies of marihuana and two individually wrapped baggies containing several sheets of colored perforated paper which he thought contained LSD. Kerr pushed the items back into appellant's pocket and handcuffed him. He finished the patdown for weapons, found none, and transported both appellant and Light to a security station operated by Seaside Security Company where the Santa Cruz police were called.

Police Officer Carr responded. Kerr told him that appellant and Light were detained on narcotics charges, and that he believed appellant had marihuana and LSD in his pocket. Carr then searched appellant and removed the drugs from appellant's pocket. Appellant was ultimately charged with possession of LSD for sale (Health & Saf. Code, SECTION

11378) and possession of marihuana (Health & Saf.Code, SECTION 11357, subd. (b)).

Appellant's motion to suppress the evidence was denied. He then pled guilty to a violation of possession of LSD (Health & Saf.Code, SECTION 11377), conditioned on no prison commitment. The marihuana charge was dismissed. The court placed appellant on probation for five years, and ordered him to serve six months in the county jail. This appeal ensued.

Contentions on Appeal

Appellant asserts that since private individuals may not search each other for contraband under California law, the evidence was illegally seized and should be excluded. Second, he contends that since the security guards were private individuals who arrested him without complying with statutes defining how private citizens may exercise the power to arrest, this court should refuse to give binding legal effect to his consent.

Alternatively, he claims that the guards were not acting in a purely private capacity since they were carrying out a police function properly reserved to the state, and because the guards were acting jointly with the police. Furthermore, he claims that the conduct of the guards must be imputed to the state because they were subject to the state's licensing and regulatory scheme. (Bus. & Prof.Code, SECTION 7544, et seq.) Therefore, a Fourth Amendment analysis is required.

As this court has recently stated, "On appeal, we review the evidence in a light favorable to the trial court's ruling on the suppression motion. . . . We uphold those express or implicit findings of fact by the trial court which are supported by substantial evidence. . . . Insofar as the evidence is uncontradicted, we do not engage in substantial evidence review, but face pure questions of law. . . . We must independently determine whether the facts support the court's legal conclusions.' [Citation.]" (People v. Brouillette (1989) 210 Cal. App.3d 842, 845–846, 258 Cal.Rptr. 635.)

[1] To the extent the facts are disputed, all presumptions, inferences and credibility assessments supporting the findings of the court below must be implied, and the trial court's findings must be upheld if supported by substantial evidence. (People v. Brouillette, supra, 210 Cal.App.3d at pp. 843–846, 258 Cal.Rptr. 633.) "Evidence, to be 'substantial' must be 'of

ponderable legal significance . . . reasonable in nature, credible, and of solid value.' [Citations.]" (People v. Johnson (1980) 26 Cal.3d 557, 376, 162 Cal.Rptr. 431, 606 P.2d 738.)

Private Action

[2] Appellant contends that if the search by the security guard was a private search, it violated section 846, which strictly limits private citizen searches to removing offensive weapons on the person of the arrestee.

"An arrest is taking a person into custody, in a case and in the manner authorized by law. An arrest may be made by a peace officer or by a private person." (SECTION 834.) A private person may arrest another for a public offense committed or attempted in his presence; for a felony, although not committed in his presence; or when a felony has been in fact committed and the private person has reasonable cause for believing the person arrested to have committed it. (SECTION 837.) A private person has the duty to take the person arrested before a magistrate or deliver him to a peace officer without unnecessary delay. (SECTION 847.)

Our courts have repeatedly held that a citizen is not authorized by section 846 to conduct a search for contraband "incidental" to the arrest, or to seize such contraband upon recovering it. "[A]bsent statutory authorization, private citizens are not and should not be permitted to take property from other private citizens." (People v. Zelinski (1979) 24 Cal.3d 357, 363, 155 Cal.Rptr. 575, 594 P.2d 1000, fn. omitted.)

Therefore, appellant argues—that although Kerr had cause to arrest "[f]or a public offense [possession of marihuana (Health & Saf.Code, SECTION 11357)] committed . . . in his presence[,]" (SECTION 837, subd. 1), he was not justified in seizing and examining the baggies.

Appellant suggests exclusion of the evidence as a proper remedy for an unlawful search by a private citizen. However, "[t]he exclusionary rules were fashioned 'to prevent, not to repair,' and their target is official misconduct. They are 'to compel respect for the constitutional guaranty in the only effectively available way—by removing the incentive to disregard it.' [Citation.] But it is no part of the policy underlying the Fourth and Fourteenth Amendments to discourage citizens from aiding to the utmost of their ability in the apprehension of criminals. If, then, the exclusionary rule is properly applicable. . . . it must be upon the basis that some type of unconstitutional police conduct occurred."

(Coolidge v. New Hampshire (1971) 403 U.S. 443, 488, 91 S.Ct. 2022, 2049, 29 L.Ed.2d 564.)

[3] Therefore, the protection of the Fourth Amendment does not extend to searches carried out by private persons. (People v. Brouillette, supra, 210 Cal. App.3d at p. 846, 258 Cal.Rptr. 635.) Appellant's remedy is civil in nature and can be pursued, as appropriate, as in any other action involving civil wrongs.

Consent

[4] Next, appellant contends that "finding consent would abrogate California's statutory scheme which strictly defines when private citizens may exercise full powers of arrest," and that this court "should refuse to give binding legal effect to [his] consent."

Appellant relies on People v. Martin (1964) 225 Cal.App.2d 91, 95, 36 Cal.Rptr. 924, for the proposition that consent given in submission to express or implied authority cannot be said to be free and voluntary and the fruits must be deemed to be inadmissible. In Martin, two Los Angeles Police Department narcotics officers made an arrest beyond the city limits, and sought and received consent to search. At that time, a police officer for one geographical district had no official power to arrest outside that district. The court of appeal therefore held that the officers merely had the powers of private citizens and no authority to search beyond removal of all offensive weapons from the person of the arrestee. The court excluded the evidence.

However, in that case, the police officers were asserting the power of the state when they identified themselves as police officers, arrested Martin, immediately questioned him about his "scabs," ordered him to remove his jacket so they could see his tracks, and then asked for and received permission and his cooperation in searching his hotel room.

Here, if the security guards were acting in a private capacity, the exclusionary rule does not apply. In a case where private investigators, hired by a father to discover what happened to his two missing sons, stopped and searched the automobile of a defendant later convicted of the sons' murder, the court said: "[a]lthough their conduct was outrageous, unquestionably tortious, and no doubt violative of several penal statutes, those are not the questions here. The question we confront is whether [substantial evidence supports] the trial court's findings [that] the investigators were serving a private . . . rather than a public interest. . . . ' (People v. De Juan)

State Action

I Public Purpose

[5] Next, appellant contends that the state is involved in the security guards' actions because they were operating jointly with the police and because they acted solely for a public purpose.

The guards' duties were to patrol the boardwalk, and not to generally enforce laws. However, he asserts that when the guards questioned him, searched him for contraband, and then arrested him, they were acting for a public purpose.

Appellant relies on People v. Zelinski, supra, 24 Cal.3d at pages 366–368, 155 Cal.Rptr. 675, 594 P.2d 1000, in which the Supreme Court held that if private security personnel were not acting in a purely private capacity but were fulfilling a public function in bringing violators of the law to public justice, they were asserting the power of the state, and were therefore subject to the constitutional proscriptions that secure an individual's right to privacy.

In Zelinski, the court relied on United States v. Price (1966) 383 U.S. 787, 794, footnote 7, 86 S.Ct. 1152, 1156–1157, foot-note 7, 16 L.Ed.2d 267, for the proposition that "a person does not need to be an officer of the state to act under color of law and therefore be responsible, along with such officers, for actions prohibited to state officials when such actions are engaged under color of law. [Citations.]" (24 Cal.3d at p. 367, 155 Cal.Rptr. 575, 594 P.2d 1000.) However, the court held that "exclusion of the illegally seized evidence is required by article 1, section 13 of the California Constitution." (People v. Zelinski, supra, 24 Cal.3d at p. 368, 155 Cal.Rptr. 575, 594 P.2d 1000.)

Zelinski is a pre-Proposition 8 case. This court recently wrote: "The enactment of California Constitution, article 1, section 28, subdivision (d) (Proposition 8) on June 8, 1982, permits us to suppress evidence only if that result is compelled by the United States Constitution; a violation of the California Constitution is no longer a basis for exclusion. [Citation.] In interpreting the United States Constitution, as in the case of all federal law, we are bound by the decisions of the United States Supreme Court and find persuasive authority in the decisions of other federal courts. [Citation.] We are also bound by the decisions of the California

Supreme Court." (People v. Brouillette, supra, 210 Cal.App.3d at p. 846, 258 Cal.Rptr. 635.) *Only if this search may be fairly characterized as state action does the exclusionary rule apply.* (*Id.* at p. 846, 258 Cal.Rptr. 635.)

The Ninth Circuit recently held: "to the extent Zelinski expanded the concept of state action under the California Constitution beyond federal law, it was abrogated by Proposition 8." (Collins v. Womancare (9th Cir.1989) 878 F.2d 1145, 1154.) "***Zelinski directly conflicts with and is superseded by Lugar*** [***v. Edmondson Oil Co.*** *(1982) 457 U.S. 922, 102 S.Ct. 2744, 73 L.Ed.2d 482*]." (Ibid.)

Under federal law, searches and seizures by private security employees have traditionally been viewed as those of a private citizen and consequently not subject to Fourth Amendment proscriptions (United States v. Lima (D.C.App.1980) 424 A.2d 113, 118).

Although the United States Supreme Court has not considered the constitutional status of private police forces (Collins v. Womancare, supra, 878 F.2d at p. 1150), Lugar v. Edmondson Oil Co., Inc., supra, 457 U.S. 922, 937, 102 S.Ct. 2744, 2753, mandates a two-prong test to determine whether state action is involved in the deprivation of a federal right.

First, the deprivation must be caused by the exercise of some right or privilege created by the state or by a rule of conduct imposed by the state or by a person for whom the state is responsible. Second, the party charged with the deprivation must be a person who may fairly be said to be a state actor. Lugar explains that "[t]his may be because he is a state official, because he has acted together with or has obtained significant aid from state officials, or because his conduct is otherwise chargeable to the State." (457 U.S. at p. 937, 102 S.Ct. at p. 2754.)

Turning to this case, the first question is whether the deprivation of appellant's right to be free from unreasonable searches and seizure resulted from the exercise of a right or privilege created by the state and which was traditionally exclusive to the state.

In Zelinski, the California Supreme Court said: "the store employees arrested defendant pursuant to the authorization contained in Penal Code section 837, and the search which yielded the narcotics was conducted incident to that arrest. Their acts, engaged in pursuant to the statute, were not those of a private citizen acting in a purely private capacity. Although the search exceeded lawful authority, it was nevertheless an integral part of the exercise of sovereignty allowed by the state to private citizens. In arresting the offender, the store employees were utilizing the coercive power of the state to further a state interest. Had the security guards sought only the vindication of the merchant's private interests they would have simply exercised self-help and demanded the return of the stolen merchandise. Upon satisfaction of the merchant's interests, the offender would have been released. By holding defendant for criminal process and searching her, they went beyond their employer's private interests." (People v. Zelinski, supra, 24 Cal.3d at p. 367, 165 Cal.Rptr. 575, 594 P.2d 1000, emphasis added, fn. omitted.)

For the first prong of the Lugar test, it is important to determine whether the state, in enacting statutes describing the circumstances in which citizens may arrest, was creating in citizens a right or privilege which was traditionally exclusive to the state.

Federal courts have not so held. "Arrest has never been an exclusively governmental function. Not all state authorized coercion is government action." (Spencer v. Lee (7th. Cir.1989) 864 F.2d 1376, 1380.) "There have been citizen arrests for as long as there have been public police, indeed much longer. In ancient Greece and Rome, and in England until the nineteenth century, most arrests and prosecutions were by private individuals." Ibid.

In United States v. Lima, Supra, 424 A.2d at page 120, in discussing a District of Columbia citizen's arrest statute, the court said: "Neither can it be argued that Congress intended to make the citizen an agent of the state for the purposes of making arrests by enacting a statute codifying the citizen common law power of arrest. [Citation.] Congress' intent by enacting this statute was to define and restrict the private citizen's common law right to arrest. . . . By so limiting the citizen's power of arrest, Congress recognized that 'law enforcement should generally be carried out by professionals.' [Citations.] A citizen's arrest power presumes that a law-abiding citizen for his own personal purposes may desire to stop criminal activity just as a merchant has a personal interest in deterring theft of his goods. Consequently, Congress has recognized these legitimate private interests of apprehending persons committing certain crimes within their presence. The fact that a private person makes a citizen's arrest does not automatically transform that individual into an agent of the state. His conduct is not actionable for any deprivation under color of law of rights, privileges or immunities secured by the Constitution."

Since the issue of what constitutes action under color of state law is ultimately one of federal, not state law (Gorenc v. Salt River Project Agr. Imp. & Power (9th Cir. 1989) 869 F.2d 503, 505), it appears that appellant has not satisfied the first prong of the Lugar test by showing that the right to arrest was traditionally exclusive to the state.

2. *Joint Operation*

[6] Appellant's next contention is that the security guards were operating jointly with the police, and that their action should be imputed to the state.

Appellant refers us to our analysis in Brouillette (distinguishing Zelinski), where we stated that "[t]he security guards here did not make an arrest or in any other way assert the power of the state. They merely inspected lost property [finding marihuana and cocaine] and called the police. The decision reached by the trial court [suppressing the evidence] required an implicit finding that the security guards asserted the power of the state when they took the particular action of inspecting the wallet, but that is not supported by substantial evidence. There was evidence to support the findings that the security guards dressed like police and are looked upon by others as representing police authority, and that they assisted the police by calling the deputy sheriff to the mall and allowing Brouillette to come to the mall office to be arrested when she perhaps thought that she was coming to collect her wallet. There was nothing to show that they made the inspection of the wallet as agents of the state." (People v. Brouillette, supra, 210 Cal.App.3d at p. 847, 258 Cal.Rptr. 635.)

Therefore, appellant contends, if we consider the same factors that we did in Brouillette, we should come to the conclusion that the security guards in the instant case were asserting the power of the state.

First, he asserts, the security guards acted jointly with the local police in that the private police maintained "Station 2," the detention center, but the public police used it also. In addition, appellant charges that since the guards had access to police radios, they should have used them and called the police, rather than "doing the dirty work of the invasive search" first.

Second, the guards exercised the authority of the state by arresting appellant, handcuffing him, and searching him. Third, the officers were clothed in the indicia of state authority. They looked like state-authorized police officers. They wore uniforms of light green pants, "duty belts," and tan shirts with badges and shoulder patches reading "Security, Santa Cruz Beach Boardwalk." They carried handcuffs, batons, and two-way radios. They also carried police radios. Furthermore, they patrolled an area used by the public which was not posted with "no trespassing" signs, and which provided access to a public beach. When these guards accosted appellant, they did not identify themselves as private security guards.

Finally, the guards did not act for a purely private purpose. Appellant and his companions were not harming Seaside Land Company's property. The officers were not afraid of appellant. Rather than protecting their employer's property by telling appellant and his companions to leave, since the Boardwalk was closed for business, they acted for the sole purpose of law enforcement: to get evidence of crime. "They wanted to find contraband: all their questions to Mr. Taylor were directed to that end. Since the Officer's [sic] sole purpose was to act in a law enforcement capacity, the Fourth Amendment must apply to their activities."

" '[T]he joint action inquiry focuses on whether the state has "so far insinuated itself into a position of interdependence with the private entity] that it must be recognized as a joint participant in the challenged activity. . . . " ' [Citation.] Joint action therefore requires a substantial degree of cooperative action." (Collins v. Womancare, supra, 878 F.2d at p. 1154.) "[M]erely complaining to the police does not convert a private party into a state actor. [Citations.] Nor is execution by a private party of a sworn complaint which forms the basis of an arrest enough to convert the private party's acts into state action. [Citation.]" (*Id.* at p. 1155.) There was no joint action where a private party, besides effecting the citizen's arrest, also transported the arrestee to the police station, attempted to persuade police to file charges, and swore out a complaint against the arrested party. (Ibid)

In light of the foregoing cases, the facts presented by appellant fail to establish that the state has " ' "so far insinuated itself into a position of interdependence with [Seaside Security employees] that it must be recognized as a joint participant in the challenged activity." ' [Citation.]" (Collins v. Womancare, supra, 878 F.2d at p. 1135.)

First, the impetus for the arrests came from the security guards. The evidence showed that the actions of the security guards sprang solely from their observations at the time. Next, appellant presented no evidence that the Seaside Security Company had contracts or agreements with the city, the county, or the state. There was no evidence from which this court can infer a "prearranged plan, customary procedure, or policy that substituted the judgment of a private party for that of the police. . . . " (Carey v. Continental Airlines, Inc. (10th Cir.1987) 823 F.2d 1402, 1404.) In short, there was no indication in the record that the state agents failed to use independent judgment or in any way coerced or encouraged the security guards to effect the citizen's arrest. (See San Francisco Arts & Athletics v. U.S. O.C. (1987) 483 U.S. 5'22, 538, 107 S.Ct. 2971, 2@82, 97 L.Ed.2d 427, 449–450.)

Furthermore, there is no evidence in the record to establish that the security guards' uniform was in any way similar in color to that of the Santa Cruz Police Department. The guards wore badges and shoulder patches marked "security." They did not carry guns. Although they did not identify themselves verbally as security guards, they did not verbally claim to be police officers. The evidence showed that their private purpose was to patrol Seaside Land Company's property. There was no evidence either establishing or negating specific instructions. Thus, there is no reason to conclude that their duties were limited to deterring crimes against property such as vandalism, littering, or trespass. (SECTION 594, 374.4, 602.)

Although the security guards made an arrest, federal cases cited ante disagree with Zelinski's assertion "that store detectives when they make an arrest do not act in a purely private capacity but 'assert the power of the state.'" (People v. Brouillette, supra, 210 Cal.App.3d at p. 847,-258-Cal.Rptr. 635 citing People v. Zelinski, supra, 24 Cal.3d at pp. 366, 368, 155 Cal.Rptr. 575, 594 P.2d 1000.) The Lugar test, requiring a showing of deprivation of a state created right by persons who can be shown to be state actors, was not satisfied.

[7] Finally, the mere fact that California licenses security guards and regulates their conduct does not transform them into state agents. (United States v. Lima, supra, 424 A.2d at pp. 120–121.) Security guards are required to take a course in exercise of power to arrest. (Bus. & Prof. Code, SECTION 7545.1, 7545.2.) The state emphasizes, in its pamphlet Powers to Arrest[,] Security Guard Training (1987 Rev.) Department of Consumer Affairs, Bureau of Collection and Investigative Services, page 8, "A security guard is not a police officer. Guards do not have the same job duties as police officers; they do not have the same training; and they do not have the same powers according to law." A security guard arrests with the same power as any other citizen. (*Id.* at p. 14.)

Substantial evidence in the record supports the finding of the trial court.

Disposition

The judgment is affirmed.

Chapter 5

SELF-INCRIMINATION AND PRIVATE SECURITY (MIRANDA)

The Fifth Amendment reads, in part as follows:

> "No person shall be compelled in any criminal case to be a witness against himself."

The privilege of electing not to incriminate oneself and the exclusionary rule protect us by not allowing in evidence at a trial confessions that have been extracted from a defendant by "Star-Chamber" or third degree methods. The case law has evolved to the Miranda rule, which provides that before a confession or admission of a defendant may be admitted into evidence, the government has the burden of proving that no custodial interrogation of the defendant took place before warnings were given to the defendant to the effect that one does not have to answer questions, that if one does, the answers may be used in a court of law, that one has the right to the presence of an attorney, and if one cannot afford an attorney the government must provide an attorney. Miranda v. Arizona 384 U.S. 436 (1966).

Prior to Miranda, the only question to be decided to determine whether a confession was admissible as evidence at a trial was whether or not the confession was given voluntarily (i.e., free from physical or psychological duress or coercion). The Miranda rule did not replace the test of voluntariness; it added the requirement that a confession or admission be voluntary. Therefore, under current law, the question of whether a confession or admission by a defendant to police officers while in custody is admissible requires affirmative answers to each of the following tests:

1. Were proper Miranda warnings given or waived?
2. Was the confession or admission voluntary?

The following lengthy case was decided by the Massachusetts Supreme

Judicial Court, setting forth the applicability of the above mentioned problems to private citizens (i.e., private security persons).

Commonwealth v. Mahnke
Supreme Judicial Court of Massachusetts, 1975
(*cert. denied,* 425 U.S. 959 (1976)
368 Mass. 662, 335 N.E.2d 660

TAURA, Chief Justice. The events which frame the central issues in this case arise from legal and illegal efforts of the family and friends of a young woman (the victim) to provide an explanation for her mysterious disappearance in September of 1970. On December 9, 1971, her body was discovered in a shallow grave near the parking lot of a Sears, Roebuck and Company (Sears) store in the Fenway area of Boston. The defendant, a boyfriend of the victim, was indicted for her murder in the first degree. Before trial, the defendant moved to suppress, inter alia, (1) statements he had made on December 9, 1971 to members of a "concerned group" of citizens who had abducted, imprisoned and interrogated him, (2) certain evidence which had come to light through information contained in the aforementioned statements, and (3) a statement given to police from a hospital bed the following day. After a lengthy voir dire, the trial judge granted the defendant's motions in part and denied them in part. The defendant was convicted of murder in the second degree and was sentenced to life imprisonment.

In the present appeal, under G.L. C.278, § 33A–33G, the defendant argues four specific assignments of error, chiefly related to the refusal of the judge to exclude from the trial all evidence of his abduction and subsequent police interrogation.

At the outset, we briefly summarize the subsidiary facts developed at the voir dire and reported in the careful and detailed initial and supplementary findings of the experienced trial judge. We accept, as we must, the trial judge's resolution of conflicting testimony (Commonwealth v. Valcourt 333 Mass. 706, 710, 133 N.E.2d 217 (1956); Commonwealth v. Femino, 352 Mass. 508, 513, 226 N.E.2d 248 (1967); Commonwealth v. D'Ambra, 357 Mass. 260, 262–263, 258 N.E.2d 74 (1970), and will not disturb his subsidiary findings if they are warranted by the evidence (See Commonwealth v. Murphy, 362 Mass. 542, 547, 289 N.E.2d 571 (1972). However, ultimate findings and conclusions of law, particularly those of constitutional dimensions, are open for our independent review in this appeal (*Id.* at 551, 289 N.E.2d 571 (Hennessey, J., concurring). See Commonwealth v. Kleciak, 350 Mass. 679, 685–689, 216 N.E.2d 417 (1966); Commonwealth v. Cook, 351 Mass. 231, 235, 218 N.E.2d 393 (1966), cert. denied, 385, U.S. 981, 87 S.Ct. 529, 17 L.Ed.2d 443 (1966). Additional facts in the case are discussed below as they become relevant to the several issues of law being considered.

The Police Investigation. On September 16, 1970, the day following the victim's disappearance, her parents reported her disappearance to the Boston Police, who immediately undertook an investigation. In the course of the early investigation, the defendant was twice interviewed by detectives from Division 4 of the Boston Police. The police did not suspect that a crime had been committed, but they did suspect that the victim was hiding somewhere in the Boston area and that the defendant had knowledge of where she was hiding, which he refused to divulge. Their suspicions were aroused by the several inconsistent stories which the defendant told in the September 16 interrogation regarding the events of the previous evening. The second interview, held September 24, with the defendant's attorney present, had as its primary purpose a discussion of whether, and in what circumstances, the defendant might take a lie detector test. In fact, the defendant never took the test.

The police investigations continued, but failed to discover the cause of the victim's disappearance or her location. In early December, 1970, Detective Stanley Gawlinski, attached to the office of the District Attorney for Suffolk County, was assigned to the case on a full time basis. After repeated urging by the victim's father Gawlinski arranged a meeting with the defendant for December 22 in the law office of the defendant's attorney. The defendant, in the presence of his attorney, described the relationship with the victim and repeated the last story he had related to the police on September 16. In April, 1971, again at the father's suggestion, Gawlinski arranged to have Muddy River in the Fenway area dragged for the victim's body. When this search proved unavailing, Gawlinski conceded that he had exhausted his leads and consigned the case to the inactive file at the district attorney's office. Thereafter, Gawlinski maintained only sporadic contact with the victim's family and limited his investigations to leads which were supplied by interested persons. Even this limited contact ceased in August, 1971, after an unpleasant conversation in which he reprimanded the father for an attempt by some young men to question the defendant at his place of work.

Private Efforts. Throughout the course of the police investigation, the father and his son were impatient with police investigations and unwilling to place sole reliance on them. The father worked with three private investigators and utilized the voluntary assistance of a large number (perhaps as many as 100) of family or neighborhood friends. Of these friends, a core group of the son's friends, styled the "concerned group" by the judge, were the most persistent workers. Included in the concerned group were Gary Fisher, James Ferreri, Frank Fontacchio, John (Jay) Campbell and Joseph (Jay) Heard, participants in the abduction of the defendant.

The private efforts were principally directed toward a program of surveillance designed to determine the pattern of the defendant's movements. Ultimately, the surveillance program was used to provide an opportunity to put questions to the defendant under conditions that would compel responses. There were a number of attempts to question the defendant. In September, 1970, before reporting the disappearance to the police, the father and son sought out the defendant on the campus of Northeastern University, where he was a student, questioned him, and took him on a tour of the Fenway district, in which, it could be supposed, the defendant met or was to have met the victim on the night of September 15. On two subsequent occasions, members of the concerned group accosted the defendant at Northeastern University and attempted, unsuccessfully, to detain him. In December, 1970, two members of the concerned group, Fontacchio and Campbell, appeared in the reception area of the office of the defendant's attorney while the meeting between the defendant and Gawlinski was in progress and inquired whether the defendant was within. They later followed the defendant and his mother. In August, 1971, Ferreri and Fontacchio were thwarted in an attempt to confront the defendant in the office of Henry F. Bryant & Son Inc., where he was a summer employee.

The Abduction. On December 8, 1971, the defendant drove to Mt. Ida Junior College in order to meet a young woman with whom he had a date. He arrived about 7:30 P.M. A surveillance group, consisting of the father, Fisher, Ferreri and Fontacchio, followed him in two cars. After the defendant had parked his car and entered a building, Ferreri and Fontacchio concealed themselves in heavy foliage near the defendant's car. When the defendant returned to his car, Ferreri emerged from the bushes, grabbed the defendant, and demanded to question him. As the defendant struggled to free himself, Ferreri, described as a "big, strong, husky youth," struck him near the left eye. The defendant fell and lost his glasses. Fontacchio approached and he and Ferreri guided the defendant into the back seat of an Oldsmobile. The father, who had moved from the Oldsmobile to the second car, raced the engine to divert the attention from the defendant's calls for help. While Fisher drove the Oldsmobile, Ferreri maintained a headlock on the defendant so that his head was below the level of the front seat. With the defendant under secure restraint, Fisher drove to his uncle's hunting cabin in Worthington, Massachusetts, in the western part of the state, 128 miles from Mt. Ida Junior College. Though the surveillance for the night of December 8 had undoubtedly been prearranged, the judge was persuaded and found that the idea to remove the defendant to a remote, isolated hunting cabin was "spontaneous and unpremeditated."

On reaching the cabin, Fisher gained entrance by breaking a pane of glass. The defendant was placed on a couch in the room farthest from the front door and ice packs were applied to the severe bruises on his face which had resulted from Ferreri's blow. At approximately 11:30 P.M. Ferreri and Fontacchio departed for Boston. Fisher, armed with a bread knife which he exhibited to the defendant, remained in the room with the defendant. The judge found that they dozed intermittently.

Interrogation of the defendant commenced on the return of Ferreri with Jay Campbell about 6 A.M. Questioning by the group continued for over six hours. During that time, the defendant admitted nothing. The questioning was repetitious and insistent. The interrogators used extremely rough language and occasionally threatened the defendant's life. The judge was satisfied, however, that no physical force was applied. Finally, at approximately 12:30 P.M. the defendant said that he wanted to speak to Ferreri alone. Ferreri wanted Campbell present at any further conversation and the defendant finally agreed.

Alone in the room with these two, the defendant, after receiving assurances that he would not be harmed, related facts pertaining to the victim's death: He met her on the night of September 15 at a bus stop near the Sears store. When she told him that she was pregnant and that he was the father, he denied the responsibility and accused her of having relations with a man in California. She slapped him and he struck her in retaliation. She fell, hit her head on the curb, and lay motionless. After mouth-to-mouth resuscitation failed to revive her, the defendant realized she was dead. He carried her down a hill to some abandoned railroad tracks, wrapped her in a blanket he found there, dug a shallow grave with his shoes, and buried her. The defendant declined to specify the exact location of the body and would say only that the gravesite was in the area near the Sears store. However, he was willing to lead the group to the body.

The interrogation ceased once the defendant had made these statements. The judge found that a spirit of relative friendliness supplanted the former hostile, strained relationship between the defendant and his captors. The defendant expressed relief at having finally disclosed his secret and referred to Ferreri and Campbell as friends. When the rest of the group returned, Ferreri persuaded the others to trust the defendant to lead them to the body. They tidied up the cabin and departed for Boston about 4:15 P.M.

As the group emerged from the cabin with the defendant it encountered two hunters, David Tyler, the chief of police of Worthington, and Reino Liimatainen. Earlier in the day, Tyler questioned Fisher about his occupation of the cabin. Though Fisher had partially satisfied Tyler as to his right to be there, Tyler had remained somewhat suspicious. At 4:15 P.M. Tyler questioned Fisher once again. Liimatainen, who harbored his own suspicions, slipped shells into the chambers of his shotgun and, in a loud voice, said, "If there is any funny business I will blow your guts out." The judge found that the entire party, including the defendant, could hear this and that the group was under the hunter's "control" at this point. Fisher evidently allayed Tyler's suspicions once again, for the episode ended with the group's driving away in two cars. As they left, the defendant remarked to Ferreri, "See, I could have gotten away if I wanted to, but I didn't."

The defendant directed Ferreri to drive to the Sears parking lot. They arrived in darkness at approximately 6:30 P.M.

The defendant described the gravesite to Ferreri as an overgrown area near an abandoned railroad spur below a grouping of three windows in a Metropolitan District Commission maintenance shed. Ferreri, alone, walked down a hill to the tracks. Unable to find the gravesite, he returned to the parking lot, where the others had remained, and told the defendant, "You will have to come down with me." The defendant refused and stated that the place was "spooked" and that they would kill him if he went down there. He handed the defendant a pocketknife for protection. Whereupon, Ferreri started down and was followed by the defendant, who held the open knife. The defendant refused to proceed the full distance to the grave, but he did point out its location. The defendant then returned to the parking lot. Ferreri, joined by Fontacchio and Campbell, ascertained that a body was buried at the place indicated.

Ferreri then drove the defendant to a point a short distance from his home.

While Ferreri had been searching the track area the first time, the defendant found himself momentarily alone with Heard and casually acknowledged that he had killed the victim. In response to the question from Heard, he said that he was not worried about the consequences because the abductors would be hostile witnesses whose testimony would not stand up in court, and because his grandmother would hire a certain well-known lawyer who would get him off. Asked how he had expected to get away with it at the time, the defendant replied that he had thought the rainfall on September 15 would prevent police dogs from discovering the body.

Subsequent Events: Police Reinvolvement. Sometime that evening the group notified the victim's family that her body had been found. About 11:30 P.M. the father telephoned Gawlinski, who had just returned home from attending college at Northeastern University, described the location of the body, and gave a somewhat cryptic, incomplete account of the events leading up to the discovery. After Gawlinski finished his telephone conversation with the father, his wife informed him that the defendant's attorney had tried to reach him that night. Gawlinski did not return the attorney's calls. He informed his partner in the case and a private investigator the father had hired that the body has been discovered and, after some delay, drove to the gravesite.

About 3:00 A.M. Gawlinski and other officers went to the defendant's home. From there, they proceeded to the Massachusetts General Hospital, where the defendant had been admitted as a patient. At the hospital, after securing permission to speak to the defendant, two officers went to his room with a police stenographer while Gawlinski remained downstairs.

The defendant was interrogated from 3:30 A.M. until 7:30 A.M. Before questioning him, the police gave the defendant the Miranda warnings. The defendant did not request counsel or respond to the precise question whether he understood the warnings. On at least four occasions, he did ask to have his parents present. Nevertheless, the police continued their questioning. The defendant did not respond to some questions; others were answered in a halting manner. The judge found that the defendant showed intelligent discrimination and some control over the course of the interrogation. Ultimately, the defendant allegedly made a statement which, in substance, reiterated the story he had related to the concerned group in the cabin.

About 7:30 A.M., on December 10, the interrogating officers left the hospital and met Gawlinski at the entrance. At 8:30 A.M. one of them, Sergeant Daley, wrote down his recollection of the defendant's statement. The following morning, December 11, the defendant was discharged from the hospital. He was indicted on December 15, 1971.

Principal Motions and Assignments of Error. After the voir dire hearing on motions to suppress, the judge ruled that all statements which the defendant had made to his kidnappers prior to the departure of the party from the cabin at 4:15 P.M. were to be suppressed and inadmissible at trial because they were the product of coercion. In this respect, the judge attached no significance to the fact that the defendant was coerced by private persons and not by police. However, he ruled that later statements to the kidnappers and "statements and actions leading to the discovery of the body of the deceased near . . . (the Sears store in) the early evening of December 9, 1971" would be admissible. These statements and actions he found to be voluntary and the result of the exercise of the defendant's "free will." The defendant assigns this ruling as error.

The defendant also moved to suppress the statements allegedly made by him to the police at the Massachusetts General Hospital on the morning of December 10, 1971. The judge ruled that as the police had knowingly denied the defendant the benefit of advice of his counsel the statement was not admissible in the Commonwealth's case in chief. Nevertheless, he ruled on the authority of Harris v. New York, 401 U.S. 222, 91S.Ct. 643, 28 L.Ed.2d 1 (1971), that the Commonwealth could introduce the statement by way of impeachment if the defendant testified. The defendant, who testified at voir dire but not at trial, assigns the latter ruling as an error.

Miranda Warnings by the Concerned Group

We disagree with the defendant's contention that the failure of his kidnappers to appraise him of his Miranda rights requires suppression of all statements made on December 9, 1971. In Miranda v. Arizona, 384 U.S. 436, 444, 461, 86 S.Ct. 1602, 16 L.Ed.2d 694 (1966), the Supreme Court formulated a series of prophylactic rules (see Michigan v. Tucker, 417 U.S. 433, 443, 94 S.Ct. 2357, 2363, 41 L.Ed.2d 182, 1974) designed "to secure the privilege against self-incrimination" from overreaching and coercion during custodial interrogation. Custodial Interrogation was defined as "questioning initiated by law enforcement officers after a person has been taken into custody or otherwise deprived of his freedom of action in any significant way." Miranda v. Arizona, supra, 384 U.S. at 444, 86 S.Ct. (1967), *cert. denied,* 391 U.S. 968, 88 S.Ct. 2039, 20 L.Ed.2d 881 (1969). In the instant case, the kidnappers were not law enforcement officers. They were private citizens embarked on an illegal enterprise. The Miranda rules do not extend to their activities. See United States v. Antonelli, 343, F.2d. 335, 337 (2d Cir. 1970), and authorities cited; United States v. Boldon, 461 F.2d. 998 (8th Cir. 1972); United States v. Casteel, 476 F.2d. 152 (10th Cir. 1973). Nevertheless, the defendant argues that the "connection" among the kidnappers, the father, and Gawlinski "clothed the actions of the kidnappers with police authority." Again, we disagree. Of course, the police may not accomplish through private proxies what they cannot do directly. If the defendant had shown that the group of kidnappers was "functioning as an instrument of the police" (United States v. Brown, 466 F.2d. 493, 495 [10th Cir. 1972]; cf. Coolidge v. New Hampshire, 403 U.S. 443, 487, 91 S.Ct. 2022, 29 L.Ed.2d 564 [1971]), or acting as an agent of the police pursuant to a scheme to elicit statements from the defendant by coercion or guile (cf., e.g., Commonwealth v. White, supra, 353 Mass. at 416, 232 N.E.2d 335; Commonwealth v. Martin, 357 Mass. 190, 193, 257 N.E.2d 444 [1970]), the statements would have to be suppressed for failure to give Miranda warnings. However, we agree with the judge that the subsidiary facts developed at voir dire supported the conclusion that the defendant did not establish such a police connection. It is true that Gawlinski worked closely with the victim's father in the initial stages of his investigation (this was to be expected). It is also true that he was aware of the father's deepening bitterness and frustration that, despite his awareness, he did not order the father and his associates to refrain from further investigation and repeatedly professed himself willing to follow any leads which private efforts uncovered. Yet, when considered in all the circumstances, these facts are insufficient to establish police connivance in, and responsibility for, the events of December 8 and 9. Gawlinski vehemently opposed any conduct which would harm the defendant or interfere with his liberty. He cautioned the father against any "rough stuff" and threatened to prosecute anyone who violates the law. In August, 1971, after the incident at Henry F. Bryant & Son, Inc., Gawlinski reprimanded the father. The two had harsh words, and communication between them, which had been sporadic since April, lapsed completely until December 9. Moreover, Gawlinski was not shown to have had foreknowledge of the kidnapping plan and first learned of its occurrence at 11:30 P.M. on December 9. In these circumstances, despite whatever encouragement the kidnappers may have felt they had received from Gawlinski's talk about possible leads, we cannot say that they acted as agents or instruments of the police in extracting statements from the defendant and that the absence of Miranda warnings required suppression of those statements.

Voluntariness of Statements Made after 4:15 PM to the Abductors

1. Since the Miranda rules are not opposite to the statements made by the defendant to his abductors, the admissibility of these statements at trial is governed by the due process standard of voluntariness. Delle Chiaie v. Commonwealth, 327 N.E.2d 696 (1975); Davis v. North Carolina, 384 U.S. 737, 740 86 S.Ct. 485, 27 L.Ed.2d 524 (1971). A conviction founded in whole or in part on statements which are the product of physical or psychological coercion deprives the defendant of his right to due process of law under the Fourteenth Amendment and, as a consequence, is invalid. Rogers v. Richmond, 365 U.S. 534, 540–541, 81 S.Ct. 735, 5 L.Ed.2d 760 (1961); Jackson v. Denno, 378 U.S. 368, 376, 84 S.Ct. 1774, 12 L.Ed.2d 908 (1964). See Commonwealth v. Harris, 364 Mass. 236, 303 N.E.2d 115 (1973). Such convictions are invalid irrespective of the truth or falsity of the statements admitted. "The use of coerced confessions . . . is forbidden because the method used to extract them offends constitutional principles" (Lego v. Twomey, 404 U.S. 477, 485, 92 S.Ct. 619, 624, 30 L.Ed.2d 618 [1972]) and because "declarations procured by torture (or other coercive means) are not premises from which a civilized forum will infer guilt." Lyons v. Oklahoma, 322, U.S. 596, 605, 64 Richmond, supra, 365 U.S. at 540–541, 81 S.Ct. 735; Jackson v. Denno, supra, 378 U.S. at 385–386, 84 S.Ct. 1774. Cf. Stein v. New York, 346 U.S. 156, 192 73 S.Ct. 1077, 97 L.Ed. 1522 (1953).

There is no easy acid test for voluntariness. Judicial determinations must rest on more than a mere "color matching" comparison of analogous cases. Reck v. Pate, 367 U.S. 433, 442, 81 S.Ct. 1541, 6 L.Ed.2d 948, (1961). In each case, the court must assess the *totality of relevant circumstances* to ensure that the defendant's confession was a free and voluntary act which had overborne his will. Clewis v. Texas, 386 U.S. 707, 708, 87 S.Ct. 1338, 18 L.Ed.2d 423 (1967). Procunnier v. Atchley 400 U.S. 446, 453, 91 S.Ct. 485, 27 L.Ed.2d.

The burden of proof is on the government to show such voluntariness by a preponderance of the evidence. Jackson v. Denno, 378 U.S. 368,

376–377, 84 S.Ct. 1774, 12 L.Ed.2d 908 (1964); Lego v. Twomey, 404 U.S. 477, 489, 92 S.Ct. 619, 30 L.Ed.2d 618 (1972).

2. These principles apply even though the statements were extracted by private coercion unalloyed with any official government involvement. We have not squarely decided this point previously, but it is implicit in our decisions in Commonwealth v. White, 353 Mass. 409, 417–418, 232 N.E.2d 881 (1967), cert. den., 391 U.S. 968, 88 S.Ct. 2039, 20 L.Ed.2d 881 (1968) (voluntariness test applied to confession made to private parties after two statements to police which were inadmissible under Miranda), Commonwealth v. Wallace, 356 Mass. 92, 96–97, 248 N.E.2d 246 (1969) (statements to Canadian police), and Commonwealth v. Martin, 357 Mass. 190, 193, 257 N.E.2d 444 (1970). The Supreme Court of the United States has not spoken to the question but it has involved the usual analysis where pressure was exerted by the private persons while the defendant was nominally in official custody. See Thomas v. Arizona, 356 U.S. 390, 78 S.Ct. 885, 2 L.Ed.2d 863 (1958) (private citizen, a member of a posse, abused a prisoner who later confessed to the authorities). A number of State courts have applied the due process analysis to circumstances in which the only claimed coercion leading to confessions was private. See, e.g., Palmore v. State, 244 Ala. 227, 12 So. 2d 854 (1943); State v. Christopher, 10 Ariz. App. 169, 457 P.2d 356 (1969); People v. Haydel, 12 Cal. 3d 190, 115 Cal. Aptr. 394, 524 P.2d 866 (1974); Lawton v. State, 152 Fla. 821, 13 So. 2d 211 (1943).

Underlying the above-cited decisions in this jurisdiction and other jurisdictions is the fundamental recognition that a statement obtained through coercion and introduced at trial is every bit as offensive to civilized standards of adjudication when the coercion flows from private hands as when official depredations elicit a confession. Statements extracted by a howling lynch mob of a lawless private pack of vigilantes from a terrorized, pliable suspect are repugnant to due process mandates of fundamental fairness and protection against compulsory self-incrimination. See People v. Berve, 51 Cal. 2d 286, 290, 332 P.2d 97 (1958).

3. When, as in the instant case, several statements given at different times by the defendant must be evaluated for voluntariness, a finding that an earlier statement was involuntary does not necessarily require suppression of the later statements. "The admissibility of the later confession depends on the same test—is it voluntary. Of course, the fact that the earlier statement was obtained from the prisoner by coercion is to be considered in appraising the character of the later confession. The effect

of earlier abuse may be so clear as to forbid any other inference than that it dominated that mind of the accused to such an extent that the later confession is involuntary . . . " Commonwealth v. White, 353 Mass. 409, 417, 232, N.E.2d 335, 241, (1967), *cert. denied,* 391 U.S. 968, 88 S.Ct. 2039, 20 L.Ed.2d 881 [1968], quoting from Lyons v. Oklahoma, 322 U.S. 596, 603, 64 S.Ct. 1208, 88 L.Ed. 1481 (1944). It is equally true, however, that the defendant may have been under no compulsion at the time of the later statements and may have felt no effect of the earlier abuse at the time. The later statements, then, would be admissible. The United States Supreme Court has never held that "making a confession under circumstances which preclude its use, perpetually disables the confessor from making a usable one after those conditions have been removed." United States v. Bayer, 331 U.S. 532, 541, 67 S.Ct. 1394, 1398, 91 L.Ed. 1645 (1947).

Two lines of analysis emerge from the case law and guide our analysis of the voluntariness of the defendant's post-4:15 statements. We are still required to look to the "totality of the circumstances". Clewis v. Texas 386 U.S. 707, 710, 87 S.Ct. 1338, 18 L.Ed.2d 423 (1967); Darwin v. Connecticut, 391 U.S. 346, 349, 88 S.Ct. 1488, 20 L.Ed.2d 630 (1968). See United States v. Bayer, supra, 331 U.S. at 540–541, 67 S.Ct. 1394). However, these lines of analysis furnish convenient, commonsense approaches to ordering and evaluating the necessary elements of the circumstances which bear on the voluntariness of the later statements. In the first line of analysis, the court must look for a "break in the stream of events," the coercive circumstances which extracted earlier statements, "sufficient to insulate the (subsequent) statement from the effect of all that went before." Clewis v. Texas, supra, 386 U.S. at 710, 87 S.Ct. at 1340. The focus of this line of analysis is on external constraints, continuing or new, which may have overborne the defendant's will. When circumstances no longer coerce the defendant, a break in the stream has occurred. The second line of analysis looks more specifically to the effect of the previous confession on the defendant's will. To be admissible, subsequent statements may not be "merely the product of the erroneous impression that the cat was already out of the bag" (Darwin v. Connecticut, 391 U.S. 346, 351, 88 S.Ct. 1488, 1491, 20 L.Ed.2d 630 (1968) (Harlan, J. concurring and dissenting) because one coerced confession has let the secret "out for good". United States v. Bayer, 331 U.S. 532, 540, 67 S.Ct. 1394, 91 L.Ed. 1654 (1947).

Pursuant to our order of January 8, 1975, the judge has filed supplementary findings addressing the issue of voluntariness as elucidated by these lines of analysis. After a detailed recitation of the evidence and the facts found by him, he concluded that the post-4:15 P.M. statements made by the defendant to his abductors were voluntary and admissible. We believe such a conclusion was warranted.

Break in the Stream of Events. The judge quite correctly ruled that statements obtained by the concerned group from the defendant prior to the departure from the cabin were involuntary because "induced by threats, duress, intimidation, fear and at least some violence (the original striking of the defendant at Mt. Ida)." The defendant, held incommunicado (see, e.g., Rogers v. Richmond, 365, U.S. 534, 536, 81 S.Ct. 735, 5 L.Ed.2d 760 [1961]) by his violent law-breaking captors (see, e.g., Brown v. Mississippi, 297 U.S. 278, 56 S.Ct. 461, 80 L.Ed. 682 [1936]) in a remote hunting cabin, was subjected to continuous rough questioning and threats (see, e.g., Lynumn v. Illinois, 372 U.S. 528, 83 S.Ct. 917, 9 L.Ed.2d 922 [1963]) designed to overcome his resistance and extract by psychological compulsion what he would not give freely. These circumstances are "so inherently coercive that . . . (their) very existence is irreconcilable with the possession of mental freedom (by the person) . . . against whom (the) full coercive force is brought to bear." Ashcraft v. Tennessee, 322 U.S. 143, 154, 64 S.Ct. 921, 926, 88 L.Ed. 1192 [1944]; Reck v. Pate, 367 U.S. 433, 442, 81 S.Ct. 1541, 6 L.Ed.2d 948 [1961]).

However, as the trial judge found on sufficient evidence, once the defendant had admitted his connection with the death, all hostility and intimidation ceased. The defendant's captors no longer threatened him or sought to elicit further information through their rough persistent questioning. A particular relationship of friendship and mutual trust seems to have arisen between Ferreri and the defendant. Thus, though the defendant remained captive while the concerned group discussed their next move, the atmosphere of coercion had been dispelled to a large extent.

After the group had left the cabin, even the vestige of coercion inherent in the group's control over the defendant's person vanished. Numerous opportunities for escape were presented to the defendant. The defendant eschewed these opportunities, though, as the trial judge found on ample evidence, he "knew he could have effected an escape." The defendant could have made some protest or sign when the group was within range of the hunters' guns. The warning about "funny business," issued by Liimatainen, was an invitation to outcry by the defendant. Yet he chose not to seek assistance. Similarly, on the trip back to Boston, the defendant made no attempt to attract attention at the Massachusetts

Turnpike tollbooths through which the group passed. While Fontacchio and Campbell, the other members of the concerned group in the car, dozed, the defendant conversed in a friendly manner with Ferreri, the driver. At the Weston toll, the defendant contributed part of the necessary payment because Ferreri lacked sufficient funds. When the group reached the Sears parking lot, the defendant again let pass opportunities for escape. He did not attempt to escape to the nearby MBTA station or to mingle with shoppers traversing the parking lot. He could have but did not create a disturbance which would have drawn public attention to his plight.

Rather, he acted like a man who felt sufficiently in control of his circumstances to make a free choice. Initially, he refused to go down to the burial site, but he agreed when armed with the only weapon then in evidence. Even then, he exercised his will and halted short of the precise site. He gave Ferreri directions to the body and, while Ferreri searched, engaged in casual incriminating conversation with Heard. His statements to Heard exhibited a bravado and lack of fear which were indicative of mental freedom of action.

Given the opportunities for escape, the lack of physical restraint and the defendant's possession of the weapon, we believe that the judge had ample justification for his finding that the defendant's statements and actions were not products of coercion exerted after he left the cabin. These factors separate the later statements from the coercive circumstances surrounding the earlier ones. Cf. Clewis v. Texas, 386 U.S. 707, 710, 87 S.Ct. 1338, 18 L.Ed.2d 423 (1967). This is not a case such as Leyra v. Denno, 347 U.S. 556, 74 S.Ct. 716, 98 L.Ed. 948 (1954), or Beecher v. Alabama, 389 U.S. 35, 88 S.Ct. 189, 19 L.Ed.2d 35 (1967), in which the later statements were extracted by part of a continuous coercive process. This is not a case such as Reck v. Pate, 367 U.S. 433, 81 S.Ct. 1541, 6 L.Ed.2d (1961); Clewis v. Texas, 386 U.S. 707, 87 S.Ct. 1338, 18 L.Ed.2d (1967), or Darwin v. Connecticut, 391 U.S. 346, 88 S.Ct. 1488, 20 L.Ed.2d 630 (1968) in which the defendant remained in official custody without access to potentially friendly faces or intercession for the duration of the "stream of events." The objective evidence of the defendant's behavior after leaving the cabin substantiates the judge's finding that the mere continuation in the presence of the concerned group did not coerce the defendant or render his post-4:15 P.M. statements involuntary.

Cat Out of the Bag. The cat-out-of-the-bag line of analysis requires the exclusion of a statement if, in giving the statement, the defendant was motivated by the belief that, after a prior coerced statement, his effort to withhold further information would be futile and he had nothing to lose by repetition or amplification of the earlier statements. Such a statement would be inadmissible as the direct product of the earlier coerced statement. The primary exposition of the underlying proposition by the United States Supreme Court occurs in United States v. Bayer, 331 U.S. 532, 540–541, 67 S.Ct. 1394, 1398, 91 L.Ed. 1654 (1947). Mr. Justice Jackson wrote: "Of course, after an accused has once let the cat out of the bag by confessing, no matter what the inducement, he is never thereafter free of the psychological and practical disadvantages of having confessed. He can never get the cat back in the bag. The secret is out for good. In such a sense, a later confession always may be looked upon as fruit of the first."

However, Mr. Justice Jackson qualified his statement of the principle: "But this Court has never gone so far as to hold that making a confession under circumstances which preclude its use, perpetually disables the confessor from making a usable one after those conditions have been removed."

Mr. Justice Harlan returned to the point in his opinion (concurring in part and dissenting in part) in Darwin v. Connecticut, 391 U.S. 346, 350–351, 88 S.Ct. 1488, 20 L.Ed.2d 630 (1968). He wrote: "A principle reason why a suspect might make a second or third confession is simply that, having already confessed once or twice, he might think he has little to lose by repetition. If a first confession is not shown to be voluntary, I do not think a later confession that is merely a direct product of the earlier one should be held to be voluntary. It would be neither conducive to good police work, nor fair to a suspect, to allow the erroneous impression that he has nothing to lose to play the major role in a defendant's decision to speak a second or third time . . . I would remand for further proceedings, in order to give the prosecution the opportunity to show that the third confession was not merely the product of the erroneous impression that the cat was already out of the bag". *Id.* at 350–351, 88 S.Ct. at 1490–1491.

The evidence supports the supplementary finding of the judge that there was "no 'cat out of the bag' aspect to . . . the defendant's post-4:15 P.M. statements and actions." The judge was warranted in finding that the defendant did not yield further information out of a conviction that his first coerced statement had damned him and in finding that subsequent admissions were not attributable to a feeling that nothing further would be lost by repetition. As the judge found, the defendant "evidenced no fear of culpability" after the statements in the cabin and did not believe what he said in the cabin would have serious adverse effect. In his conversation with Heard, the defendant disclaimed any fear that the statements made under coercion would lead to his conviction. He stated that a (specific) good lawyer would discredit his abductors' testimony and secure his acquittal in any subsequent proceeding. He may have thought he had "little to lose" (Darwin v. Connecticut, 391 U.S. 346, 350, 88 S.Ct. 1488, 20 L.Ed.2d 630 (1968) (Harlan, J.) through further admissions, but not because he feared the use of his previous statements. He may have thought he had "little to lose" based on an actual belief that he could not be convicted. Perhaps he thought the kidnappers believed and accepted his story that the victim's death was accidental.

The post-4:15 P.M. statements and actions appear to be attributable to the peculiar friendship which the defendant formed with Ferreri or to relief at having divulged his secret at last. Neither of these sentiments is the sentiment against which the cat-out-of-the-bag analysis would guard. Fear, continuation of coercive effects, and a sense of the futility of attempting to "get the cat back in the bag" are the objects of the analysis. See Darwin v. Connecticut, supra, at 350, 88 S.Ct. at 2012; Harrison v. United States, 392 U.S. 219, 224–226, 88 S.Ct. 2008, 20 L.Ed.2d [1968]).

In these circumstances, we cannot say, contrary to the judge's findings, that the post-4:15 P.M. statements and actions were involuntary because they were products of earlier statements. Cf. United States v. Gorman, 355 F.2d 151, 157 (2d Cir. 1967), *cert. denied,* 384 U.S. 1024, 86 S.Ct. 1962, 16 L.Ed.2d 1027 (1966).

4. In holding the post-4:15 P.M. statements made to the abductors admissible, we do not in any way approve the illegal and reprehensible manner in which they were obtained. Justice Kaplan's dissent begins with a statement which focuses attention on the "dangerous vigilantism" evident in this case and which indicates that such vigilantism must not be condoned. We join with him in vigorous condemnation of the violence, kidnapping and intimidation practiced by the members of the concerned group. Regardless of the nature of the crime alleged to have been committed by the defendant, there can be no justification for such unlawful conduct. Such conduct, apart from its illegality, is contrary to all acceptable norms of human behavior. It cannot be countenanced in any form. The rule of law and lawful procedures must be followed.

Having said this much, we must add that it is also the duty of this court to follow settled rules of law in its review of the facts of the trial judge. It is settled (and undisputed) that an appellate court cannot disturb the judge's findings of subsidiary facts if they are supported by the evidence. In like manner, the court may not draw inferences contrary to those of the trial judge which were derived from his subsidiary findings and from oral testimony. See Glover v. Waltham Laundry Co., 235 Mass. 330, 333, 127 N.E. 420 (1920). There is a very real and practical reason for the rule: The appellate court did not conduct the trial or the voir dire. It has neither heard the witnesses nor seen all of the evidence. It lacks the exposure to appearance and demeanor on the witness stand which assists the trial judge in his evaluation of veracity and resolution of conflicting testimony.

In the instant case, none of the dissenters is willing to say that the judge below was plainly wrong in his findings. Each purports to accept the basic "historical or subsidiary facts" found below but then reaches a result inconsistent with the trial judge's factual finding that the defendant was "completely free from fear" after the encounter with the hunters. Justice Kaplan returns to the record in order to decide the defendant's state of mind throughout the period following the departure from the cabin. He concludes (contrary to the trial judge's findings) that "the defendant remained under the heel of the kidnappers" and that his "statements at the Sears parking lot were . . . made within continuing constraint and compulsion." Justice Hennessey, while unwilling to draw these further inferences, nevertheless finds that the Commonwealth has not proved that the defendant's admissions were voluntary by a fair preponderance of the evidence. He refuses to be bound by the judge's inference . . . "that is synonymous with voluntariness."

Is it now open to this court to disregard the trial judge's findings and to come to a contrary conclusion? We think no. A decision as to the voluntariness of the defendant's admission involves determination of his state of mind at the time they were made. State of mind is a question of fact. See Kelley v. Jordan Marsh Co., 278 Mass. 101, 106, 197 N.E. 299 (1932); Commonwealth v. Holiday, 349 Mass. 126, 128, 206 N.E.2d 691 (1965). It can be established by the defendant's direct testimony or through reasonable inferences drawn from other proved facts and demeanor evidence. In the instant case, the defendant testified directly to the precise question at issue—namely, his state of mind at the time he agreed to disclose the gravesite to the concerned group. He testified that he had agreed to lead the group to the body in order to get out of the cabin. He claimed that members of the group had told him that he would never leave the cabin alive if he did not tell them the location of the body. Thus, it was his story that fear engendered his cooperation with his captors, his disclosure of the gravesite and his other admissions. However, this testimony cannot be of any significance here and cannot be employed to support inferences contrary to those of the trial judge. The trial judge, who had the opportunity to observe all of the witnesses, evaluated the defendant's testimony and rejected it. The judge observed the defendant on the stand, his appearance and his mannerisms; the tone of his voice and his attitude as he was examined and cross-examined; his facial expressions and his general demeanor. In short, the trial judge's primary function on this issue (voluntariness) was to ascertain the defendant's state of mind—whether he was telling the truth as to the reasons he gave for his decision to reveal the gravesite (and as to his state of mind). The trial judge, in rejecting the defendant's testimony, necessarily found that he was not telling the truth. This was a finding of fact based on oral testimony of the defendant and of other witnesses. An appellate court cannot find to the contrary.

This is not to say that merely because the judge disbelieved the defendant's testimony he could, without additional evidence, find the reverse to be true. His finding of the reverse must be supported by other relevant evidence. Here there was extensive testimony, as fully delineated elsewhere in this opinion, tending to demonstrate the change of mood and relationship found by the judge below. It was more than sufficient to sustain the government's burden of proof. The judge's finding of voluntariness must stand.

Statement to the Police at Hospital: The Harris v. New York Problem

1. The judge quite properly suppressed all statements made to the police in the The Massachusetts General Hospital on December 10 for purposes of the prosecution's case in chief. Police conduct at the hospital was clearly inconsistent with the standards for custodial interrogation established by Miranda v. Arizona, 384 U.S. 436, 86 S.Ct. 1602, 16 L.Ed.2d 694 (1966). It is true that an officer read the requisite Miranda warnings to the defendant and then requested that the defendant read the Miranda warning card. However, none of the officers apprised the defendant of his lawyer's efforts to speak to Gawlinski or informed the attorney that a custodial interrogation of his client was in progress. Gawlinski, who was most familiar with the case and who knew both that the defendant had had counsel for many months and that counsel wished urgently to

contact a responsible police official, conspicuously absented himself from the interrogation. The judge stated that "conduct on the part of prosecuting officers was at least heedless, if not deliberate and I can conclude only that it was a course of conduct calculated to circumvent ... (the defendant's) constitutional rights to have the benefit, aid and counsel of his attorney."

The Miranda safeguards encompass more than a simple explanation to a suspect that he has a right to remain silent and a right to counsel. The suspect must "be afforded the opportunity to exercise these rights throughout the interrogation.... He ... (is) entitled to know of his counsel's availability and with that knowledge, to make the choice (to forgo the benefits of counsel) with intelligence and understanding". Commonwealth v. McKenna, 355 Mass. 313, 324, 244 N.E.2d 560, 566 [1969]). In previous cases, we have noted that police may not thwart counsel who seeks to confer with a client (Commonwealth v. McKenna, supra, at 325–326, 244 N.E.2d 560) and have held inadmissible statements elicited by the police in the absence of counsel after an attorney has entered the case when no intentional and knowing waiver of the right to counsel was proved (Commonwealth v. Murray, 359 Mass. 541, 544–546, 269 N.E.2d 641 [1971]). Cf. Commonwealth v. Cain, 361 Mass. 224, 227–229, 279 N.E.2d 706 (1972). Similarly, in the instant case, the defendant's statements in the hospital were inadmissible for the prosecution's case in chief.

Nevertheless, we hold that the defendant's statements, if voluntary and trustworthy, were available to impeach his testimony if he took the stand. Harris v. New York, 401 U.S. 222, 91 S.Ct. 643, 28 L.Ed.2d 1 (1971), and Oregon v. Hass, 420 U.S. 714, 95 S.Ct. 1215, 43 L.Ed.2d 570 (1975), are controlling.

In Harris v. New York, the defendant took the stand and denied having sold heroin to an undercover officer. On cross-examination, he was asked whether he had made certain statements to the police shortly after his arrest. The transcript of the interrogation showed that the police had not advised the defendant of his right to appointed counsel at the time. Despite this infringement of the Miranda safeguards (Miranda v. Arizona, supra, 384 U.S. at 444, 86 S.Ct. 1602), *the Supreme Court held that the statements had been properly admitted to impeach the defendant's testimony.* The court rejected the argument that under Miranda "evidence inadmissible against an accused in the prosecution's case in chief is barred for all purposes". Harris v. New York, supra, 401 U.S. at 224, 91

S.Ct. at 645. In the court's view, a valid policy consideration, the possibility that the defendant might deliver perjurious testimony, outweighed the extra measure of deterrence to unconstitutional police action which might be achieved by total exclusion of such evidence. Mr. Chief Justice Burger wrote for the court: *"Every criminal defendant is privileged to testify in his own defense, or to refuse to do so. But that privilege cannot be construed to include the right to commit perjury.... The shield provided by Miranda cannot be perverted into a license to use perjury by way of defense, free from the risk of confrontation with prior inconsistent utterances." Id.* at 225–226, 91 S.Ct. at 645–646. The court noted, however, that there had been no claim that the statements made to police were coerced or involuntary and that "the trustworthiness of the evidence (must) satisfy legal standards." *Id.* at 224, 91 S.Ct. at 645.

In Oregon v. Hass, the court again spoke to the issued whether evidence obtained by the police without strict compliance with Miranda standards was admissible for impeachment purposes. After his arrest for bicycle theft, Hass was given the Miranda warnings. He admitted that he had stolen two bicycles but was uncertain which one was the subject of the investigation. He and a police officer then departed for the place where he had left one of the stolen bicycles. On the way, Hass commented that he "was in a lot of trouble" and wanted to telephone his attorney. The police officer replied that Hass could use the telephone after they returned to the "office." Thereafter, Hass guided the police officer to the bicycle and pointed out the locations of the houses from which he had stolen the two bicycles. At trial, Hass's statements to the police officer after his request for counsel were admitted only as to the credibility of his testimony. The Oregon Court of Appeals reversed his subsequent conviction and the Supreme Court of Oregon affirmed the reversal. The United States Supreme Court, on the authority of Harris v. New York, reversed. The court reiterated its concern that exclusionary rules could "free (the defendant) from the embarrassment of impeachment evidence from ... (his) own mouth" (Oregon v. Hass, 420 U.S. 714, 723, 95 S.Ct. 1215, 1221, 43 L.Ed.2d 570) and emphasized, as it had in Harris, the valuable aid which the defendant's statements would provide to the jury in assessing his credibility. *Id.* at 722, 95 S.Ct. at 1221. The court found no "valid distinction" between the situation in Harris, which involved defective Miranda warnings, a violation of a prophylactic rule, and the situation in Hass, which involved the failure to afford a suspect his full constitutional right to counsel after his attempt to exercise that right.

The court added, however, that "if, in a given case, the officer's conduct amounts to an abuse, that case, like those involving coercion or duress, may be taken care of when it arises measured by the traditional standards for evaluating voluntariness and trustworthiness." *Id.* at 723, 95 S.Ct. at 1221.

We believe the Harris and Hass exception to the exclusionary rule of Miranda and like cases permits introduction of the defendant's statements (if they are voluntary and trustworthy) to impeach his direct testimony. Functionally, the violation of the defendant's rights in the instant case is closely analogous to that in Harris and Hass. In each case, the deprivation of rights stems from the failure of police to provide a suspect with counsel to whom he was entitled. Just as Harris received no assistance from the appointed counsel to whom he was entitled and Hass did not have a timely opportunity to consult counsel whom he had requested, so the defendant here did not benefit from the assistance of counsel who urgently wished to reach him.

We are not persuaded that factual distinctions between the instant case and Harris and Hass are sufficient to shift the balance struck in the two Supreme Court cases between impeachment of perjurious testimony and deterrence of improper police conduct. The exclusionary rules fashioned in Miranda and like cases deter "impermissible police conduct" (see Harris v. New York, *supra,* 401 U.S. at 225, 91 S.Ct. 643) by excluding from trial any evidence which was improperly obtained. Michigan v. Tucker, 417 U.S. 433, 447, 94 S.Ct. 2357, 41 L.Ed.2d 182 (1974) Cf. United States v. Calandra, 414 U.S. 338, 347, 94 S.Ct. 613, 38 L.Ed.2d 561 (1974). An exception to the exclusionary rules in the instant case is no more an encouragement to such misconduct (or slackening of the deterrent effect of the rules) than are the exceptions promulgated in Harris and Hass. Such encouragement may be thought to arise from the police officer's knowledge that a lawyer will likely advise his client to make no statement while in custody and the further knowledge that a statement elicited in the absence of counsel will at least be available for impeachment of testimony. Yet, in Hass, where the suspect had actually requested counsel and, thus, the incentive for continuation of interrogation without adherence to constitutional requirements, if there were an impeachment exception to the exclusionary rule, would be at a maximum, the court held that the interest in deterring such police conduct was outweighed by the general interest in impeachment of perjurious testimony. In the instant case, by contrast, the police could not know that the defendant would ask to see his attorney. If he had been informed that his attorney wished to see him, the defendant might have chosen to proceed without counsel—to reject the offer. After all, the police had "given" the defendant his Miranda warnings. He was aware of the fact that his parents had engaged an attorney to represent him. It was open to him at any time to halt the inquiry and request the attorney. Instead, the defendant intermittently asked for his parents and continued to answer questions when they did not arrive. In view of the uncertainty in the defendant's response to the information that his attorney wished to see him, an exception to the exclusionary rule in the instant case presents lesser incentives to police misconduct than were present in Hass, and there is a correspondingly less substantial interest in an exclusionary rule for deterrence.

Accordingly, we hold that, as in Hass, the interest in impeachment of perjurious testimony here outweighed the interest in deterrence of police misconduct and that those of the defendant's statements which were voluntary and trustworthy were properly available to impeach his testimony if he had taken the stand.

2. We think the judge was warranted in finding that the statements made by the defendant to the police at the hospital were voluntary.

Having concluded that the defendant's post-4:15 P.M. statements to his abductors were separated from his earlier statements to them by a break in the stream of events and that these later statements were not made because the cat was out of the bag, we believe that the statements in the hospital were also sufficiently separated from the coercive conditions which had extracted the statements in the cabin and were also not the product of the cat-out-of-the-bag effect. The statements in the hospital were elicited by different people, police officers uninvolved in the original abduction, in a different place. See Lyons v. Oklahoma, 322 U.S. 596, 602, 64 S.Ct. 1208, 88 L.Ed. 1481 (1944). Cf. Miranda v. Arizona, 384 U.S. 436, 496, 86 S.Ct. 1602, 16 L.Ed.2d 694 (1966). By the time of his questioning in the hospital, the defendant had had an opportunity to consult his family (cf. Reck v. Pate, 367 U.S. 433, 441, 81 S.Ct. 1541, 6 L.Ed.2d 948 [1961]) and had been out of the control of his captors for quite some time (cf. Beecher v. Alabama, 389 U.S. 35, 38, 88 S.Ct. 189, 19 L.Ed.2d 35 [1967]; Darwin v. Connecticut, 391 U.S. 346, 349, 88 S.Ct. 1488, 20 L.Ed.2d 630 [1968]). It does not appear from the evidence that the statements in the cabin caused him to make admissions to the police. As noted above, the defendant did not believe his statements could be used against him. In the interrogation by police, he did not immediately confess, as might a man who felt he had nothing to lose. Rather, he maintained some control over the session and answered only selected questions.

Further, we believe that the trial judge found correctly that the police interrogation, itself, did not overbear the defendant's will and did not extract an involuntary statement from him. The trial judge found the following significant subsidiary facts on ample evidence. The defendant is an intelligent and educated young man. See Commonwealth v. Pratt, 360 Mass. 708, 713–714, 277 N.E.2d 517 (1972); Lisenba v. California, 314 U.S. 219, 239–241, 62 S.Ct. 280, 86 L.Ed. 166 (1941). (cf., e.g., Fikes v. Alabama, 352 U.S. 191, 196, 77 S.Ct. 281, 1 L.Ed.2d 246 (1957); Payne v. Arkansas, 356 U.S. 560, 567, 78 S.Ct. 844, 2 L.Ed.2d 975 (1958). At the time of his interrogation, he was neither dazed nor bewildered (cf. Leyra v. Denno, 347 U.S. 566, 560, 74 S.Ct. 716, 98 L.Ed. 948 (1954), nor drugged (cf. Beecher v. Alabama, 389 U.S. 35, 38, 88 S.Ct. 189, 19 L.Ed.2d (1967), nor too sick or weak to resist questioning (see Commonwealth v. Sousa, 350 Mass. 591, 598, 215 N.E.2d 910 (1966) (cf. Reck v. Pate, 367 U.S. 433, 443, 81 S.Ct. 1541, 6 L.Ed.2d 948 (1961); Beecher v. Alabama, supra). He was physically and mentally alert. Aside from the injury to his eye, he showed no evidence of physical disability or impairment of physical or mental functions. Before questioning commenced, the officers informed the defendant of his Miranda rights. See Davis v. North Carolina, 384 U.S. 737, 740, 86 S.Ct. 1761, 16 L.Ed.2d 895 (1966); Procunier v. Atchley, 400 U.S. 446, 453, 91 S.Ct. 485, 27 L.Ed.2d 524 (1971). During the questioning, the police officers were courteous. They did not threaten the defendant (cf. Harris v. South Carolina, 338 U.S. 68, 70, 69 S.Ct. 1354, 93 L.Ed. 1815 (1949) (threat to the defendant concerning his mother); Beecher v. Alabama, supra, 389 U.S. at 36, 88 S.Ct. 189) or attempt to induce admissions by deception (cf. Spano v. New York, 360 U.S. 315, 323, 79 S.Ct. 1202, 3 L.Ed.2d 1265 [1959]). The questioning was not unduly lengthy or prolonged (cf. Ashcraft v. Tennessee, 322 U.S. 143, 153–154, 64 S.Ct. 921, 88 L.Ed. 1192 (1944); Watta v. Indiana, 338 U.S. 49, 53, 69 S.Ct. 1347, 93 L.Ed. 1801 (1949); Clewis v. Texas, 386 U.S. 707, 709, 87 S.Ct. 1338, 18 L.Ed.2d 423 [1967]) and, throughout the questioning, the defendant maintained the above-mentioned control over the proceedings (see Commonwealth v. Cook, 351 Mass. 231, 235, 218 N.E.2d 292 (1966), *cert. denied,* 385 U.S. 981, 87 S.Ct. 529, 17 L.Ed.2d 443 (1966); Stein v. New York, 346 U.S. 156, 186, 73 S.Ct. 1077, 97 L.Ed. 1522 (1953)). At his insistence, the stenographer was dismissed. He did not answer every question, but chose those to which he would reply.

In these circumstances, we cannot say that the statements which finally emerged were involuntarily given. Accordingly, the statements were properly ruled available for impeachment of testimony under the rule of Harris and Hass.

Review Pursuant to G.L. C.278, § 33E

Having determined that there was not constitutional error in the admission of evidence at trial, we turn now to the additional review of the record and law, which is our duty in all capital cases. General Laws C.278, § 33E, as amended through St. 1974, C.457, provides in relevant part, "In capital case . . . the supreme judicial court shall transfer to that court the whole case for its consideration of the law and the evidence. Upon such consideration the court may, if satisfied that the verdict was against the law or the weight of the evidence, or because of newly discovered evidence, or for any other reason that justice may require (a) order a new trial or (b) direct the entry of a verdict of a lesser degree of guilt, and remand the case to the superior court for the imposition of sentence." The statute "gives us the power and duty exercised by a trial judge on a motion for a new trial" (Commonwealth v. Baker, 346 Mass. 107, 109, 190 N.E.2d 555, 557 [1963]) but also reserves for our consideration the broader issue whether the verdict rendered represents a miscarriage of justice or whether a lesser degree of guilt would be more constant with justice. Commonwealth v. Baker, supra; Commonwealth v. Williams, 364 Mass. 145, 301 N.E.2d 683 (1973). See Commonwealth v. Jones, 323 N.E.2d 726 (1975). This latter power is a power which the trial court does not have. Commonwealth v. Baker, supra; Commonwealth v. Bearse, 358 Mass. 481, 485, 265 N.E.2d 496 (1970).

The record before us contains little direct evidence from which a finder of fact could construct an account of the events which immediately preceded the victim's death. There were no witnesses to the conversation and violence between the victim and the defendant. The jury undoubtedly reached their verdict, a verdict warranted by the evidence, by drawing a chain of inferences from the relationships among the witnesses, the defendant and the victim and from the defendant's statements and actions immediately before and simultaneously with the discovery of the body. The principal direct evidence concerning the killing, the defendant's admissions to members of the concerned group in the cabin and to the police in the hospital, was, of necessity, excluded from the trial and had no place in the jury's deliberations. This evidence, itself, is suspect because of the coercive circumstances in which the admissions were elicited (see Jackson v. Denno, 378 U.S. 368, 386–388, 84 S.Ct. 1774, 12 L.Ed.2d 908 (1964) and the subsequent implicit repudiation of the admissions by the defendant in his voir dire testimony.

Nevertheless, despite this relative paucity of reliable direct evidence concerning the victim's death, we believe that justice requires that we reduce the verdict of murder in the second degree to manslaughter. The thrust of the evidence is that the killing lacked the element of malice aforethought necessary to support a verdict of murder.

In reaching this conclusion, we rely in large measure on the account of the killing given by the defendant to the concerned group in the cabin. Although this evidence was correctly excluded from the jury's consideration, it may be considered by us in the exercise of our authority under G.L. C.278, § 33E. Cf. Commonwealth v. Smith, 357 Mass. 168, 182, 258 N.E.2d 13 (1970). To repeat, the defendant's story was that, after an argument, the victim provoked him with a slap which he answered impulsively and angrily with a return blow. Her death then followed in an unexpected manner as she fell and hit her head on the curb. This version of the events will not support a finding of malice aforethought. The defendant never formed a specific intention to kill the victim. Rather he struck in almost-reflexive response to her provocation, and such passion as he felt did not achieve the intensity of a desire to kill. Though the defendant undoubtedly intended to inflict some injury on the deceased, this intention was "palliated by the existence of . . . (the) mitigating circumstances" (Commonwealth v. Mangum, 357 Mass. 76, 85, 256 N.E.2d 297, 303 [1970]) represented by the prior slap and provocation. Nor could death reasonably be expected to follow the defendant's blow. According to common experience there is no "plain and strong likelihood that death will follow" a simple blow with the hand administered to a healthy adult—even if the victim is spattered pavement. See Commonwealth v. Chance, 174 Mass. 245, 252, 54 N.E. 551 (1899); Commonwealth v. Gordon, 307 Mass. 155, 158, 29 N.E.2d 719 (1940), cf. Commonwealth v. Gricus, 317 Mass. 403, 411, 58 N.E.2d 241 (1944). Such a battery which causes death is manslaughter. Commonwealth v. Sostilio, 325 Mass. 143, 145, 89 N.E.2d 510 (1949); Commonwealth v. Campbell, 352 Mass. 387, 397, 226 N.E.2d 211 (1967) See, generally, Perkins, A Re-examination of Malice Aforethought, 43 Yale L.J. 537, 552–555 [1934]).

Although other reconstructions of the events of that night are possible and some will support a finding of malice, we have accepted the defendant's story insofar as it precludes a finding of malice aforethought and suggests an accidental, unintended death, because it comports well with the other evidence concerning the defendant, the victim, and their relationship. The defendant appears to be a reasonably normal, mature and intelligent engineering student. In his life prior to the evening of the victim's death, he had not manifested any violent tendencies and had not had any prior involvement with the law. His ongoing relationship with the victim was of some duration and was characterized, it seems, by reciprocal affection. Although the smooth continuation of the relationship was evidently disturbed by the victim's trip to California, her relationship with a man there, and the defendant's consequent jealousy, there is not evidence in the record that his feelings of jealousy had so overmastered his affectionate inclination toward the victim that he would at any time have considered taking steps to bring about her death. Certainly, there is no substantial indication in the record that he went to their meeting that night with the premeditated intent to kill or to employ violence against the victim. Cf. Commonwealth v. Kendrick, 351 Mass. 203, 210–211, 218 N.E.2d 408 (1966). Further, there is no indication that their relationship had so deteriorated that he would have undertaken to kill or attack savagely the object of his affections even if he had been enraged at being asked to bear the consequences of her infidelity—a pregnancy. In the context of their relationship, the defendant's story of one hasty unfortunate blow rings true.

The case is remanded to the Superior Court where the verdict of murder in the second degree and the sentence previously imposed are to be vacated. A verdict of guilty of manslaughter shall be entered and sentence shall be imposed thereon. So ordered.

Comment

The Mahnke case, albeit lengthy, is extraordinary in its relevance to the purpose and goals of this book as mentioned in the introduction and its thoughts provoking potential for discussion. I shall limit my comments to the former.

For our purposes, the Mahnke case firmly establishes (as of today) two basic principles:

A. For a statement or confession of a defendant in the custody of a private security person who has made a lawful arrest to be admissible in evidence in a court of law, the prosecution does not have to establish that the Miranda warnings were given to the defendant or waived by him prior to interrogation, unless the private security person was functioning as an instrument of the police.

B. For a statement or confession of a defendant to a private security person to be admissible evidence in a court of law, the prosecution must establish that the statement or confession was the *voluntary* act of defendant.

A. We have heard much about the "French Connection." Let's look at the facts as to the "Police Connection." Whether or not the vigilante group was so connected to the police as to render inadmissible the defendant's statements because this group did not give the Miranda warnings was the legal issue. What facts did the Supreme Judicial Court of Massachusetts consider relevant on this legal issue?

1. Detective Gawlinski's close work with victim's father during initial stages of this investigation.
2. Gawlinski's failure to order the father and the group to refrain from investigation (Both of these facts are quite normal, and it would seem that a police officer who did not act accordingly would be subject to criticism.)
3. Gawlinski cautioned against "rough stuff," and demanded obedience to the law.
4. Gawlinski reprimanded the father, and thereafter communication between police and the group ceased.
5. No evidence that Gawlinski had knowledge of the kidnapping, etc.

These basic facts led the court to decide that the concerned group was not acting as an instrument of the police and that, therefore, the rule of Miranda did not apply in this case.

B. The prosecution, before a confession is admissible as evidence in a court of law, must establish that the confession was voluntary, not in violation of the due process clause of the Fourteenth Amendment to the U.S. Constitution. What are some facts that the court considers, from the "totality of circumstances," to determine voluntariness?

1. The defendant was kidnapped by a group.
2. The defendant was physically abused.

3. The defendant was held incommunicado at a distant place.
4. The defendant was threatened with a deadly weapon.

Considering these facts from the totality of circumstances, the court decided that the defendant's admissions and statements while at the cabin and immediately prior thereto were not voluntary and, therefore, not admissible.

But, what about Mahnke's statements and confession made after 4:15 P.M.? These subsequent statements presented another question of their voluntariness and, therefore, their admissibility.

In analyzing the circumstances surrounding the defendant's statements after leaving the cabin area, the court employs two tests:

1. Break-in-the-stream-of-events test (*external*)
2. Cat-out-of-the-bag test (*internal*)

The break-in-the-stream-of-events test seeks to determine whether the defendant was still under any *external constraints.* If not, a break in the stream of events has occurred and the confession *may* be admissible.

The facts that the court found to be determinative of this issue were the following:

1. The defendant's failure to take advantage of opportunities to escape.
2. The defendant contributed to a turnpike toll payment.
3. The lack of physical restraint on the defendant.
4. The defendant was given a deadly weapon.

The court concluded, "These factors separate the later statements from the coercive circumstances surrounding the earlier ones"; therefore, on to the "internal" test!

The cat-out-of-the-bag test seeks to determine what effect the earlier statements and confessions had on his mind, on his free will. Did they cause the defendant to believe that his earlier statements had doomed him and that, therefore, subsequent ones could do him no further harm? The court decided that the defendant felt that his earlier statements and confession did not doom him, the significant factor being that the defendant, after the stream of events had been broken, had stated in effect that his lawyer would destroy the legal effect, if any, of his earlier confession.

Commonwealth v. Tynes
400 Mass. 369, 510 NE 2d

Before HENNESSEY, C.J., and LIACOS, NOLAN, LYNCH and O'CONNOR, JJ. LIACOS, Justice.

The defendant was convicted by a jury of six on one count of operating a motor vehicle while under the influence of intoxicating liquor, his second such offense within a six-year period. See G.L. c. 90, section 24 (1)(a)(1) (1984 ed.). Prior to trial, he moved to suppress testimony concerning incriminating statements he had made on the day of his arrest. That motion was denied.

Testimony was taken at a pretrial hearing on the defendant's motion to suppress. John J. Hagan stated that at all relevant times he was employed as a police officer in the town of Littleton. He resided, however, in Holliston where, on the morning of March 30, 1985, he went jogging, dressed in a sweat suit and not showing any badge or insignia of office as a policeman. Near Phipps Hill, at 11 A.M., Hagan noticed a line of automobiles stopped at an intersection. When the light turned green, one of these vehicles remained stationary, and others were forced to drive around it. The vehicle was in gear, and the engine was running. Hagan observed the defendant at the wheel, apparently unconscious or asleep. After rapping on a window and getting no response, Hagan opened the door on the driver's side and immediately detected an odor of alcohol inside. He shook the defendant, who remained unresponsive. Hagan noted a very strong odor of alcohol on the defendant's breath. He asked a passerby to summon an ambulance.

At this point, the defendant roused himself. Hagan asked if he was all right; the defendant said "yes." Hagan asked whether he was ill or had any history of fainting or epilepsy. The defendant said "no." Hagan asked whether he knew who and where he was. The defendant gave his name and said "he was coming from Framingham and he was going home." The vehicle then started to move. Hagan reached in and "put the vehicle into the parked position." The defendant reached for the keys, but Hagan removed them from the ignition.

Hagan questioned the defendant further. In response to questions, the defendant admitted that he had been drinking on the morning in question, that he had lost consciousness due to drinking and lack of sleep, and that his drinking had "affected his operation to drive." When a Holliston police officer arrived on the scene, Hagan "conveyed [his] observations" to the officer, including his opinion that the defendant had been driving while under the influence of intoxicating liquor.

Hagan never identified himself to the defendant as a police officer, nor did he arrest the defendant or advise him of his rights. He testified that it was his understanding that his jurisdiction as an officer extended only to Littleton and contiguous towns, not including Holliston. He became involved, not as a police officer but as a certified emergency medical technician and as a "concerned citizen." On cross-examination, Hagan conceded that he did not return the automobile keys to the defendant, and he admitted that he would not have given Tynes his keys, if asked; but he said that the defendant was at all times free to leave on foot, if he chose.

The Holliston police officer, Charles Todd, testified that he arrested the defendant and advised him of his rights while driving the defendant in a cruiser to the Holliston police station. The defendant did not testify at the suppression hearing. In light of the uncontested testimony of Hagan and Todd, the judge found that Hagan had acted as a private citizen when querying the defendant; the defendant had not been in custody when Hagan questioned him; and "the Defendant's statements were voluntary, intelligently given."

[1] In this appeal, the defendant argues that (1) suppression of his pretrial statements was compelled by Miranda v. Arizona, 384 U.S. 436, 86 S.Ct. 1602, 16 L.Ed.2d 694 (1966); (2) the prosecutor's closing statement was prejudicial because it implied, incorrectly, that drinking and driving (without more) is a crime in Massachusetts; (3) the judge's instructions misstated the Commonwealth's burden of proof as enunciated in Commonwealth v Connolly, 394 Mass. 169, 474 N.E.2d 1106 (1985); (4) the judge's use in his instructions of this court's statement of the legislative purpose behind G.L. c. 90, section 24 (1984 ed.) was inflammatory; and (5) in the alternative, the standard defined in *Connolly* should be revised so as to permit conviction under G.L. c. 90, section 24, only on proof that intoxication caused the defendant to operate his vehicle in an "unsafe" manner. We transferred this case from the Appeals Court on our own motion, and we affirm.

[2]1. *The Miranda question.* "In Miranda v. Arizona, 384 U.S. 436, 444, 461, [86 S.Ct. 1602, 1612, 1620–21, 16 L.Ed.2d 694] (1966), the Supreme Court formulated a series of prophylactic rules . . . designed 'to secure the privilege against self-incrimination' from overreaching and coercion during custodial interrogation. Custodial interrogation was defined as

'questioning initiated by ***law enforcement officers*** after a person has been taken into custody or otherwise deprived of his freedom of action in any significant way' (emphasis supplied). Miranda v. Arizona, supra, at 444 [86 S.Ct. at 1612]." (Citation omitted.) Commonwealth v. Mahnke, 368 Mass. 662, 676, 335 N.E.2d 660 (1975), *cert. denied,* 425 U.S. 959, 96 S.Ct. 1740, 48 L.Ed.2d 204 (1976). The judge found that the defendant was not in custody when Hagan asked him questions and, implicitly, that there was no violation of Miranda in this case because its strictures apply only to custodial interrogation by law enforcement officers or their "private proxies." Mahnke, supra 368 Mass. at 677, 335 N.E.2d 660. Hagan performed in neither capacity when he interrogated the defendant. There was no error.

It is undisputed that Hagan wore no badge of officer; nor did he give any verbal indication that he was employed anywhere as a police officer. Therefore, we see no reason to suppose that the defendant's will was affected in any way by that force of "compulsion [which is] inherent in custodial surroundings," Miranda v. Arizona, supra 384 U.S. at 458, 86 S.Ct. at 1619; as a consequence, the animating concerns of Miranda are simply not implicated here. See Berkemer v. McCarty, 468 U.S. 420, 442, 104 S.Ct. 3138, 3151–52, 82 L.Ed.2d 317 (1984) (where lone police officer detains motorist, asks modest number of questions, and requires performance of field sobriety test[s] at location visible to passersby, motorist is not "in custody" for purposes of Miranda). See also Commonwealth v. Bryant, 390 Mass. 729, 736–737, 459 N.Ed.2d 792 (1984).

More than this, the record shows that Hagan did not suppose himself to possess a police officer's authority to arrest or otherwise to detain the defendant. Indeed, this court has recently held that "[w]hen a police officer makes a warrantless arrest outside of his jurisdiction, and not in 'fresh and continued pursuit' of the suspect within the meaning of G.L. c. 41, section 98A, then he acts as a private citizen . . . " Commonwealth v. Grise, 398 Mass. 247, 250, 496 N.E.2d 162 (1986), quoting Commonwealth v. Gullick, 386 Mass. 278, 282, 435 N.E.2d 348 (1982). "When police officers leave their jurisdiction 'they cease[] to be officers . . . ' " *Id.* Thus, from the standpoint of the law, Hagan acted as he portrayed himself—in the capacity of a private citizen, to whose acts Miranda does not apply.

The defendant argues, however, that we should view Hagan as acting in the role of an adjunct or assistant to the Holliston police and not as an ordinary citizen. Without question, "the police may not accomplish through private proxies what they cannot do directly." Mahnke, supra.

Statements may be suppressed for failure to give Miranda warnings where the interrogator "was 'functioning as an instrument of the police' (United States v. Brown, 466 F.2d 493, 495 [10th Cir.1972]; cf. Coolidge v. New Hampshire, 403 U.S. 443, 487 [91 S.Ct. 2022, 2048–49, 29 L.Ed.2d 564 (1971)], or acting as an agent of the police pursuant to a scheme to elicit statements from the defendant by coercion or guile . . . " Mahnke, supra.

This argument is not persuasive. The mere fact that Hagan helped the local police is insufficient to render him an agent or an instrument of the police. This is so, not only because Hagan's efforts were no different from what would be desired or expected on the part of any private citizen, but also because there is no evidence that the Holliston police even knew about Hagan's opportunity to interrogate the defendant prior to its occurrence. Commonwealth v. Mahnke, supra 368 Mass. at 677–678, 335 N.E.2d 360. The motion to suppress was properly denied.

Comment

Commonwealth v. Tynes involved an off-duty police officer, out of his jurisdiction, confronted by a potential driving under the influence situation where he believed that he could not arrest.

The evidence seems to indicate that the officer was concerned about the driver's safety and well-being. He tried to summon help, but controlled the driver; talked to him and did not give Miranda warning as he had no indication of his status; he questioned the driver and would not let him drive by seizing his keys. (1) Defendant was not in custody. (2) Officer was not acting as an agent of the Holliston police; they were unaware of his status.

Motion to suppress was properly denied.

Commonwealth v. Harmon
410 Mass 425, 573 N.E.2d, 490 (1991)

ABRAMS, Justice.

The defendant, Raymond Harmon, was convicted of murder in the first degree and armed robbery in the beating death of Frederick Slavin. On appeal, the defendant claims that the trial judge erred (1) by admitting the testimony of a fellow prison inmate concerning inculpatory statements made by the defendant, (2) by failing to suppress the defendant's statements to police and certain physical evidence, and (3) by denying defense counsel's request to recall two state witnesses. We affirm. The defendant also asks that we exercise our power under G.L. c. 278, section 33E (1988 ed.), to reverse his conviction for murder in the first degree. We conclude that there is no reason to exercise our power under G.L. c. 278, section 33E, in the defendant's favor.

The jury could have found the facts as follows. Frederick Slavin, who was seventy-five years old at the time of his death, worked for a package store in Lowell. He stacked supplies and delivered goods to customers. Slavin also made a practice of cashing checks for friends and customers. It was thus not unusual for Slavin to be carrying several thousand dollars in cash as he made his deliveries. Slavin cashed checks for the defendant on at least two occasions. On the morning of November 14, 1985, the package store received a telephone order for a case of beer to be delivered to the rear door of 241 Pawtucket Street. Slavin left the package store shortly after 1 P.M. and stopped at a bank. He withdrew $8000, and left the bank with the cash in a brown paper lunch bag. Shortly after 2 P.M. Slavin's body was discovered at the rear of 241 Pawtucket Street. His death was caused by several blows to the head. The paper bag containing $8000 in cash lay near the body, but Slavin's front pant pockets had been turned inside out and were empty.

At 10:30 on the evening, the defendant was at the apartment of David Mullamphy with John Tarrant, Barbara Peaslee, and Raymond Grenier. Police Inspector Durkin arrived at the apartment with three other police officers. Durkin knocked on the door, and the defendant admitted the officers. He had been drinking, but did not appear intoxicated. Durkin noticed a pair of dungarees draped over a washing machine in the kitchen. The dungarees were wet, and had a brown stain on one leg. The defendant indicated that the pants belonged to him. After a short time, Durkin asked the defendant if he was willing to go to the police station, and the defendant agreed to go. At one point, the defendant began staggering as he walked from the police car to the police station. Durkin told him to "knock it off," and the defendant walked normally the rest of the way to the police station. When they reached the police station, Harmon signed a card acknowledging that he had been given and understood the warning required by Miranda v. Arizona, 384 U.S. 436, 86 S.Ct. 1602, 16 L.E.2d 694 (1966). Durkin then questioned the defendant about his movements during the day. Durkin asked if he could retrieve the wet dungarees from the apartment, and the defendant replied, "Go ahead." He signed a consent form authorizing the police to perform a chemical test on the pants. Testing later showed the stain to be blood of the same type as the victim's blood. The defendant signed a second "Miranda" card, and then gave a statement to Durkin. Durkin typed out the statement and the defendant signed it. The defendant left the police station early the next morning.

In May, 1986, the defendant was indicted for the murder of Slavin. At that time, he was serving a sentence at the Massachusetts Correctional Institution, Cedar Junction, on an unrelated charge. While at Cedar Junction, the defendant encountered a fellow inmate, Jose Otero, whom he had met during a previous incarceration. The two held several conversations, and the defendant told Otero that he had committed the murder. Otero took some notes on the information revealed by the defendant, and telephoned Durkin to tell him what he had learned. Otero testified for the Commonwealth at trial.

Testimony of Jose Otero. Before trial, the defendant moved to suppress Otero's testimony. The motion was denied. On appeal, the defendant claims that admission of Otero's testimony as to their prison conversations violated his state and federal rights to counsel.

[1,2] A criminal defendant's right to be represented by counsel may be violated by "indirect and surreptitious" interrogations by government agents as well as overt interrogations by uniformed police officers. Massiah v. United States, 377 U.S. 201, 206, 84 S.Ct. 1199, 1203, 12 L.Ed.2d 246 (1964). See Commonwealth v. Rodwell, 394 Mass. 694, 698–699, 477 N.E.2d 385 (1985). Where the government has entered into an arrangement with a prison inmate agreeing to pay him for incriminating evidence elicited from another inmate, an agency relationship may have been established. See United States v. Henry, 447 U.S. 264, 100 S.Ct. 2183, 65 L.Ed.2d 115 (1980). However, an inmate who has not entered into any agreement with the government, and who reports incriminating evidence to police out of conscience or even "an unencouraged hope to curry favor" is not acting as a government agent. Thomas v. Cox, 708 F.2d 132, 136 (4th Cir.), cert. denied, 464 U.S. 918, 104 S.Ct. 284, 78 L.Ed.2d 262 (1983); United States v. Watson, 894 F.2d 1345, 1348 (D.C.Cir.1990); Lightbourne v. Dugger, 829 F.2d 1012, 1021 (11th Cir. 1987), cert. denied, 488 U.S. 934, 109 S.Ct. 329, 102 L.Ed.2d 346 (1988); United States v. Taylor, 800 F.2d 1012, 1016 (10th Cir. 1986), cert. denied 484 U.S. 838, 108 S.Ct. 123, 98 L.Ed.2d 81 (1987). See Commonwealth v. Rodwell, supra 394 Mass. at 698–699, 477 N.E.2d 385. "An individual's actions will not be attributed to the State if no promises are made for that individual's help and if nothing was offered

to or asked of the individual." Commonwealth v Rancourt, 399 Mass. 269, 274, 503 N.E.2d 960 (1987).

[3] At the suppression hearing, the judge heard testimony from Otero and Durkin, as well as from other witnesses. He issued written findings detailing the facts of the relationship between the defendant and Otero and Durkin. On appeal, we accept those findings of fact absent clear error. Commonwealth v. Yesilciman, 406 Mass. 736, 743, 550 N.E.2d 378 (1990). However, we make an independent determination as to whether Otero was functioning as a government agent by applying constitutional principles to facts. See Commonwealth v. Rancourt, supra 399 Mass. at 273–274, 503 N.E.2d 960; Commonwealth v. Haas, 373 Mass. 545, 550, 369 N.E.2d 692 (1977), S.C., 398 Mass. 806, 501 N.E.2d 1154 (1986).

[4] The judge's findings are as follows. Otero was in prison at the time of Slavin's murder. Durkin had arrested Otero on the charges that led to his sentence. Durkin also had arrested Otero on at least four other occasions during the previous four years. In May, 1986, Otero was transferred from Cedar Junction to the South Eastern Correctional Center (SECC), a medium security prison. From prison Otero called Durkin collect, two or three times a month. Otero had no visitors at SECC, and regarded Durkin as a "friend and advisor." Durkin kept Otero informed about Otero's brothers and sisters in Lowell. Otero was transferred from SECC back to Cedar Junction because of disciplinary infractions. Otero began working as a cook in the kitchen at Cedar Junction. There he encountered the defendant, an acquaintance from a previous incarceration in Billerica, who was also working in the kitchen. During one of his telephone calls to Durkin, Otero mentioned that he was working with "the guy who killed the old man." Durkin told him to "keep his ears open." After the defendant told Otero about the murder, Otero began to keep notes of his conversations with the defendant. In mid-October, the defendant told Otero that he had killed Slavin by beating him, and by hitting Slavin's head against a rock. Two days later Otero telephoned Durkin and told him that the defendant had revealed the details of the murder. Durkin responded that such knowledge was of no use to him unless Otero was willing to testify to it. Otero said that he needed to think it over. The next day Otero called back and told Durkin that he was willing to testify. Durkin arranged meetings with police and an assistant district attorney to take Otero's statement and retrieve Otero's notes. Immediately after meeting police, Otero was placed in segregation for his own protection.

Otero testified that Slavin had cashed checks for him, and that "the old man didn't deserve what [the defendant] had done to him." He denied having been offered any promises, inducements, or rewards for his testimony. The assistant district attorney stated that he told Otero that he would request that Otero's parole board hearing be moved up from mid-December to late November.

The facts found by the judge are supported by the evidence at the suppression hearing and at trial. Nothing in these facts lends credence to the defendant's conclusion that Otero was functioning as a government agent. Nothing in the record indicates that Durkin or other officials entered into any agreement with Otero. No money or benefit was promised to Otero, expressly or implicitly, as an inducement or reward for information about the defendant. The only action that can be attributed to the government is Durkin's suggestion that Otero "keep his ears open." Such a suggestion, especially when offered after Otero already had come forward with information, does not suffice to establish an agency relationship. See Lightbourne v. Dugger, supra; Commonwealth v. Rancourt, supra. We conclude, therefore, that Otero was not functioning as a government agent when he spoke with the defendant in prison. The defendant's right to counsel was not violated.

Comment

Held snitch was not an agent of the police. "Miranda forbids coercion, not mere strategic deception."

Hoffa v. United States

Joseph A. Fanelli, Washington, D.C., for petitioners.

Fred M. Vinson, Jr., and Nathan Lewin, Washington, D.C., for respondent.

Mr. Justice STEWART delivered the opinion of the Court.

Over a period of several weeks in the late autumn of 1962 there took place in a federal court in Nashville, Tennessee, a trial by jury in which James Hoffa was charged with violating a provision of the Taft-Hartley Act. That trial, known in the present record as the Test Fleet trial, ended with a hung jury. The petitioners now before us—James Hoffa, Thomas Parks, Larry Campbell, and Ewing King—were tried and convicted in 1964 for endeavoring to bribe members of that jury. The convictions were affirmed by the Court of Appeals. A substantial element in the government's proof that led to the convictions of these four petitioners was contributed by a witness named Edward Partin, who testified to several incriminating statements which he said petitioners Hoffa and King had made in his presence during the course of the Test Fleet trial. Our grant of certiorari was limited to the single issue of whether the Government's use in this case of evidence supplied by Partin operated to invalidate these convictions. 382 U.S. 1024, 86 S.Ct. 645, 15 L.Ed.2d 538.

The specific question before us, as framed by counsel for the petitioners, is this:

> Whether evidence obtained by the Government by means of deceptively placing a secret informer in the quarters and councils of a defendant during one criminal trial so violates the defendant's Fourth, Fifth and Sixth Amendment rights that suppression of such evidence is required in a subsequent trial of the same defendant on a different charge.

At the threshold the government takes issue with the way this question is worded, refusing to concede that it " 'placed' the informer anywhere, much less that it did so 'deceptively.' " In the view we take of the matter, however, a resolution of this verbal controversy is unnecessary to a decision of the constitutional issues before us. The basic facts are clear enough and a lengthy discussion of the detailed minutiae to which a large portion of the briefs and oral arguments was addressed would serve only to divert attention from the real issues before us.

The controlling facts can be briefly stated. The Test Fleet trial, in which James Hoffa was the sole individual defendant, was in progress between October 22 and December 23, 1962, in Nashville, Tennessee. James Hoffa was president of the International Brotherhood of Teamsters. During the course of the trial he occupied a three-room suite in the Andrew Jackson Hotel in Nashville. One of his constant companions throughout the trial was the petitioner King, president of the Nashville local of the Teamsters Union. Edward Partin, a resident of Baton Rouge, Louisiana, and a local Teamsters Union official there, made repeated visits to Nashville during the period of the trial. On these visits he frequented the Hoffa hotel suite, and was continually in the company of Hoffa and his associates, including King, in and around the hotel suite, the hotel lobby, the courthouse, and elsewhere in Nashville. During this period Partin made frequent reports to a federal agent named Sheridan concerning conversations he said Hoffa and King had had with him and with each other, disclosing endeavors to bribe members of the Test Fleet jury. Partin's reports and his subsequent testimony at the petitioners' trial unquestionably contributed, directly or indirectly, to the convictions of all four of the petitioners.

The chain of circumstances which led Partin to be in Nashville during the Test Fleet trial extended back at least to September of 1962. At that time Partin was in jail in Baton Rouge on a state criminal charge. He was also under a federal indictment for embezzling union funds, and other indictments for state offenses were pending against him. Between that time and Partin's initial visit to Nashville on October 22 he was released on bail on the state criminal charge, and proceedings under the federal indictment were postponed. On October 8, Partin telephoned Hoffa in Washington, D.C., to discuss local union matters and Partin's difficulties with the authorities. In the course of this conversation Partin asked if he could see Hoffa to confer about these problems, and Hoffa acquiesced. Partin again called Hoffa on October 18 and arranged to meet him in Nashville. During this period Partin also consulted on several occasions with federal law enforcement agents, who told him that Hoffa might attempt to tamper with the Test Fleet jury, and asked him to be on the lookout in Nashville for such attempts and to report to the federal authorities any evidence of wrongdoing that he discovered. Partin agreed to do so.

After the Test Fleet trial was completed, Partin's wife received four monthly installment payments of $300 from government funds, and the state and federal charges against Partin were either dropped or not actively pursued.

Reviewing these circumstances in detail, the government insists the fair inference is that Partin went to Nashville on his own initiative to discuss union business and his own problems with Hoffa, that Partin ultimately cooperated closely with federal authorities only after he discovered evidence of jury tampering in the Test Fleet trial, that the payments to Partin's wife were simply in partial reimbursement of Partin's subsequent out-of-pocket expenses, and that the failure to prosecute Partin on the state and federal charges had no necessary connection with his services as an informer. The findings of the trial court support this version of the facts, and these findings were accepted by the Court of Appeals as "supported by substantial evidence." 349 F.2d at 36. But whether or not the government "placed" Partin with Hoffa in Nashville during the Test Fleet trial, we proceed upon the premise that Partin was a government informer from the time he first arrived in Nashville on

October 22, and that the government compensated him for his services as such. It is upon that premise that we consider the constitutional issues presented.

Before turning to those issues we mention an additional preliminary contention of the government. The petitioner Hoffa was the only individual defendant in the Test Fleet case, and Partin had conversations during the Test Fleet trial only with him and with the petitioner King. So far as appears, Partin never saw either of the other two petitioners during that period. Consequently, the government argues that, of the four petitioners, only Hoffa has standing to raise a claim that his Sixth Amendment right to counsel in the Test Fleet trial was impaired, and only he and King have standing with respect to the other constitutional claims. Cf. Wong Sun v. United States, 371 U.S. 471, 487–488, 491–492, 83 S.Ct. 407, 417–418, 419–420, 9 L.Ed.2d 441; Jones v. United States, 362 U.S. 257, 259–267, 80 S.Ct. 725, 730–734, 4 L.Ed.2d 697. It is clear, on the other hand, that Partin's reports to the agent Sheridan uncovered leads that made possible the development of evidence against petitioners Parks and Campbell. But we need not pursue the nuances of these "standing" questions, because it is evident in any event that none of the petitioners can prevail unless the petitioner Hoffa prevails. For that reason, the ensuing discussion is confined to the claims of the petitioner Hoffa (hereinafter petitioner), all of which he clearly has standing to invoke.

It is contended that only by violating the petitioner's rights under the Fourth Amendment was Partin able to hear the petitioner's incriminating statements in the hotel suite, and that Partin's testimony was therefore inadmissible under the exclusionary rule of Weeks v. United States, 232 U.S. 383, 34 S.Ct. 341, 58 L.Ed. 652. The argument is that Partin's failure to disclose his role as a government informer vitiated the consent that the petitioner gave to Partin's repeated entries into the suite, and that by listening to the petitioner's statements Partin conducted an illegal "search" for verbal evidence.

[1–3] The preliminary steps of this argument are on solid ground. A hotel room can clearly be the object of Fourth Amendment protection as much as a home or an office. United States v. Jeffers, 342 U.S. 48, 72 S.Ct. 93, 96 L.Ed. 59. The Fourth Amendment can certainly be violated by guileful as well as by forcible intrusions into a constitutionally protected area. Gouled v. United States, 255 U.S. 298, 41 S.Ct. 261, 65 L.Ed. 647. And the protections of the Fourth Amendment are surely not limited to tangibles, but can extend as well to oral statements. Silverman v. United States, 365 U.S. 505, 81 S.Ct. 679, 5 L.Ed.2d 734.

[4] Where the argument falls is in its misapprehensions of the fundamental nature and scope of Fourth Amendment protection. What the Fourth Amendment protects is the security a man relies upon when he places himself or his property within a constitutionally protected area, be it his home or his office, his hotel room or his automobile. There he is protected from unwarranted governmental intrusion. And when he puts something in his filing cabinet, in his desk drawer, or in his pocket, he has the right to know it will be secure from an unreasonable search or an unreasonable seizure. So it was that the Fourth Amendment could not tolerate the warrantless search of the hotel room in Jeffers, the purloining of the petitioner's private papers in Fouled, or the surreptitious electronic surveillance in Silverman. Countless other cases which have come to this Court over the years have involved a myriad of differing factual contexts in which the protections of the Fourth Amendment have been appropriately invoked. No doubt the future will bring countless others. By nothing we say here do we either foresee or foreclose factual situations to which the Fourth Amendment may be applicable.

In the present case, however, it is evident that no interest legitimately protected by the Fourth Amendment is involved. It is obvious that the petitioner was not relying on the security of his hotel suite when he made the incriminating statements to Partin or in Partin's presence. Partin did not enter the suite by force or by stealth. He was not a surreptitious eavesdropper. Partin was in the suite by invitation, and every conversation which he heard was either directed to him or knowingly carried on in his presence. The petitioner, in a word, was not relying on the security of the hotel room; he was relying upon his misplaced confidence that Partin would not reveal his wrongdoing. As counsel for the petitioner himself points out, some of the communications with Partin did not take place in the suite at all, but in the "hall of the hotel," in the "Andrew Jackson Hotel lobby," and "at the courthouse."

Neither this Court nor any member of it has ever expressed the view that the Fourth Amendment protects a wrongdoer's misplaced belief that a person to whom he voluntarily confides his wrongdoing will not reveal it. Indeed, the Court unanimously rejected that very contention less than four years ago in Lopez v. United States, 373 U.S. 427, 83 S.Ct. 1381, 10 L.Ed.2d 462. In that case the petitioner had been convicted of attempted bribery of an internal revenue agent named Davis. The Court was divided with regard to the admissibility in evidence of a surreptitious electronic recording of an incriminating conversation Lopez had had in his private office with Davis. But there was no dissent from the view that testimony about the conversation by Davis himself was clearly admissible.

As the Court put it, "Davis was not guilty of an unlawful invasion of petitioner's office simply because his apparent willingness to accept a bribe was not real. Compare Wong Sun v. United States, 371 U.S. 471, 83 S.Ct. 407, 9 L.Ed.2d 441. He was in the office with petitioner's consent, and while there he did not violate the privacy of the office by seizing something surreptitiously without petitioner's knowledge. Compare Gouled v. United States, supra. The only evidence obtained consisted of statements made by Lopez to Davis, statements which Lopez knew full well could be used against him by Davis if he wished.***" 373 U.S. at 438, 83 S.Ct. at 1387, 10 L.Ed.2d 462. In the words of the dissenting opinion in Lopez, "The risk of being overheard by an eavesdropper or betrayed by an informer or deceived as to the identity of one with whom one deals is probably inherent in the conditions of human society. It is the kind of risk we necessarily assume whenever we speak." *Id.,* 373 U.S. at 465, 83 S.Ct. at 1402, 10 L.Ed.2d 462. See also Lewis v. United States, 385 U.S. 206, 87 S.Ct. 424, 17 L.Ed.2d 312.

[5] Adhering to these views, we hold that no right protected by the Fourth Amendment was violated in the present case.

The petitioner argues that his right under the Fifth Amendment not to "be compelled in any criminal case to be a witness against himself" was violated by the admission of Partin's testimony. The claim is without merit.

[6] There have been sharply differing views within the Court as to the ultimate reach of the Fifth Amendment right against compulsory self-incrimination. Some of those differences were aired last Term in Miranda v. State of Arizona, 384 U.S. 436, 499, 504, 526, 86 S.Ct. 1602, 1640, 1643, 1654, 16 L.Ed.2d 694. But since at least as long ago as 1807, when Chief Justice Marshall first gave attention to the matter in the trial of Aaron Burr, all have agreed that a necessary element of compulsory self-incrimination is some kind of compulsion. Thus, in the Miranda case, dealing with the Fifth Amendment's impact upon police interrogation of persons in custody, the Court predicated its decision upon the conclusion "that without proper safeguards the process of in-custody interrogation of persons suspected or accused of crime contains inherently compelling pressures which work to undermine the individual's will to

resist and to compel him to speak where he would not otherwise do so freely.***" 384 U.S., at 467, 86 S.Ct. at 1624, 16 L.Ed.2d 694.

[7] In the present case no claim has been or could be made that the petitioner's incriminating statements were the product of any sort of coercion, legal or factual. The petitioner's conversations with Partin and in Partin's presence were wholly voluntary. For that reason, if for no other, it is clear that to right protected by the Fifth Amendment privilege against compulsory self-incrimination was violated in the case.

The petitioner makes two separate claims under the Sixth Amendment, and we give them separate consideration.

[8] During the course of the test Fleet trial, the petitioner's lawyers used his suite as a place to confer with him and with each other, to interview witnesses, and to plan the following day's trial strategy. Therefore, argues the petitioner, Partin's presence in and around the suite violated the petitioner's Sixth Amendment right to counsel, because an essential ingredient thereof is the right of a defendant and his counsel to prepare for trial without intrusion upon their confidential relationship by an agent of the government, the defendant's trial adversary. Since Partin's presence in the suit thus violated the Sixth Amendment, the argument continues, any evidence acquired by reason of his presence there was constitutionally tainted and therefore inadmissible against the petitioner in this case. We reject this argument.

In the first place, it is far from clear to what extent Partin was present at conversations or conferences of the petitioner's counsel. Several of the petitioner's Test Fleet lawyers testified at the hearing on the motion to suppress Partin's testimony in the present case. Most of them said that Partin had heard or had been in a position to hear at least some of the lawyers' discussions during the Test Fleet trial. On the other hand, Partin himself testified that the lawyers "would move you out" when they wanted to discuss the case, and denied that he made any effort to "get into or be present at any conversations between lawyers or anything of that sort," other than engaging in such banalities as "how things looked," or "how does it look?" He said he might have heard some of the lawyers' conversations, but he didn't know what they were talking about, "because I wasn't interested in what they had to say about the case." He testified that he did not report any of the lawyers' conversations to Sheridan, because the latter "wasn't interested in what the attorneys said." Partin's testimony was largely confirmed by Sheridan. Sheridan did testify, however, to one occasion when Partin told him about a group of prospective character witnesses being interviewed in the suite by one of the petitioner's lawyers, who "was going over" some written "questions and answers" with them. This information was evidently relayed by Sheridan to the chief government attorney at the Test Fleet trial.

The District Court in the present case apparently credited Partin's testimony, finding "there has been no interference by the government with any attorney-client relationship of any defendant in the case." The Court of Appeals accepted this finding. 349 F.2d at 36. In view of Sheridan's testimony about Partin's report of the interviews with the prospective character witnesses, however, we proceed here on the hypothesis that Partin did observe and report to Sheridan at least some of the activities of defense counsel in the Test Fleet trial.

The proposition that a surreptitious invasion by a government agent into the legal camp of the defense may violate the protection of the Sixth Amendment has found expression in two cases decided by the Court of Appeals for the District of Columbia Circuit, Caldwell v. United States, 92 U.S. App.D.C. 355, 205 F.2d 879, and Coplon v. United States, 89 U.S.App.D.C. 103, 191 F.2d 749. Both of those cases dealt with government intrusion of the grossest kind upon the confidential relationship between the defendant and his counsel. In Coplon, the defendant alleged that government agents deliberately intercepted telephone consultations between the defendant and her lawyer before and during trial. In Caldwell, the agent, "[i]n his dual capacity as defense assistant and Government agent***gained free access to the planning of the defense. ***Neither his dealings with the defense nor his reports to the prosecution were limited to the proposed unlawful acts of the defense: they covered many matters connected with the impending trial." 92 U.S.App.D.C., at 356, 205 F.2d at 880.

We may assume that the Coplon and Caldwell cases were rightly decided, and further assume, without deciding, that the government's activities during the Test Fleet trial were sufficiently similar to what went on in Coplon and Caldwell to invoke the rule of those decisions. Consequently, if the Test Fleet trial had resulted in a conviction instead of a hung jury, the conviction would presumptively have been set aside as constitutionally defective. Cf. Black v. United States, 385 U.S. 26, 87 S.Ct. 190, 17 L.Ed.2d 26.

But a holding that it follows from this presumption that the petitioner's conviction in the present case should be set aside would be both unprecedented and irrational. In Coplon and Caldwell, the Court of Appeals held that the government's intrusion upon the defendant's relationship with his lawyer "invalidates the trial at which it occurred." 89 U.S. App.D.C., at 357, 205 F.2d at 881. In both of those cases the court directed a new trial, and the second trial in Caldwell resulted in a conviction which this Court declined to review. 95 U.S.App.D.C. 35, 218 F.2d 370; 349 U.S. 930, 75 S.Ct. 773, 99 L.Ed. 1260. The argument here, therefore, goes far beyond anything decided in Caldwell or in Coplon. For if the petitioner's argument were accepted, not only could there have been no new conviction on the existing charges in Caldwell, but not even a conviction on other and different charges against the same defendant.

It is possible to imagine a case in which the prosecution might so pervasively insinuate itself into the councils of the defense as to make a new trial on the same charges impermissible under the Sixth Amendment. But even if it were further arguable that a situation could be hypothesized in which the government's previous activities in undermining a defendant's Sixth Amendment rights at on trial would make evidence obtained thereby inadmissible in a different trial on other charges, the case now before us does not remotely approach such a situation.

This is so because of the clinching basic fact in the present case that none of the petitioner's incriminating statements which Partin heard were made in the presence of counsel, in the hearing of counsel, or in connection in any way with the legitimate defense of the Test Fleet prosecution. The petitioner's statements related to the commission of quite separate offense—attempted bribery of jurors—and the statements were made to Partin out of the presence of any lawyers.

Even assuming, therefore, as we have, that there might have been a Sixth Amendment violation which might have made invalid a conviction, if there had been one, in the Test Fleet case, the evidence supplied by Partin in the present case was in no sense the "fruit" of any such violation. In Wong Sun v. United States, 371 U.S. 471, 83 S.Ct. 407, 9 L.Ed.2d 441, a case involving exclusion of evidence under the Fourth Amendment, the Court stated that "the more apt question in such a case is 'whether, granting establishment of the primary illegality, the evidence to which instant objection is made has been come at by exploitation of that illegality or instead by means sufficiently distinguishable to be purged of the primary taint.' Maguire, Evidence of Guilt, 221 (1959)." 371 U.S. at 488, 83 S.Ct. at 417, 9 L.Ed.2d 441.

Even upon the premise that this same strict standard of excludability should apply under the Sixth Amendment—a question we need not decide—it is clear that Partin's evidence in this case was not the consequence of any "exploitation" of a Sixth Amendment violation. The petitioner's incriminating statements to which Partin testified in this case were totally unrelated in both time and subject matter to any assumed intrusion by Partin into the conferences of the petitioner's counsel in the Test Fleet trial. These incriminating statements, all of them made out of the presence or hearing of any of the petitioner's counsel, embodied the very antithesis of any legitimate defense in the Test Fleet trial.

[9] The petitioner's second argument under the Sixth Amendment needs no extended discussion. That argument goes as follows: Not later than October 25, 1962, the government had sufficient ground for taking the petitioner into custody and charging him with endeavors to tamper with the Test Fleet jury. Had the government done so, it could not have continued to question the petitioner without observance of his Sixth Amendment right to counsel. Massiah v. United States, 377 U.S. 201, 84 S.Ct. 1199, 12 L.Ed.2d 246; Escobedo v. State of Illinois, 378 U.S. 478, 84 S.Ct. 1758, 12 L.Ed.2d 977. Therefore, the argument concludes, evidence of statements made by the petitioner subsequent to October 25 was inadmissible, because the government acquired that evidence only by flouting the petitioner's Sixth Amendment right to counsel.

[10,11] Nothing in Massiah, in Escobedo, or in any other case that has come to our attention, even remotely suggests this novel and paradoxical constitutional doctrine, and we decline to adopt it now. There is not constitutional right to be arrested. The police are not required to guess at their peril the precise moment at which they have probable cause to arrest a suspect, risking a violation of the Fourth Amendment if they act too soon, and a violation of the Sixth Amendment if they wait too long. Law enforcement officers are under no constitutional duty to call a halt to a criminal investigation the moment they have the minimum evidence to establish probable cause, a quantum of evidence which may fall far short of the amount necessary to support a criminal conviction.

[12] Finally, the petitioner claims that even if there was no violation—"as separately measured by each such Amendment"—of the Fourth Amendment, the compulsory self-incrimination clause of the Fifth Amendment, or of the Sixth Amendment in this case, the judgment of conviction must nonetheless be reversed. The argument is based upon the Due Process Clause of the Fifth Amendment. The "totality" of the government's conduct during the Test Fleet trial operated, it is said, to "'offend those canons of decency and fairness which express the notions of justice of

English-speaking peoples even toward those charged with the most heinous offenses' (Rochin v. [People of] California, 342 U.S. 165, 169 [72 S.Ct. 205, 208, 96 L.Ed. 183])."

The argument boils down to a general attack upon the use of a government informer as "a shabby thing in any case," and to the claim that in the circumstances of this particular case the risk that Partin's testimony might be perjurious was very high. Insofar as the general attack upon the use of informers is based upon historic "notions" of "English-speaking peoples," it is without historical foundation. In the words of Judge Learned Hand, "Courts have countenanced the use of informers from the time immemorial; in cases of conspiracy, or in other cases when the crime consists of preparing for another crime, it is usually necessary to rely upon them or upon accomplices because the criminals will almost certainly proceed covertly.***" United States v. Dennis, 2 Cir., 183 F.2d 201, at 224.

This is not to say that a secret government informer is to the slightest degree more free from all relevant constitutional restrictions than is any other government agent. See Massiah v. United States, 377 U.S. 201, 84 S.Ct. 1199, 12 L.Ed.2d 246. It *is* to say that the use of secret informers is not *per se* unconstitutional.

[13] The petitioner is quite correct in the contention that Partin, perhaps even more than most informers, may have had motives to lie. But it does not follow that his testimony was untrue, nor does it follow that his testimony was inadmissible. The established safeguards of the Anglo-American legal system leave the veracity of a witness to be tested by cross-examination, and the credibility of his testimony to be determined by a properly instructed jury. At the trial of the case, Partin was subjected to rigorous cross-examination, and the extent and nature of his dealing with federal and state authorities were insistently explored. The trial judge instructed the jury, both specifically and generally, with regard to assessing Partin's credibility. The Constitution does not require us to upset the jury's verdict.

Affirmed.

Mr. Justice WHITE and Mr. Justice FORTAS took no part in the consideration or decision of these cases.

Mr. Chief Justice WARREN, dissenting.

Comment

In standard procedure, defense counsel argues that each and every possible Constitutional Request was violated and the court painstakingly discusses each issue. The court held that with respect to incriminating statements attributed to Hoffa, none were the product of compulsion or coercion, and were entirely voluntary, therefore no violation by private person of the Fifth Amendment occurred.

INDEX OF CASES